The National Debt

ALSO BY ROBERT E. KELLY

Baseball for the Hot Stove League:
Fifteen Essays
(McFarland, 1989)

Baseball's Best:
Hall of Fame Pretenders Active in the Eighties
(McFarland, 1988)

The National Debt

From FDR (1941) to Clinton (1996)

by
ROBERT E. KELLY

with a foreword by Jeff Jacoby

McFarland & Company, Inc., Publishers
Jefferson, North Carolina, and London

Acknowledgments: This book could not have been produced without the research, editing assistance, and support of my wife, Margaret Rodden Kelly. A close friend (and deeply concerned citizen), Leo Dioguardi, planted the seed of creation with his remark: "You should write a book on national debt."

Economists from local colleges and elsewhere were gracious with advice about sources of information. And people contacted via e-mail at various U.S. government departments (Labor, Treasury, Commerce, Budgets, etc.) were enormously helpful as direct sources of historical data.

The patience, guidance, and support of friends and colleagues made perseverance possible. It was and is deeply appreciated.

Library of Congress Cataloguing-in-Publication Data

Kelly, Robert E., 1926–
 The national debt : from FDR (1941) to Clinton (1996) / by
Robert E. Kelly.
  p. cm.
 Includes bibliographical references and index. ∞
 ISBN 0-7864-0622-4 (library binding : 50# alkaline paper)
 1. Debts, Public—United States. 2. Budget deficits—
United States. 3. Government spending policy—United
States. I. Title.
HJ8119.K45 2000
336.3'4'097309045—dc21   99-52888
                                              CIP

British Library Cataloguing-in-Publication data are available

Manufactured in the United States of America

McFarland & Company, Inc., Publishers
 Box 611, Jefferson, North Carolina 28640
  www.mcfarlandpub.com

To the memory of
Hugh and Rose Rodden,
and
James and Mildred Kelly,
long ago settled with their Maker,
loving parents and devoted citizens
of their beloved United States of America.

Contents

Those who expect to reap the blessings of freedom
must ... undergo the fatigue of supporting it.—Thomas Paine

Liberty means responsibility. That is why
most men dread it.—George Bernard Shaw

Liberty exists in proportion
to wholesome restraint.—Daniel Webster

The history of liberty is a history of limitations of
government power, not the increase of it.—Woodrow Wilson

Interest works day and night, in fair weather and
in foul. It gnaws at a man's substance with
invisible teeth.—Henry Ward Beecher

Foreword
by Jeff Jacoby

"I place economy among the first and most important of republican virtues," wrote Thomas Jefferson, "and public debt as the greatest of dangers."

When President Jefferson left office in 1809, the public debt of the United States was $57 million. Today it approaches $4 trillion. If Jefferson was right—if public debt is indeed the greatest of dangers—then the 70,000-fold increase in the nation's indebtedness since his day must mean that the American people are in grave peril indeed.

During the Jefferson administration, the federal government's debt shrank. The $57 million debt Jefferson bequeathed to his successor was 31 percent lower than the $83 million debt John Adams had bequeathed to him. To modern Americans, this will sound astonishing. It would not have to our great-grandparents (or to theirs). In reducing public debt, Jefferson was typical of peacetime presidents during the first 150 years of U.S. history. Only in recent decades have Americans been conditioned to believe that it is normal for the country's indebtedness to defy gravity and always rise.

How did we get from there to here?

America's descent into $4 trillion of public indebtedness did not "just happen." It began during World War II, when Washington embarked on massive deficit spending in order to finance the immense enterprise of defeating Germany and Japan. Even as federal borrowing soared, so did federal tax collections. The government's revenue in 1940 was $6.5 billion; by 1944, it had risen to $211 billion. When Pearl Harbor was attacked, the average American lost only 7 percent of his earnings to federal taxes. Just three years later, the government was helping itself to more than 28 percent of the average taxpayer's salary.

Revenues swelled in part because millions of unemployed Americans went back to work as the depression ended. But they also swelled because income tax rates went through the ceiling. The top marginal rate in 1944

1

was a staggering 94 percent. And there was a change of even greater consequence during the war years: Income tax withholding was born. For the first time, the federal government began confiscating money from working Americans *before* it showed up in their pay envelope. Without the urgency of the war, Congress could never have gotten away with inflicting so severe a tax regime on the public. By the time the war ended, it was too entrenched to repeal.

Tax withholding meant that money now poured into Washington year-round. A permanent pool of cash filled the Treasury, tempting politicians to spend as they had never been tempted before. A succession of presidents and Congresses chipped away at the time-honored understanding that broad swaths of economic and social activity were outside the scope of federal authority. The New Deal led to the Fair Deal led to the New Frontier led to the Great Society. Social welfare programs—from Social Security to the GI Bill, from Aid to Families with Dependent Children to farm price supports, from Medicare to food stamps—began mushrooming in the national budget.

Although tax rates were trimmed by 1950, they remained much higher than they had been before the war. The sharp decline in debt that had followed every previous war did not materialize after World War II. And as the political class grew more and more practiced in the art of winning favor (and votes) by spending other people's money, it came to rely ever more on running up the federal tab.

All government spending is financed in one of two ways: through taxes or through borrowing. The difference between them is akin to the difference between paying for a purchase with a debit card and using a credit card. The one immediately deducts the price from your bank account, which means you have to have the money on hand to make the purchase. The other postpones the date that payment actually must be made. Deficit spending enabled politicians to distribute goodies to their constituents and allies without having to raise taxes to pay the price—that is, without having to first collect the cash from the voters receiving the benefits.

But it is one thing to finance the Second World War by accumulating debt; it is something else to rely on deficits to pay for a "war" on poverty. The Second World War, and the extraordinary burdens it imposed on the federal budget, came to an end. But the welfare state goes on and on. Each year's budget is tens of billions of dollars higher than its predecessor. Each State of the Union message is studded with new schemes for spending. Each Congress—even the Republican-controlled Congresses of the late 1990s—spends more money than the Congress it replaced.

"I'm going to build me the God-damnedest, biggest, chromium-platedest, formaldehyde-stinkingest free public hospital the all-Father ever let live," bellows Willie Stark in Robert Penn Warren's *All the King's Men*. "Boy,

I tell you, I'm going to have a cage of canaries in every room that can sing Italian grand opera, and there ain't going to be a nurse hasn't won a beauty contest and every doorknob will be 18-carat gold, and by God, every bedpan will have a Swiss music box attachment to play 'Turkey in the Straw' or the 'Sextet from Lucia,' take your pick."

All the King's Men—a work of fiction, it should be noted—was written in 1946. But the Willie Starks we have always with us, and Washington in 1999 is loaded with them. The federal government may not yet be paying for musical bedpans. But it does pay farmers not to grow crops, it does fund museums built to honor Lawrence Welk, it does subsidize McDonald's to advertise Chicken McNuggets overseas, and it does underwrite catfish farms in Arkansas. And none of those, sad to say, is fictional.

In this volume, Robert E. Kelly traces, with admirable sure-footedness, the path that led the United States into a $4 trillion indebtedness. What animates his sweeping history of our public debt is his insistence that mountainous levels of government debt did not create themselves and were not created by events. They were created by men and women who knew what they were doing and ought to be held accountable for their handiwork. This book appears at a propitious moment: Thanks to a booming economy, government revenues have grown so energetically that Washington is actually running a surplus. For the first time in years, the political discourse is not about how to reduce the deficit. The budget is in the black, and the politicians now debate how to spend the surplus.

There are only two respectable positions: The excess money should be spent either to pay down the national debt or to lighten the heavy yoke of taxes under which most Americans strain. My own preference is for tax cuts, since—assuming the right taxes are cut—they help keep the government from growing still larger by removing some revenue from political control; increase incentives to work, save, and invest; and thereby make the economy grow faster. Others may argue, for different reasons, that reducing government indebtedness should take priority.

But it is clear that the *worst* of all options would be an increase in federal spending. In current dollars, government expenditures are at an all-time peak; as a percentage of national wealth, they are close to the record high. Every dollar Washington spends is another dollar unavailable for ordinary Americans—especially the American who earned that dollar—to spend. There is an inverse relationship between the size of the federal budget and the scope of individual liberty. As the budget has grown, our freedom has shrunk. That increased spending has also fueled the growth of the nation's public debt only means that our children's freedom has shrunk as well as our own.

"Voters must get angry," Robert Kelly concludes. "They must vote. They must remove from office those who do not talk straight; elect those who will cut spending, reduce the size of government, lower debt, and return to

Americans the right to live their own lives." But before they do any of those things, they must stop thinking of government as the solver of all their problems. Americans never thought that in Thomas Jefferson's day. Which goes a long way toward explaining why the national debt when he was in the White House was less than one-70,000th of what it is today.

Jeff Jacoby
March 1999

Mr. Jacoby is a columnist for the Boston Globe.

Introduction

"National debt" as a descriptive term means different things to different people. It is important to define the "debt" that one is talking about.

The number that flashes on some billboards or appears in most newspapers is total debt, the gross value of all U.S. securities issued to government and to private owners. In 1996 it amounted to $5.2 trillion, divided as follows:

National Debt (in trillions of dollars)

Owner	Amount
U.S. Govt. bodies	$1.5
Held by the public	3.7
Total	$5.2

Federal trust funds, mostly Social Security, are required by law to invest in U.S. securities, which explains the holdings of the government in the above table. This study focuses on public holdings only—$3.7 trillion in 1996. These public holdings will be referred to consistently as "public debt" or "debt."

Why did it to grow so big? Is it dangerous? How do we measure it? Who did it?

This book responds to such questions, and it will probe others that relate to America's most underreported domestic nightmare—runaway debt.

The Cause of the Problem

The *Treasury Home Page* (Internet, February 19, 1997) offers this explanation for the persistent growth of public debt: "a legacy of war, economic recession and inflation."

That description from such an authoritative source is incomplete and misleading to an astonishing degree. People, not external events, are responsible

5

for the increase in public debt. Specifically, six people created and nurtured the development of a welfare state under the cover of war, inflation, and recession. In four decades, they transformed the great American experiment into a form of American socialism.

The Media

Contemporary press coverage hovers over the story of the annual budget and the associated deficit that soon will be, say political leaders, a thing of the past. Not much emphasis is focused by the media on additions to debt in the interim period.

This is unbelievable.

Interest (1996) is almost as expensive as *Defense*; and is 50 percent greater than Medicare costs. How can so large a cost be ignored? Better yet, why is it ignored? Could it be because the discussion of it necessarily places the size of the debt before the public?

Politicians' avoidance of such topics is understandable. But how can journalists bemoan with a straight face the size of various line items in the budget and at the same time ignore one of the largest and most unproductive expenditures of all? The solution to the debt problem will be made easier if the media become more vigorous in their pursuit of this question.

Concentrating on annual deficits is like worrying about the five dollars borrowed last week and ignoring the size of the mortgage that is beyond one's ability to carry. To be sure, current debts must be paid or lowered to a painless level, as one prepares to deal with a debt crisis, but procedure must not be confused with substance. When current deficits are gone, long-term debt remains. Deficits are the hurdles that precede debt reduction.

In the sense that it is part of the whole problem, it is appropriate that progress made in dealing with deficits be followed by the media. But they should not overlook the dangers and penalties associated with a debt level that has been too large, for too long, for the wrong reasons.

Coverage has improved. The *Wall Street Journal, U.S. News, Fox News Sunday*, and the *Boston Globe* are among major news outlets that have given increasing coverage to the problem of public debt. A continuation of this trend must be a fundamental part of pressures applied to politicians who will otherwise allow the problem to drift or worsen.

Political Converts

Washington is buzzing about the possibilities of budget surpluses and some politicians are planning to spend the excess cash. Others seek to restore purdent debt management and hope to control spending and reduce debt. Failing that, they will propose significant tax reduction as a defense against the obsessive spenders in Washington. This power struggle between those who seek an ever-expanding role for government, and those in search of prudent debt management and more limited government, has been building for a decade. The outcome will reverberate in the world for decades to come.

Just as Reagan in the 1980s changed thinking relative to annual deficits, so it may be that in the 2000s dual principles of federal finance practiced by our Founding Fathers may be reapplied: borrow for war, repay in peace.

Who Will Solve the Problem?

The people and the media will solve the problem, or it will not be solved at all.

Political leaders add to the public debt problem but will not fix it, or even lessen it. The appetite for power and prestige motivates behavior in most of them. Active proponents of ever-expanding federal power are popular in today's culture, more so than thoughtful, restrained types who argue for a smaller federal role. These facts of life sterilize politicians as problem solvers: spending equals victory at the polls, economizing equals defeat, and winning equals power, the aphrodisiac of the politician.

Citizens must solve the problem of paralyzing public debt by (1) getting beyond generalizations (recessions did it) to the truth (people did it), (2) learning that they are threatened by the problem, (3) making realistic solutions a popular cause for politicians to adopt. And the media must cooperate by keeping the focus on the issue until a solution path has been found.

Education

Those with the background, talent, and time should improve upon the simple offerings in this book and broadcast their knowledge about the dangers of extended debt and the need for political action to the widest possible audience in the most understandable terms of which they are capable.

Average Americans do not learn about the economy from charts or from self-serving political speeches on economics. They turn instead to favored columnists, books, commentators, professors, executives, periodicals, and conversations with family, friends, and associates, sources that express ideas in ways that, to them, are truthful and understandable.

But whatever the source, citizens owe it to themselves to seek out and study the views of their most objective sources of information on current affairs. It would be a tragedy of history if the great American culture were destroyed by the tamperings of do-gooders and the indifference of the public.

The Objective

This study hopes to meet that test of acceptability enunciated above: truthful and understandable. The trail of public debt from George Washington through Franklin D. Roosevelt (1940) will be cursorily traced. From Roosevelt (1941) through William J. Clinton, the analysis will be presented in detail. The source and condition of public debt will be traced and examined through the prism of one with no political past, present, or future, each chapter aspiring to be a link in the thin chain of understanding forged by thoughtful columnists and authors, part of an effort that may someday motivate citizens to the acceptance of the thesis that the level of public debt is an important problem that endangers them and all Americans.

Why Begin with FDR?

Succeeding Herbert Hoover, FDR was elected in 1932. Under his leadership the government assumed many new duties, presumably to help a citizenry reeling under the unrelenting attack of an economic depression that began in 1929.

Over a period of time, FDR introduced a blitz of intrusive programs managed by new federal agencies: AAA (Agricultural Adjustment Administration), CCC (Civilian Conservation Corps), WPA (Works Progress Administration), TVA (Tennessee Valley Authority), NRA (National Recovery Administration), FSA (Farm Security Administration) that were directed against the immediate pains of the Great Depression. The programs did not work, but new relationships forged during those years between the people and Washington remained, and they paved the way for the social service activities that now make up the *Human Resources* cost center.

So it is fitting that FDR, the president who sank the footings for a socially active federal government, serves as the touchstone of this study. For good or ill, the Great Depression and FDR's reaction to it changed the fundamental idea of what a federal government should be in the United States of America.

Why 1941?

Figures are readily available for 1941. More importantly, FDR's social programs were minor budget items in 1941 and the buildup of *Defense* for World War Two was in its infancy.

Analytical Technique

Apart from pure administrative functions and related costs, federal spending represents projects and programs approved by federal politicians. *The focus here is not on what was approved but, rather, on what was financed.* The analytical period used is a four-year presidential term.

When a deficit exists, expenditures are too high or the deficit was planned. Whatever the reason, it will be herein allocated to *Defense, Interest, Government,* or *Human Resources*, which will be referred to as cost centers. In any period the deficit may be caused by underfunding of one or more of the cost centers.

The first responsibility of government is to protect the nation; the second, to protect its currency. A weak America with an out-of-favor dollar is a nothing. From these statements there arises an axiom that is followed throughout this book: *Defense* and *Interest* get first bite of the revenue apple. Other analytical principles followed are:

• To contribute to a deficit is to add to public debt, a statement of the obvious to many but not to all. Interviews reveal that to some citizens, public debt equals the sum total of private debt.

• If a deficit exists, and *Defense* increased over the previous period at a faster rate than revenue, then *Defense* is held responsible for the deficit to the extent of that excessive increase. For example, if revenue increases 15 percent, *Defense* is allowed a 15 percent increase. Under techniques being employed, growth beyond that rate will contribute to a deficit. The same procedure is applied to growth in *Interest*.

• If *Defense/Interest* do not grow as fast as revenue, all unexpended federal receipts are deemed to be available for *Government/Human Resources*.

• Funds available for *Government/Human Resources* versus spending by those cost centers in the previous period, represents the rate of allowable growth beyond which one or both of the cost centers will add to the deficit.

• In the allocation of responsibility for deficits, there are nuances that are handled and explained within each presidential period.

Conclusion

Holding politicians accountable for spending beyond the limits of the revenue stream is not a harsh standard to apply when measured against fiscal restraints that are commonplace in the home and in industry. If anything, the federal government should be the most niggardly of all of our institutions.

Since the 1960s, federal revenue has never increased less than 24.8 percent in a four-year period. In the high inflation years of Jimmy Carter, it increased 69.6 percent. Spending, not a lack of revenue, has been the fundamental problem since the mid-1950s. When and where the spending aberrations occurred will be presented in the remaining chapters.

Society, according to conservative thought, is the marriage of what was, what is, and what is to be. Ancestors teach us, reason guides us, children make us responsible.

In the handling of America's resources, have political leaders since Roosevelt acted prudently? We shall see.

Notes

This book contains many tables expressing dollar amounts. These amounts are expressed *in the dollars of the period indicated.* Direct comparisons that ignore the impact of inflation are therefore invalid.

Public debt amounts prior to 1940 were taken from a listing of "Historical Information" published by the Bureau of Public Debt. Thereafter amounts were taken from Table 7.1, "Federal Debt at the End of the Year," included in the publication *Historical Tables; Budget of the United States Government, Fiscal Year 1997,* U.S. Government Printing Office.

Chapter 1

Background, 1789–1940

A Look at the Presidents

GEORGE WASHINGTON (1789–1796)

Burdened with war debt of $75-$80 million during his two terms in office. But according to John Steele Gordon, author of *Hamilton's Blessing,* by 1794, the United States "had the highest credit rating in Europe" thanks to wise presidential leadership and the skillful management of the first secretary of the Treasury, Alexander Hamilton.

JOHN ADAMS (1797–1800)

Took on an $83.7 million public debt and a growing economy. America moved into the nineteenth century with a debt of about $83 million.

THOMAS JEFFERSON (1801–1808)

Westward expansion was symbolized by the Louisiana Purchase. Public debt was reduced to $65 million.

JAMES MADISON (1809–1816)

The British impressed our seamen, interfered with our vessels in international waters and excited Indian uprisings in the West, all of which led to the War of 1812. Public debt rose to $127 million.

JAMES MONROE (1817–1824)

The last of the Revolutionary War officers. Spain owned Florida at the time and exercised no control over the Seminole Indians, who regularly raided American settlements in Georgia. The Seminole War (1817–1818) and the purchase of Florida were the results. The Monroe Doctrine (1823) was a warning to Spain, Russia, and others to stay out of the Western Hemisphere. Debt dropped to $90 million.

JOHN QUINCY ADAMS (1825–1828)

Andrew Jackson won the popular vote for president in 1824 in a race between four candidates; Adams was second. None of the four won a majority of the electoral vote, and the House was directed to choose. Adams emerged as the victor. He proposed great improvements to national transportation systems and opened the Chesapeake and Ohio canals. Debt dropped to $67.5 million.

ANDREW JACKSON (1829–1836)

Americans pushed west and treated Indians harshly. Jackson vetoed the charter of the national bank. Land speculation, inflation, and a banking crisis followed. Public debt was almost eliminated, having dropped to $38 thousand.

MARTIN VAN BUREN (1837–1840)

Jackson's banking policy was behind the Panic of 1837, but Van Buren paid for it. The Seminole Indian problem still festered in Florida. Texas applied for statehood. Debt increased to $4 million.

WILLIAM HENRY HARRISON (1841)

Caught a cold while delivering his inaugural address and died April 4, 1841.

JOHN TYLER (1841–1844)

Vice president to Harrison. He succeeded to the presidency in April 1841. A treaty was signed with Great Britain settling the boundaries of Maine, a sore spot to both countries that had caused skirmishes. Texas became a state. The Seminole Indian question was settled. Public debt increased to $33 million.

JAMES POLK (1845–1848)

Westward expansion increased tensions between Mexico and the United States that resulted in the Mexican War (1846–1848). Debt went up to $47 million.

ZACHARY TAYLOR (1849–1850)

Died of food poisoning July 9, 1850.

MILLARD FILLMORE (1850–1852)

Vice president to Taylor. He succeeded to the presidency in 1850. California admitted to the Union as part of the Compromise of 1850, an agreement that postponed a civil war over the question of slavery but had little else to commend it. Public debt rose to $66 million.

Franklin Pierce (1853–1856)

Bought land from Mexico that completed the boundaries of Arizona and New Mexico. The public debt dropped to $32 million.

James Buchanan (1857–1860)

A major insurance company went bankrupt in 1857, an event followed by bank failures and a deep depression. The slavery issue reached its peak of intensity. Before Buchanan's term ended, South Carolina, Georgia, Florida, Alabama, Louisiana, Mississippi, and Texas seceded from the Union. Public debt rose to $64.8 million.

Abraham Lincoln (1861–1865)

The Civil War. Four more states seceded from the Union: Virginia, North Carolina, Arkansas, and Tennessee. The first shot of the war was fired on April 12, 1861; Lee surrendered on April 9, 1865. Lincoln was assassinated on April 14, 1865. Public debt skyrocketed to $2.7 billion.

Andrew Johnson (1865–1868)

Vice president to Lincoln. He succeeded to the presidency in 1865 and presided over the bitter aftermath of the war. Squabbled with Congress over the limits of presidential authority and was impeached, tried, and acquitted. The 13th Amendment outlawing slavery was passed. Alaska was purchased from Russia. Three years after the war public debt was $2.6 billion, five times higher than it was in 1862.

Ulysses S. Grant (1869–1876)

The victorious general. Presidential pressure was required to protect the civil rights of blacks against unreconstructed rebels. Postwar problems brought a domestic depression for five years. The 15th Amendment to the Constitution, protecting the right to vote, was ratified. Colorado entered the Union. Debt went down to $2.2 billion.

Rutherford B. Hayes (1877–1880)

Federal troops were removed from the South. Public debt was $2.1 billion.

James Garfield (1881)

Assassinated July 2, 1881, by Charles Guiteau, a former political supporter.

CHESTER ARTHUR (1881–1884)

Vice president to Garfield. He succeeded to the presidency in 1881. Arthur created the modern Civil Service system. Under his administration, Civil War debt began to tumble. Debt dropped to $1.8 billion.

GROVER CLEVELAND (1885–1888)

Active in administrative affairs. Public debt, $1.7 billion.

BENJAMIN HARRISON (1889–1892)

Six more states entered the Union: North Dakota, South Dakota, Idaho, Wyoming, Montana, and Washington. Public debt, $1.6 billion.

GROVER CLEVELAND (1893–1896)

The second time around. Business failures in 1893 brought financial panic and a four-year depression. Utah joined the Union. Public debt, $1.8 billion.

WILLIAM MCKINLEY (1897–1901)

The Hawaiian Islands were annexed. Spain's attempts to maintain influence in Cuba kept tensions between Spain and the United States acute. To settle the issue, America declared war against Spain in April 1898. By August 1898, the Atlantic and Pacific Spanish fleets were destroyed. In December a treaty was signed, and Cuba became independent. Puerto Rico and Guam were ceded to the United States. The Philippine Islands were sold to America for $20 million. On September 6, 1901, McKinley was shot by an unemployed millworker. A week later McKinley died. Public debt, $2.1 billion.

THEODORE ROOSEVELT (1901–1908)

A vice president under McKinley, Theodore Roosevelt succeeded to the presidency in 1901 and then in 1904 won the election to continue in service. Land needed to construct the Panama Canal was bought from Panama. Roosevelt, the Great Conservationist, created the national park system and funded irrigation projects in the West. A brief financial panic took place in 1907–1908. Public debt rose to $2.6 billion.

WILLIAM TAFT (1909–1912)

The last nation-building president. New Mexico and Arizona joined the Union and completed the formation of the contiguous 48 states. Debt went up to $2.9 billion.

WOODROW WILSON (1913–1920)

In 1913 the 16th Amendment to the Constitution, authorizing income taxes, was ratified. To mitigate his financing problems, Wilson turned to the income tax which thereafter became the nation's primary taxing vehicle. By the end of the war, marginal rates reached as high as 77 percent. The cost of World War One lifted the public debt to a height of $27.4 billion. After the war, obedient to history, debt dropped. It was down to $26.0 billion at the end of Wilson's term.

WARREN HARDING (1921–1923)

Died in August 1923 of complications following pneumonia. He founded the Bureau of Budgets, which was supposed to place restraints on government spending. Andrew Mellon, Treasury secretary under Harding and the next two presidents, was a proponent of limited government, low taxes, and economic growth. Tax rates were dropped, spending cut. Revenues held up, and the wealthy paid more at lower marginal rates than they did at higher rates. The public debt was $22.3 billion.

CALVIN COOLIDGE (1923–1928)

Vice president Calvin Coolidge succeeded Harding and later won the 1924 presidential election. Public debt fell to $17.6 billion

HERBERT HOOVER (1929–1932)

Became president when severe economic problems were imminent. The Federal Reserve Bank was wounded in 1929 by the death of its leader, Benjamin Strong. The organization failed to act when the panic hit Wall Street in October 1929, and when the recession set in, the Federal Reserve did not lower interest rates. In the meantime, actions by President Hoover dealing with tariffs and unwise tax increases turned, some say, a recession into the Great Depression.

Debt had gone as low as $16 billion in the 1920s but was returned to $19 billion by the time Hoover left Washington. *From that time until the present, no president has left office with a smaller debt than the one that greeted him, except for Harry Truman (1949–1952).*

FRANKLIN D. ROOSEVELT (1933–1940)

When Franklin D. Roosevelt (FDR) took office, pains of the Great Depression were visible on the countenance of Herbert Hoover and in the numbers of the budget. At the end of FDR's first term (1936), debt was $33.8 billion; in 1940, the end of his second term, it was $42.8 billion. Yet in 1940, with nothing but personality and a message of hope going for him, FDR ran for a third term (which was legal at the time). He beat Wendell Willkie by five million votes. Taxes and debt per capita hit an all-time high on his watch, but voters loved him. The entertainment business had Houdini; politics had FDR.

Conclusion

Franklin D. Roosevelt was the 32d president of the United States; William J. Clinton is the 42d. Prior to FDR, federal government was a minor presence in the average American's life, confining itself to defense, infrastructure, foreign policy, remote economic guidance, tax collection, and modest assistance to citizens in times of stress. Taxes were low, debt increased only when emergencies or expansion opportunities arose, and it declined thereafter.

FDR broke with the past. He planned deficits and sought an expanded role for the federal government. And his vision, perhaps appropriate for that time, emboldened liberal disciples of later years to break similarly with tradition—to ignore long-established principles of debt management. That vision (planned deficits and an expanded role for government in domestic matters) legitimized in the minds of social engineers the subsequent *unfunded* growth in federal domestic spending. Over the decades, budgets have spun out of control. Debt and interest, for wrong reasons, have skyrocketed.

Whether true to FDR's inner beliefs or to distortions of them, the fiscal legacy of his first term, especially as later interpreted by President Lyndon Baines Johnson, serves as the primal cause of the unacceptable level of national debt that faces us today.

Chapter 2

Franklin D. Roosevelt, 1941–1944

Charles J. Guiteau, an active supporter of James A. Garfield in the presidential election of 1880, traveled to Washington after the contest in search of a diplomatic post he thought he deserved. Turned away as unqualified, Guiteau sought revenge against the man upon whom he had spent his loyalty, James A. Garfield. On July 2, 1881, he shot Garfield twice. After three operations, the president died on September 19, 1881, and he was succeeded by Vice President Chester A. Arthur. By June 1882, Guiteau was tried, found guilty, and hanged.

In the same year, in Hyde Park, New York, Franklin D. Roosevelt (FDR) was born.

In another time it might have been said that the blood of kings poured through FDR's veins. He was a fourth cousin of Presidents Ulysses S. Grant and Zachary Taylor, a fifth cousin of President Theodore Roosevelt, and a seventh cousin of Prime Minister Winston Churchill, with whom he shared some of the headiest moments in the history of relationships.

Franklin D. Roosevelt's bloodline, as blue as it gets, was political from the beginning. Nicholas Roosevelt was involved in New York politics in the late 1600s. Isaac Roosevelt, a wealthy sugar refiner, served in the New York state senate; FDR's great-grandfather, James, in the state assembly.

By the time Franklin's father James arrived on the scene, the family fortune was intact, requiring only prudence to assure a high lifestyle. Father James managed his estate, served on the proper boards of directors, invested wisely, and lived well as a country squire, traveling to and fro in his private railroad car.

Father James' second wife, Sara Delano, was 26 years younger than he, and Franklin was their only son. At her death in 1941, she left $920,000 to Franklin (equivalent to $10 million in 1996 dollars). Sara ruled her son's financial well being for most of his life.

Franklin Roosevelt was brought up as the privileged child of parents who, as a measure of their snobbery, looked down on the Vanderbilts. He learned the basics from tutors and at 14 entered Groton. Governor Theodore Roosevelt (soon to be vice president) spoke at Franklin's graduation from Groton in 1900 and was president of the United States when Franklin got out of Harvard in 1904.

Franklin Roosevelt was a mediocre student. Following Harvard, he spent three years at Columbia Law School, but when he passed the bar examination in 1907, he dropped out and never graduated. With his new wife, whom he married in 1905, Roosevelt moved to New York, where he joined a law firm and disappeared from public life until his election as a state senator in 1911. His political career was on the move, over mother Sara's objections.

While serving in the New York senate, Roosevelt threw his support behind presidential candidate Woodrow Wilson, and in 1913 he was rewarded with an appointment as assistant secretary of the navy. He resigned to become the vice presidential nominee of the Democratic ticket in 1920, which was headed by James M. Cox. They were swamped almost two to one in the popular vote by the Republican pair, Warren G. Harding and Calvin Coolidge.

Defeat in 1920 moved Roosevelt temporarily out of the public spotlight. An attack of poliomyelitis that paralyzed his legs in 1921 could have made his absence permanent, but it didn't. Something in his blood, something in that "spoiled brat" background gave him the strength and gumption to persevere. In 1924 at the Democratic convention he made the speech nominating Alfred E. Smith for president. (John W. Davis got the nomination and was beaten badly by Calvin Coolidge. Smith prevailed in 1928 but was trounced by Herbert Hoover in the presidential election.)

Roosevelt returned to the practice of law in 1924, working on the fringes of the political system until his breakthrough in 1929 as governor of New York. From this mighty perch, he lambasted Hoover's regime and won his party's nomination. In the 1932 election, about a decade after he was stricken with polio, he whipped Hoover by more than seven million votes to become the 32d president of the United States.

Out went Prohibition, a wildly popular decision. Up went hope ("The only thing we have to fear is fear itself"). In went a large assembly of New Deal programs that were supposed to attack and defeat the Great Depression. And the careful watch began of the antics of Germany's new leader, Adolf Hitler, who in 1933 withdrew his nation from the League of Nations.

In 1941–1944, FDR was supported by House Speaker Sam Rayburn of Texas and Senate leader Alben Barkley of Kentucky, both Democrats. Together they faced a $42.8 billion public debt, summarized as follows:

Table 2.1
Unrecovered Cost[a] (In Billions of Dollars)

Civil War	$1.5
Pre-World War One	1.4
World War One	13.3
Great Depression	26.6
Debt, 1940	$ 42.8
Convert[b]	$479.7
Debt, 1996	$3732.9

a) The portion of total cost financed with debt.
b) Convert subject debt to 1996 dollars.

Several comments regarding this table are in order. During the Civil War (1861–1865), debt reached undreamed-of levels, peaking in 1866 at $2.8 billion. Under Grant, Hayes, Garfield/Arthur, Cleveland, Harrison, and Cleveland a second time, it dropped to $1.5 billion by 1891, the net cost of the Civil War passed on to future generations. When Woodrow Wilson took office in 1912, debt was about $2.9 billion. In the intervening two decades, (1891–1912) America continued to build the 48 states, fought the Spanish American War, built the Panama Canal, the national park system, etc., all of which caused public debt to climb by $1.4 billion. This was consistent with the principles established by earlier presidents: to finance unusual events with debt (and pay down later). Public debt increased to $16.2 billion by 1930, $2.9 billion of which had been incurred before the war. The net growth of debt ($13.3 billion) was related to World War One and was passed on to future presidents. Beginning with the crash of 1929 and ending with 1940 (the end of FDR's second term), the public debt went up to $42.8 billion. It was never again so low and the increase of $26.6 billion over the pre-depression level ($16.2 billion) represents a fair estimate of the cost of the Great Depression that was financed through debt.

Pre-World War Two debt ($42.8 billion) is a small part (12.8 percent) of current debt. Reasons for the buildup of additional public debt will be found in upcoming analyses of presidencies, from FDR to Clinton.

Change in Public Debt

During Roosevelt's third term, public debt increased from $42.8 billion to $184.8 billion, as follows:

Table 2.2
Change in Public Debt, 1940–1944 (In Billions of Dollars)

Public debt, 1940	$ 42.8
Deficits, 1941–1944	127.8
Total	$ 170.6
Adjustment[a]	14.2
Public debt, 1944	$ 184.8

a) Government figures come from a variety of sources and differ somewhat. This adjustment "forces" the above total to agree with the public debt amount that is reported by the Office of Management and Budget, Historical Tables, 7.1.

From the beginning, American presidents financed wars and great disasters with debt. It was entirely appropriate for FDR to do the same in 1941–1944.

Money poured into Washington during those years. The economy surged with wartime production for the military forces being drafted, trained, and equipped. Costs were huge, and deficits increased sharply as the war progressed—$20 billion in 1942, $55 billion in 1943, $48 billion in 1944. War was expensive, but FDR poured it on. Victory was the goal. The magnificent American economy responded, making the fourfold increase in debt tolerable.

In 1940, GDP (Gross Domestic Product) was $100 billion; public debt was 42.8 percent of that amount. In 1944, GDP was $211 billion. If America had continued its borrowing rate of 42.8 percent, debt in 1944 would have been $90.3 billion instead of the actual amount of $184.8 billion (above). One reason America was able to borrow the additional $94.5 billion was the fact that at least half of its borrowing capacity was still available at the outbreak of the war. America's reserve strength for military or economic emergencies is determined in part by the prudent management of its debt.

Perspectives

In FDR's third term, America was pulled into a war on two fronts against Germany and Japan. Its unemployed poured into defense-associated jobs as the economy raced to supply goods needed by the Allies, and by the rapidly expanding armed forces of the United States. FDR's declaration of war in December 1941 took minutes to speak but did what Hoover and FDR had failed to do over a period of 12 years—buried the Great Depression.

By the time America joined the Allied forces, the war was over two years old. Poland, Netherlands, Belgium, Luxembourg, Yugoslavia, and France were gone. The Balkans, Greece, Russia, and other countries were under attack.

England had turned to Winston Churchill for leadership as bombs rained down on London. Hitler was on the march. Japan was equally destructive in the Pacific. For the Allies, 1942 was a year best forgotten.

The worm turned in 1943. The Nazi attack on Russia fizzled, the first major setback for Hitler. The German dominance in Africa ended. Mussolini was deposed and Italy was invaded. By the end of the year, plans were in motion to invade Europe from England as a major first step in an all-out offensive. Douglas MacArthur, director of the Pacific effort, was also making a comeback. The war didn't end in 1944, but the going was all downhill in both theaters.

The Normandy invasion took place in June, paving the way for the ultimate destruction of the German war machine. MacArthur landed in the Philippines and planned an onslaught against Japan. It was a good time for America and a good time for Roosevelt. Whatever his deficiencies as a leader of the economy, he stood tall as a war chief, a proud figure dealing eye to eye with great leaders of the world.

On the home front, the Manhattan Project researching the atomic bomb, a venture that would resonate through the ages, was secretly underway in 1942; use of the bomb would eventually end the Japanese conflict. In 1943 all American citizens became part of the war effort when FDR imposed controls of prices and wages.

Also in 1943, the pill that would soon desensitize the public to tax increases olid into the picture—*the federal withholding tax, a mechanism that scooped earnings before they were ever seen.*

FDR was always the master politician, and before victory in Europe became final, he executed the GI Bill of Rights in 1944, a federal program that everybody applauded, even those who cynically noted that it was passed in an election year.

FDR's third term created a financial profile quite different from that of the prewar years.

Table 2.3
Financial Profile

	1940 (pop: 132.5 mil)[a]	**1942** (pop: 134.6 mil)	**1944** (pop: 133.9 mil)	**1996** (pop: 265.5 mil)
Federal Income and Outlay, in Billions of Dollars				
GDP[b]	$100.0	$158.5	$ 211.0	$7636.0
Taxes	6.5	14.6	43.7	1453.1
Spending	9.5	35.1	91.3	1560.5
Debt	42.8	67.8	184.8	3732.9
Interest	.9	1.1	2.2	241.1

	1940 (pop: 132.5 mil)[a]	1942 (pop: 134.6 mil)	1944 (pop: 133.9 mil)	1996 (pop: 265.5 mil)

Federal Income and Outlay—Proportional Comparisons, in Percentages

Taxes/GDP	7%	9%	21%	19%
Spending/GDP	10	22	43	20
Debt/GDP	43	43	88	49
Taxes/Debt	15	22	24	39
Interest/Taxes	14	8	5	17

Federal Income and Outlay Per Capita, in Dollars

Taxes	$49	$108	$326	$5473
Spending	72	261	682	5878
Debt	323	504	1380	14060
Interest	7	8	16	908

Average Per Capita Income, in Dollars[c]

	$849	$998	$1148	$24231

Federal Income and Outlay as Percentage of Avg. Per Capita Income

Taxes	6.0%	11.0%	28.0%	23.0%
Spending	8.0	26.0	59.0	24.0
Debt	38.0	51.0	120.0	58.0
Interest	.8	.8	1.3	3.7

Misery index, in percentages[d]

Prime interest	1.5%	1.5%	1.5%	8.3%
Unemployment	14.6	4.7	1.2	5.3
Inflation	.7	10.9	1.7	3.0

a) Population: U.S. Bureau of Census. b) GDP: 1940, 1942, 1944—Salem State College; other years—Federal Reserve Board, Chicago. c) Average income was not available for all years. Figures for missing years were estimated on a linear basis. d) Rates taken from several U.S. government sources.

America's public debt was about 43 percent of GDP when it entered World War Two. In four years, GDP doubled and the debt was almost its equal in size. Expenditures increased 10 times. Unemployment became a bad memory. The elasticity of the American economy and the adaptability of its people were a great thing to behold. Would America be able to meet a similar emergency by the last years of the century?

The federal government of 1941–1944 put military needs above everything else. The following graphic shows how priorities were switched as Americans pulled together to win the fight and bring American troops home.

Table 2.4
Spending Priorities

	1940	1942	1944	1996
Defense	17.9%	73.2%	86.6%	17.0%
Interest	9.5	3.1	2.4	15.5
Total	27.4	76.3	89.0	32.5
Government	29.5	13.4	8.9	6.1
Soc. Sec.	0.0	0.0	0.0	22.4
Medicare	0.0	0.0	0.0	11.2
Veterans	.6	.1	0.0	2.4
Welfare	42.5	10.2	2.1	25.4
Total	100.0	100.0	100.0	100.0

Note that amounts spent on *Government* and *Human Resources*, as a percent of total expenditures, become distorted in times of very high or very low *Defense*. For example, if *Defense* is doubled in a time of strife, the pool of spending expands and, as a percent of the total, all other items diminish in relative size. A serious level of cost expansion in nondefense areas can pass unnoticed in such circumstances.

America was isolationist in temperament and was unprepared for war in 1940. But by 1944, *Defense* was 86.6 percent of total spending. In 1996, when America is regarded as *the* military giant, *Defense* is 17.0 percent of spending. Have the lessons of history been absorbed? Has improved technology made *Defense* so inexpensive?

Transactions

Transactions during the period reveal the anatomy of a deficit which grew in four years to more than twice the size of all public debt accumulated during the previous years of American history.

Table 2.5
Transactions (In Billions of Dollars)

		1941–1944		Base[a]
Taxes		$91.0		$26.0
Less:				
Defense	$177.9		$ 6.8	
Interest	5.7		3.6	
Total		183.6		10.4
Net		-$92.6		$15.6
Less:				
Government	$22.8		$11.2	
Human Resources	12.4		16.4	
Total		35.2		27.6

	1941–1944	Base[a]
Surplus/Deficit	-$ 127.8	$12.0
Adjustment[b]	-14.2	
Total	-$ 142.0	
Debt, beg	-$ 42.8	
Debt, end	-$ 184.8	

a) 1940 levels times four—the inherited profile. b) See Table 2.2, note a.

Taxes

Taxes during the war tracked the extraordinary increase in military spending. In 1942, *Defense* increased fourfold; it more than doubled in 1943 and it was up by almost 20 percent in 1944. Taxes didn't pay for all of it, but the higher tax load was not insignificant.

Table 2.6
Tax Revenues (In Billions of Dollars)

	Total	Income	Corp.	SS[a]	Excise	Other[b]
1941pw	$8.7	$1.3	$2.1	$2.0	$2.5	$.8
1944w	43.7	19.7	14.8	3.4	4.8	1.0

p = mostly peace. w = mostly war.
a) Social Security. b) Estate and gift taxes, custom duties and fees, Federal Reserve earnings, sundry.

It is useful to stand back and appraise this increase in tax revenue (not adjusted for inflation) and note that it was collected not to soothe social ills, but to finance a war. The dual strategy during World War Two was to finance the conflict with a mixture of debt and taxes. Part of the problem was solved when the unemployment rate dropped from 14.6 percent in 1940 to a low of 1.2 percent in 1944. In any event, the combination of higher tax rates and full employment exploded tax receipts.

Taxes were not a large part of the life of Americans in 1941. Three years later about one-third of their earnings (28.4 percent) departed unseen, untouched, with a one-way ticket to Washington.

Table 2.7
Revenues and Spending

Year	Federal Dollars		Per Capita Dollars			Per Capita Percentages of Average Earnings	
	Taxes	Spending	Taxes	Spending	Avg. Earnings	Taxes	Spending
1941[a]	$9 bil.	$14 bil.	$ 65	$ 102	$ 923	7.0 %	11.1%
1944[a]	44 bil.	91 bil.	326	682	1148	28.4	59.4

a) deficit year

If personal freedom is partly measured by the ability to retain one's earnings, a large slice of liberty was sent to Washington in the war years. To most, the war justified the temporary transfer. Wars don't last forever, and patient Americans looked forward to better days.

One could assume that, given presidential history, war taxes would be returned to the people when war debt was paid. But the floodgates of revenue potential were wide open, never again to be closed. Postwar politicians quickly learned that good debt management was not compatible with their goals of social engineering and personal advancement. Unlike their political ancestors, they were more attracted to power than to debt reduction and tax relief.

What Did It?

With such a major increase in revenue, one might expect a balanced budget, but war costs are heavy. A large deficit was the cost of the bombs and planes that were deliberately financed with debt.

In a normal period, a 58 percent increase in *Interest* would draw attention; doubling the cost of *Government* would have been scandalous. Not so, however, in a period where *Defense* grows by 26 times and converts all other expenditures into petty-cash transactions.

In the 1941–1944 years, the public debt villain is easy to locate. *Uncovered military costs of World War Two were the sole cause of the $127.8 billion deficit.*

HUMAN RESOURCES

Some parts of domestic spending, inconspicuous at the time, became in later years expensive considerations; one example is pension payments to military and civil service workers. FDR added Social Security and unemployment insurance, programs that remain as major elements of modern budgets. These popular ideas were partly financed with payroll deductions and employers' taxes and were therefore separated from what would later be known as welfare programs.

During FDR's third term, Aid to Families with Dependent Children was the first foray of the federal government into the field of welfare, an example of Rooseveltian activism that would inspire future liberals to do the same, and more. The issue then (and now) was not the justness of the cause but the source of the aid—federal or local.

Under the huge umbrella of military spending in 1941–1944, the impact of such programs on budgets, current and future, was ignored.

Relative to the deficit, FDR's legacy is not so much programs that have endured as it is methods that he devised to insinuate government into the daily lives of Americans. Social Security, disability pensions, helping veterans and students, and soothing the pains of unemployment have over time been accepted as proper roles for Washington. But the ideas that supported such programs were later seized upon by liberals and expanded to embrace any hardship suffered by American citizens, an evolutionary result of which FDR might or might not have approved.

Roosevelt dignified the concept of a "passive" deficit as a tool to be used during recessions. He inaugurated the "silent" (withholding) tax without which social programs might have floundered. But can he be held responsible for the extrapolations of his students that have led to the debt crisis? On that question debate will never end.

Conclusion

War is expensive, as the deficit in 1941–1944 proved. The cost of the war was almost three times the size of the public debt of 1940 ($42.8 billion).

Table 2.8
Unrecovered Cost (In Billions of Dollars)

World War Two	$127.8

In the context of this book, FDR was a contributor to the deficits of his time for the best of reasons—World War Two.

FDR and the Great Depression have, as memories, become entangled in a positive way, as if he had solved the insoluble problem through the application of his alphabet agencies and unconventional methods. That was not, however, the case. FDR was not successful on the domestic front. The Great Depression was a raging economic fire until World War Two blew it out.

Relative to the modern problem of public debt, FDR's Social Security program is regarded by some as a problem, but only because the federal government has become a super welfare agency. Had its reach been limited to historical boundaries, financing Social Security would not have become a problem in anyone's eyes. Any other influence that FDR has had on current budget affairs is largely intangible.

Like Churchill, it is as a wartime leader that Roosevelt made a reputation that tends to uplift the value of his efforts in other matters. He was America's greatest cheerleader at home and abroad at a time when the nation needed such a man. If he didn't defeat the Great Depression—and he didn't— he did defeat other dragons of equal size.

FDR's groundbreaking attitudes toward the role of government establish him as the patriarch of the liberal movement. He has long been the target of conservatives who blame contemporary problems on his far-reaching influence. Like all myths that endure, there is some truth in this. But it is equally true that opportunities to diminish his influence have not always been pounced upon with vigor. His memory would not be as vivid had his critics been as active as he and his successors.

Chapter 3

Franklin D. Roosevelt/ Harry S Truman, 1945–1948

In 1944, Franklin D. Roosevelt was reelected to a fourth term, a circumstance that led to a constitutional amendment prohibiting more than two consecutive terms. He was a sick man, a shadow of the exuberant personality that had charmed the American public for so many years. His intimates, perhaps he himself, knew his days were numbered when on January 20, 1945, he took the now familiar oath of office. "We have learned to be citizens of the world," he said in his inaugural address, referring to lessons learned in World War Two, and "The only way to have a friend is to be one," a simple comment that laid the foundation of the Marshall Plan, the brilliant idea that under Harry Truman made possible the recovery of war-ravaged Europe.

FDR cast a large shadow and attained an international reputation that few before or after him have enjoyed. He was the only president most American soldiers had ever known. He died in April 1945. Vice President Harry Truman succeeded him.

Sam Rayburn, a Democrat from Texas, was the House Speaker; Joseph Martin, a Republican from Massachusetts, replaced him in 1947–1948. Alben Barkley, a Democrat from Kentucky, was majority leader in the Senate, and Wallace White, a Republican from Minnesota, held the position in 1947–1948.

Public debt was $184.8 billion at the beginning of FDR's last term, as follows:

Table 3.1
Summary of Deficits/Debt, 1941–1944 (In Billions of Dollars)

Years (FDR)	Total	Defense	Interest	Govt.	Human Resources
Before 1941	$ 42.8	$ 42.8[a]	$ 0.0	$ 0.0	$ 0.0
1941–44	127.8	127.8	0.0	0.0	0.0
Deficits	$ 170.6	$ 170.6	$ 0.0	$ 0.0	$ 0.0
Adjust[b]	14.2				

Table 3.1 *(continued)*
Summary of Deficits/Debt, 1941–1944 (In Billions of Dollars)

	Total	Defense	Interest	Govt.	Human Resources
Debt	$ 184.8				
Convert^c	$ 1647.4				
Debt 1996	$ 3732.9				
Debt 1944					
% of 1996	44.1%				

a) Includes cost of Great Depression (see p. 19). b) Government figures come from a variety of sources and differ somewhat. This adjustment "forces" the above total to agree with the public debt amount reported by the Office of Management and Budget, Historical Tables, 7.1. c) Convert subject debt to 1996 dollars.

In 1944 it was accurate to explain America's debt in terms of external events. Soon, however, internal attitudes would show themselves to be a force even more to be feared as a source of debt. And another actor appeared on the budget stage for the first time in 1946. The president's Council of Economic Advisers was formed, many of them being followers of John Maynard Keynes, a British economist of renown.

Generally speaking, Keynes held that deficits and debt were not major concerns, that the job of government was to intervene when the economy overheated or cooled and to fine-tune the powerful machine in such a way that major hills and valleys were avoided. This point of view was the opposite of that preached by Adam Smith, the guru whose ideas had guided earlier presidents.

Given the fascination that politicians have for spending and the loose controls over it that had existed, it was troubling to see an economic philosophy appear that gave intellectual support to the greatest weakness of politicians. It was frightening also to consider that the advice to future presidents would inspire similar behavior and invite even more economic engineering in the private sector.

Change in Public Debt

Following presidential precedent, FDR and Truman financed the final costs of World War Two with debt until in 1946 public debt reached $241.9 billion. *Thereafter, and again following presidential precedent, Truman reduced public debt for two straight years.* Over the four-year period, however, deficits were more powerful than surpluses, and higher debt was bequeathed to the next president, as follows:

Table 3.2
Change in Public Debt, 1944–1948
(In Billions of Dollars)

Public debt, 1944	$ 184.8
Deficits, 1945–1948	47.6
Total	$ 232.4
Adjustment[a]	16.1
Public debt, 1948	$ 216.3

a) See Table 3.1, note b.

Working with a Republican Congress in 1947–48, Truman reduced debt $19 billion, the first time it had dropped since 1930 under Herbert Hoover. That was a positive sign as the 1945–1948 administration drew to a close.

Perspectives

War in Europe was in its mop-up stage. General Douglas MacArthur, like an inspired running back, whirled and weaved his way through the Pacific strongholds to the heart of his enemy—Tokyo. Events moved swiftly. FDR died in April and in the same month, Hitler committed suicide. In May, Germany surrendered; Japan did the same in September. War ended and reconstruction began.

In 1946, both wars moved to the bins of history as signs of "getting on with it" appeared all over the globe. The United Nations General Assembly had its first meeting in London. The Nuremberg war trials began and ended. In 1947 the Marshall Plan, an American idea to get Europe back on its feet, came into being.

Relations with Russia, tenuous throughout the war, fell apart after it when the Soviets blocked the flow of supplies to Berlin. America responded with an airlift program that lasted for almost a year.

Defense spending peaked in 1945 ($83 billion); two years later it was 85 percent lower. Price and wage controls were dropped. Pent-up demand and other factors gave President Truman an inflation problem. These and other events of significance once again substantially changed the financial profile of the United States.

Table 3.3
Financial Profile

	1940 (pop: 132.5 mil)[a]	1944 (pop: 133.9 mil)	1948 (pop: 146.7 mil)	1996 (pop: 265.5 mil)
Federal Income andOutlay, in Billions of Dollars				
GDP[b]	$ 100.0	$ 211.0	$ 275.8	$7636.0
Taxes	6.5	43.7	41.6	1453.1
Spending	9.5	91.3	29.8	1560.5
Debt	42.8	184.8	216.3	3732.9
Interest	.9	2.2	4.3	241.1
Federal Income and Outlay—Proportional Comparisons, in Percentages				
Taxes/GDP	7%	21%	15%	19%
Spending/GDP	10	43	11	20
Debt/GDP	51	88	78	49
Taxes/Debt	15	24	19	39
Interest/Taxes	14	5	10	17
Federal Income and Outlay Per Capita, in Dollars				
Taxes	$ 49	$ 326	$ 284	$ 5473
Spending	72	682	203	5878
Debt	323	1380	1474	14060
Interest	7	16	29	908
Average Per Capita Income, in Dollars[c]				
	$ 849	$ 1148	$ 1388	$ 24231
Federal Income and Outlay as Percentage of Avg. Per Capita Income				
Taxes	6.0%	28.0%	20.0%	23.0%
Spending	8.0	59.0	15.0	24.0
Debt	38	120.0	106.0	58.0
Interest	.8	1.3	2.1	3.7
Misery Index, in Percentages[d]				
Prime interest	1.5%	1.5%	1.8%	8.3%
Unemployment	14.6	1.2	3.8	5.3
Inflation	.7	1.7	8.1	3.0

a) Population: U.S. Bureau of Census. b) GDP: 1940, 1942, 1944—Salem State College; other years—Federal Reserve Board, Chicago. c) Average income was not available for all years. Figures for missing years were estimated on a linear basis. d) Rates taken from several U.S. government sources.

The 30.7 percent growth of GDP from 1944 to 1948 was an illusion. Inflation during the four-year period was 35.3 percent, more than enough to erase any real growth. It was a cooling-down period for the economy as American wartime production muscle turned toward butter and away from guns.

A livable rate of unemployment at the end of the war cycle was heartening to those who wondered if America could be healthy in peacetime. And the relationship of revenue to expenditures in 1948 gave hope that public debt, still over 75 percent of GDP, could be reduced to more acceptable levels that *would allow future presidents flexible spending options when confronted by another economic or physical war.*

As wartime spending decreased and controls were lifted, unemployment and inflation rose. By 1950 the inflation scare was over, but an unemployment rate thereafter of less than 4 percent became a rarity.

The increase in average income per capita (from $1,148 to $1,388) of 21 percent was less than the rate of inflation during the period. But taxes per capita dropped; it was a time of mixed blessings for taxpayers.

America's spending priorities changed during the war and changed again as the country wrenched itself back into a peacetime posture, never again to be what it had been and resembling little what it was to become.

Table 3.4
Spending Priorities[a]

	1940	1944	1948	1996
Defense	17.9%	86.6%	30.5%	17.0%
Interest	9.5	2.4	14.4	15.5
Total	27.4	89.0	44.9	32.5
Government	29.5	8.9	21.9	6.1
Soc. Sec.	0.0	0.0	1.9	22.4
Medicare	0.0	0.0	0.0	11.2
Veterans	.6	0.0	21.8	2.4
Welfare	42.5	2.1	9.5	25.4
Total	100.0%	100.0%	100.0%	100.0%

a) See the discussion following Table 2.4.

Priorities at the conclusion of the FDR/Truman era were remarkably different as the United States reassessed its new role at home (a more intrusive government) and abroad (a world leader). The change in all cost centers was dramatic. *Defense* was lower for obvious reasons. Higher *Interest* was no surprise, given more debt and rising inflation.

Changes in the relative size of *Government* and *Human Resources* are confused at this stage in the analysis because of the altered expenditure mix. More data, provided below, clarify these issues.

Transactions

When the war ended in 1945, it became the lot of Harry Truman to assist our allies in their rehabilitation attempts while, at the same time, he guided

America from a wartime to a peacetime economy. Reducing the military, dealing with the returning veterans, loosening wartime controls all fed into the spending plans of the federal government. The needs and challenges of the time were as radically different from the previous four years as were the postwar political leaders who handled them. Transactions for the period demonstrate the new world in which Harry Truman operated.

Table 3.5
Transactions (In Billions of Dollars)

		1945–1948		1941–1944
Taxes		$ 164.6		$ 91.0
Less:				
Defense	$ 147.6		$ 177.9	
Interest	15.7		5.7	
Total		163.3		183.6
Net		$ 1.3		-$ 92.6
Less:				
Government	$ 21.7		$ 22.8	
Hum. Resources	27.1		12.4	
Total		48.8		35.2
Net		-$ 47.6		-$ 127.8
Debt, beg		184.8		- 42.8
Total		- 232.4		-$ 170.6
Adjustment[a]		16.1		- 14.2
Debt, end		-$ 216.3		-$ 184.8

a) See Table 3.1, note b.

Taxes

The 1941–1944 period featured four years of accelerating income, with the final year being fivefold larger than the first. Revenue increased again in 1945, dropped by about 13 percent in 1946, and remained relatively stable for the next two years. The net effect was an increase in revenue in 1945–1948 of 80.9 percent over 1941–1944 .

During the war, debt increased four times. After the war, tax rates of lower income groups were reduced as the government edged to a peacetime basis, seeking equilibrium between taxes and costs, as those costs would be redefined in a postwar world.

Military spending decreased from $83 billion in 1945 to $9 billion in 1948, but for the entire period, it was still a major cost. By 1948, total outgo was less than federal revenue. The near-term possibility of debt reduction and tax reduction looked good.

The following table demonstrates the movement toward revenue stabilization that was underway in 1945–1948.

Table 3.6
Tax Revenues
(In Billions of Dollars)

	Total	Income	Corp.	SS[a]	Excise	Other[b]
1941pw	$ 8.7	$ 1.3	$ 2.1	$ 2.0	$ 2.5	$ .8
1944w	43.7	19.7	14.8	3.4	4.8	1.0
1948p	41.6	19.3	9.7	3.8	7.4	1.4

p = mostly peace. w = mostly war.
a) Social Security. b) Estate and gift taxes, custom duties and fees, Federal Reserve earnings, sundry.

In this table, the reduction in taxes appears modest because of the inflation rate (35.3 percent). Actually, the tax load per capita was significantly reduced (see below).

Taxes are paid by people. Even corporate taxes (which demagogues sell as a tax on the "rich") find their way into the cost stream and reappear to taxpayers in the form of higher prices or lower wage levels.

In 1948, taxpayers got a break. The part of a week's pay sent to Washington went down.

Table 3.7
Revenues and Spending

Year	Federal Dollars		Per Capita Dollars			Per Capita Percentages of Average Earnings	
	Taxes	Spending	Taxes	Spending	Avg. Earnings	Taxes	Spending
1941[a]	$ 9 bil.	$ 14 bil.	$ 65	$ 102	$ 923	7.0%	11.1%
1944[a]	44 bil.	91 bil.	326	682	1148	28.4	59.4
1948	42 bil.	30 bil.	284	203	1388	20.5	14.6

a) deficit year

What Did It?

The deficit in 1945–1948 was $47.6 billion. Why? From whence? Which cost centers were not financed by the 80.9 percent increase in revenue?

INTEREST

In 1945–1948, *Interest* was 72 percent as expensive as the entire cost of *Government,* 58 percent as expensive as the entire cost of *Human Resources.* It had increased by 175.4 percent over the previous four years. *Had its increase* *been limited to 80.9 percent, the cost would have been $10.3 billion, or $5.4 billion less than actual. To that extent, Interest contributed to the increase in public debt.*

Sensitive politicians should have learned a valuable lesson as a result of their experience with *Interest* during the war: A cost that is normally of minor concern *(Interest)* can become, unobservedly, a major budget item during a period of exploding federal expenditures.

GOVERNMENT

Compared with the previous four years, *Government* cost 5 percent less in 1945–1948. The drop would have been more substantial had it not been for the cost of rebuilding Europe, a venture in which America participated via the Marshall Plan (1947). Except for the line item of International Affairs, the cost reductions in the cost center were appropriate.

Since the cost of *Government* dropped in 1945–1948, it was in no way responsible for the deficit.

HUMAN RESOURCES

The cost of *Human Resources* increased by 118.5 percent, well above the rate of revenue increase (80.9 percent). A review of this cost center appears below:

Table 3.8
Human Resources
(In Billions of Dollars)

	1945–48	1941–44	% Change
Education, Training, Services, Employment	$ .4	$ 3.3	- 87.9%
Health	.8	.4	100.0
Income Security	8.9	6.8	30.9
Subtotal	$ 10.1	$ 10.5	- 3.8
Social Security[a]	$ 1.6	$ .6	166.7
Medicare[a]	0.0	0.0	0.0
Veterans	15.4	1.3	1084.6
Subtotal	$ 17.0	$ 1.9	794.7
Grand total	$ 27.1	$ 12.4	118.5%

a) Funded by employers and employees.

The GI Bill was utilized by returning veterans, causing a bloating of the Veterans line item, a temporary phenomenon. The other increases were not surprising, except for Social Security, and it was too early in that program's life to get excited about percentage increases.

Had the growth of Human Resources *been limited to the growth in income (80.9 percent), the cost would have been $22.3 billion, or $4.8 billion less than actual. To that extent this cost center was responsible for the four-year deficit.*

DEFENSE

The war ended in 1945, but one does not disassemble the strongest military machine in the world overnight. *Defense* cost $83 billion in 1945 (the most expensive war year) and dropped to $43 billion in 1946 before it finally plummeted to $9 billion in 1948. The decrease was natural but, given the unsettled condition of the world, probably too severe, leaving America where it was before the war—a military force with two guns and seven horses.

Defense dropped 17 percent below the spending of the previous four years, while revenues went up by 80.9 percent. Under general methods employed in this book, it would appear that this cost center was fully financed. But these were not ordinary times.

During the war, no attempt was made to support the conflict by taxes alone—increased public debt was a major partner in the financing project. In the postwar period, however, taxes were supposed to pay the bill. They didn't. And the reason is that final *Defense* costs continued to need debt support, especially for the years 1945 and 1946. The amount assigned to *Defense* was calculated as follows:

Table 3.9
Deficit—Defense Portion
(In Billions of Dollars)

Deficit, 1945–1948	$ 47.6
Assigned to:	
Interest	$ 5.4
Government	0.0
Human Resources	4.8
Total	$ 10.2
Assigned to Defense	$ 37.4

If the allocations to *Interest* and *Human Resources* are reasonable, the *Defense* allocation must be accepted.

Conclusion

FDR lived for four months into his fourth term, time enough to leave behind a "thank-you" to war veterans that in one form or another is with us today: the GI Bill of Rights, legislation that voiced the approval of American citizens to their fighters in the form of housing, education, employment, and health assistance. Such items made their first significant appearance in Truman's 1948 budget .

FDR/Truman passed along to the next administration new public debt of $47.6 billion, as follows:

Table 3.10
Unrecovered Cost
(In Billions of Dollars)

World War Two	$ 37.4
Interest	5.4
Government	0.0
Human Resources	4.8
Total	$ 47.6

And so ended the World War Two era and with it the passing of its leading players—FDR, Hitler, Mussolini, dead in 1945; Churchill, replaced in 1945; Tojo, dead in 1946. Of the great war leaders, only Stalin remained.

The huge presence of FDR was gone as the histrionic man with the grandiose ideas of an activist government moved to the pages of history. He had dominated the American stage for 13 years and he left behind a political philosophy which through his apostles shaped the expansion of the size and the duties of federal government until the 1980s. For so long as stories are told about the Great Depression or World War Two and for so long as Social Security checks are issued each month, the memory of FDR will be kept alive.

Harry Truman replaced FDR and surprised everybody with the courage and ability he showed during the closing year of the war. He hoped to capitalize on his new image by winning the next presidential race on his own. His opponent was Thomas Dewey of New York. Truman was a huge underdog, but he beat Dewey by more than two million votes.

Chapter 4

Harry S Truman, 1949–1952

Chester Arthur was president in 1884 when Harry S Truman was born in Lamar, Missouri, at the family home. His father, John (1851–1914), was a farmer. After his marriage to Martha Ellen Young (1852–1947), John Truman left the family farm in Jackson County, Missouri, and established his own place in Lamar with his bride. The parents survived lean days and provided a secure home life for their three children, the oldest of whom was Harry S. The "S" in his name was not the first letter of his middle name, as is the normal custom. The single letter was his full middle name.

John Truman, given to speculating on commodities, took a financial bath in 1901. After working at odd jobs, he established a second farm in 1904, but that didn't work out, and in 1906 he moved himself and his family into his mother-in-law's farm near Grandview, Missouri.

Truman went to grade school and high school in Independence, Missouri, where he was known as a hardworking student. He was considering college and a possible career as a musician (he was an accomplished pianist) after leaving high school in 1901. But his father's financial troubles put an end to those dreams. He went to work as a timekeeper. Theodore Roosevelt was president at the time, and the public debt was $2.1 billion.

For the next five years, Truman held nondescript jobs in Kansas City until family troubles pulled him in a different direction in 1906. His father couldn't run the Grandview farm alone, so Truman returned home. While working the land in 1914, John Truman injured himself, and he died soon after, never suspecting that his 30-year-old son would one day become the 33d president of the United States. Martha Truman lived long enough, however, to see her son succeed Franklin Roosevelt. Harry Truman had one prestigious relative: John Tyler was his great-uncle.

After his father's death in 1914, the management of the farm became Truman's problem. There he remained until World War One beckoned, and in 1917 he joined the army, but not before demonstrating that he was his father's son. In 1915 and 1916 he absorbed sizable losses from speculative ventures involving lead, zinc, and oil. Truman was 33 years old in 1917. Woodrow Wilson was president, and the public debt was $5.7 billion.

Truman served with the Missouri National Guard in 1905–1911, and when he joined the army in 1917, it was with the rank of lieutenant. He had an honorable military career and ended the war as commander of an artillery unit. He was discharged as a major in 1919 and returned home to establish a haberdashery in Kansas City. He was 35 years old. Wilson was still president. Reflecting the costs of war, public debt had risen to $27.4 billion, the highest in American history—about five times the 1917 level.

Marriage to his childhood sweetheart was the main event in 1919 for Truman. Elizabeth Virginia Wallace (1885–1982), a product of finishing schools, never fully approved of Truman's later political career, not even when he won the presidency. He probably spent more nights alone in the White House than any married president in history.

When the haberdashery business failed in 1922, Truman's political career began. His road to success was slow but consistent. In 1922 he was elected as a county judge. This put him in the political loop controlled by Thomas Pendergast, a controversial political operator who was to become an influential backer of Truman's career. To equip himself for his new work, Truman attended Kansas City Law School (1923–1925). He continued to grow in influence in local politics until in 1934 he ran against and defeated incumbent Senator Roscoe Patterson. Truman was 50 years old. Franklin Roosevelt was president. The public debt was $27.1 billion, about the same as it was when Truman had left the army in 1919.

In 1944, after a decade of solid service in the United States Senate that had made him a national figure, Truman reluctantly agreed to share the Democratic ticket with FDR in the Great Man's successful campaign for a fourth term.

In April 1945, Roosevelt died and was replaced by Truman, who served as a valiant and capable leader. In 1948, Truman ran under his own banner, and contrary to predictions of the pundits, he defeated the heavy favorite, Thomas Dewey, by two million votes. He retired in 1952 to Independence, Missouri, and died in 1972 after several years of illness.

During Truman's administration, Sam Rayburn of Texas ran the House; Scott Lucas of Illinois and Ernest McFarland of Arizona led the Senate, Democrats all. Public debt was $216.3 billion in 1948, summarized as follows:

Table 4.1
Summary of Deficits/Debt, 1941–1948 (In Billions of Dollars)

Years	Total	Defense	Interest	Govt.	Human Resources
Before 1941	$ 42.8	$ 42.8[a]	$ 0.0	$ 0.0	$ 0.0
1941–44 (FDR)	127.8	127.8	0.0	0.0	0.0
1945–48 (FDR/HST)	47.6	37.4	5.4	0.0	4.8

Table 4.1 *(continued)*
Summary of Deficits/Debt, 1941–1948 (In Billions of Dollars)

Years		Total	Defense	Interest	Govt.	Human Resources
	Deficits	$ 218.2	$208.0	$ 5.4	$ 0.0	$ 4.8
	Adjust[b]	- 1.9				
	Debt	$ 216.3				
	Convert[c]	$ 1408.2				
	Debt 1996	$ 3732.9				
	Debt 1948					
	% of 1996	37.7%				

a) Includes cost of Great Depression (see p. 19). b) Government figures come from a variety of sources and differ somewhat. This adjustment "forces" the above total to agree with the public debt amount reported by the Office of Management and Budget, Historical Tables, 7.1. c) Convert subject debt to 1996 dollars.

Truman avoided budget deficits despite the advice from Keynesians that surrounded him. He was from the old school, the Adam Smith school that paid its bills. His pay-as-you-go policies were continued in a Congress led by Democrats, as they were begun in 1947–1948 with Republicans. *In the 1940s and early 1950s, both sides were still inclined to reduce debt.*

In 1950, fate intervened in the form of the Korean War (1950–1953), a conflict that again put America on a wartime footing and thwarted whatever plans Truman had to reduce debt. He and the Congress supported both the war and their other programs with current tax revenues, and to that extent they deserve credit. But did the war-conscious public realize that domestic spending was burgeoning during the war? Would Americans have tolerated the high taxes needed to fund social programs absent the camouflage of a war?

Change in Public Debt

Measured against post-Eisenhower presidencies, Truman's budget performance in 1949–1952 was outstanding. But measured against pre-Roosevelt presidents, when the political ethic that governed taxing and spending behavior was rooted in the past, there was nothing remarkable about it. Reducing debt in peacetime was normal. Deficit spending was discouraged. *Democrats and Republicans alike supported such policies.*

The only four-year budget surplus in this 1941–1996 survey took place in 1949–1952 under Truman.

Table 4.2
Change in Public Debt, 1948–1952
(In Billions of Dollars)

Public debt, 1948	-$ 216.3
Surplus, 1949–1952	2.0

Table 4.2 *(continued)*
Change in Public Debt, 1948–1952
(In Billions of Dollars)

Net	-$ 214.3
Adjustment[a]	- .5
Public debt, 1952	-$ 214.8

a) See Table 4.1, note b.

No president acts alone. What he does greatly depends upon those with whom he must deal in Congress. Those who appraise the results of a president's administration must give weight to the influence of congressional leaders as well.

Table 4.3
Profile of Power, 1949–1952

Cong.	House	Senate	President
81	Rayburn (D)	Lucas (D)	Truman (D)
82	Rayburn (D)	McFarland (D)	Truman (D)

Democrats enjoyed full control of the government under Truman, but he did not get full support for Fair Deal programs. For example, his proposal for national health insurance failed. Congress in those days had within it strong conservative impulses emanating from men whose memories reached back to a time when fiscal integrity was deemed a virtue.

Perspectives

Truman began his administration in peace and left it in war. In his second year, tensions in Korea exploded. *Defense,* down to $9.1 billion in 1948, increased fivefold during the Korean War to $46.1 billion in 1952.

Russia was dangerous enough to the Allies in 1949 that they (the Allies) decided to establish the North Atlantic Treaty Organization (NATO), a formidable defensive tool accepted by 12 nations. This seemed eminently justified when, despite the attempts of America to contain atomic weapons, Russia demonstrated its own atomic capabilities in late 1949, thus electing itself to the exclusive atomic club. Truman replied in 1950 with a program designed to build the hydrogen bomb. In the same year, North Korean Communists invaded South Korea. America, with United Nations assistance, responded. Its financial profile changed again.

Table 4.4
Financial Profile

	1940	**1948**	**1952**	**1996**
	(pop: 132.5 mil)[a]	(pop: 146.7 mil)	(pop: 157.6 mil)	(pop: 265.5 mil)

Federal Income and Outlay, in Billions of Dollars

	1940	1948	1952	1996
GDP[b]	$ 100.0	$ 275.8	$ 371.4	$7636.0
Taxes	6.5	41.6	66.2	1453.1
Spending	9.5	29.8	67.7	1560.5
Debt	42.8	216.3	214.8	3732.9
Interest	.9	4.3	4.7	241.1

Federal Income and Outlay—Proportional Comparisons, in Percentages

	1940	1948	1952	1996
Taxes/GDP	7%	15%	18%	19%
Spending/GDP	10	11	18	20
Debt/GDP	51	78	58	49
Taxes/Debt	15	19	31	39
Interest/Taxes	14	10	7	17

Federal Income and Outlay Per Capita, in Dollars

	1940	1948	1952	1996
Taxes	$ 49	$ 284	$ 420	$ 5473
Spending	72	203	430	5878
Debt	323	1474	1363	14060
Interest	7	29	30	908

Average Per Capita Income, in Dollars[c]

	1940	1948	1952	1996
	$ 849	$ 1388	$ 1653	$ 24231

Federal Income and Outlay as Percentage of Avg. Per Capita Income

	1940	1948	1952	1996
Taxes	6.0%	20.0%	25.0%	23.0%
Spending	8.0	15.0	26.0	24.0
Debt	38.0	106.0	82.0	58.0
Interest	.8	2.1	1.8	3.7

Misery index, in percentages[d]

	1940	1948	1952	1996
Prime interest	1.5%	1.8%	3.0%	8.3%
Unemployment	14.6	3.8	3.0	5.3
Inflation	.7	8.1	2.0	3.0

a) Population: U.S. Bureau of Census. b) GDP: 1940, 1942, 1944—Salem State College; other years—Federal Reserve Board, Chicago. c) Average income was not available for all years. Figures for missing years were estimated on a linear basis. d) Rates taken from several U.S. government sources.

After a slow start in 1949 (10 months), the business cycle was kind to Truman. He had 38 months of steady growth in GDP to support his need for tax revenues, especially in 1951 and 1952 (Korean War, 1950–1953).

America's economy, on a quasi-wartime footing, grew by 34 percent in 1949–1952, which was about 23 percent after inflation, which was almost 6 percent per year. This represented a healthy before-tax climate for the American taxpayers.

In 1951, as Korea heated up, revenues rose 31 percent; in 1952 they rose 28 percent. Obviously, Truman and Congress decided debt was high enough. But were the taxes used for war or for programs? Were the American people informed? Was the possibility of shrinking government considered as an alternative to higher taxes?

Working with a Democrat majority in 1949–1952, Truman reduced the size of public debt in relation to GDP from 78 percent to 58 percent. Breaking with tradition, the leadership financed a war with current revenues instead of debt, by their actions recognizing that some level of debt was too high. It is important to remember that this was the mental cast of the politicians of that age.

The Truman years contain a second lesson of importance. In 1949–1952, federal revenue exceeded expenditures. In a day when some claim that balanced budgets are dangerous, it is useful to review the Truman years when the president and his congress balanced the books, paid the bills, and watched the GDP grow at an average rate of 5.6 percent.

The "misery" index in 1948 was 13.7 percent; in 1952 it was 8.0 percent— a major improvement. Unemployment and inflation were down, but the cost of money was continuing on its upward path.

Average income per capita grew by 19 percent, which was about 4.8 percent per year. Inflation took about 2 percent away, increased taxes, about 3 percent (from 20 percent to 23 percent of average income). Without considering increased costs of getting to work (more travel, more away-from-home lunches) and taxes imposed by local governments, it is obvious that taxpayers struggled in 1949–1952.

From war to peace, peace to war. So the international pendulum swung, dragging with it tensions and costs. Also, there were changes in domestic programs which, from a fiscal point of view, had their own brand of explosives, unseen behind the mask of big-bang military expenditures. Priorities, always in flux, shifted again in 1949–1952.

Table 4.5
Spending Priorities [a]

	1940	1948	1952	1996
Defense	17.9%	30.5%	68.1%	17.0%
Interest	9.5	14.4	6.9	15.5
Total	27.4	44.9	75.0	32.5
Government	29.5	21.9	7.6	6.1
Soc. Sec.	0.0	1.9	3.1	22.4

Table 4.5 *(continued)*
Spending Priorities[a]

	1940	1948	1952	1996
Medicare	0.0	0.0	0.0	11.2
Veterans	.6	21.8	7.8	2.4
Welfare	42.5	3.6	6.5	25.4
Total	100.0%	100.0%	100.0%	100.0%

a) See the discussion following Table 2.4.

The shift to a wartime budget because of the Korean conflict is obvious from the above. The relative "savings" in other cost centers is illusory for reasons explained following Table 2.4. After reviewing additional data below, the significance of the "savings" in the fiscal portrait will be clarified.

Transactions

Under remarkably different circumstances, Truman managed an overall budget surplus in 1949–1952—a deficit in the first two years (low *Defense)* of $2.5 billion and a surplus over the final two years (high *Defense*) of $4.5 billion. Federal transactions for the period are summarized below.

Table 4.6
Transactions (In Billions of Dollars)

		1949–1952		1945–1948
Taxes		$ 196.6		$ 164.6
Less:				
Defense	$ 96.6		$ 147.6	
Interest	18.7		15.7	
Total		115.3		163.3
Net		$ 81.3		$ 1.3
Government	$ 31.6		$ 21.7	
Hum. Resources	47.7		27.1	
Total		79.3		48.8
Net		$ 2.0		-$ 47.6
Debt, beg		- 216.3		184.8
Total		-$ 214.3		$ 232.4
Adjustment[a]		- .5		16.1
Debt, end		-$ 214.8		-$ 216.3

a) See Table 4.1, note b.

Taxes

Total revenue in 1949–1952 grew 19.4 percent over the total of the previous four years. The inflation rate of 12.2 percent brought the real increase in revenue down to 7.2 percent. Given the Korean War, the increase would seem too modest for the higher needs of the era until one recalls that the high tax base of World War Two had not decreased to a peacetime basis, nor had debt been lowered. From a fiscal point of view, the impact of the Korean War was to stop in its tracks the beginnings of debt reduction that might have led to tax reduction. Instead, the unadjusted tax base was used to fund current needs.

"Might have" is the qualifying phrase used above in connection with tax reduction. With Truman as president, it is a required qualifier because he was more devoted to spreading New Deal and Fair Deal programs than in returning taxes to citizens. For example, he vetoed a tax reduction bill in 1947 and did so again in 1948, but Congress overrode his veto. In his State of the Union message in 1949, Truman pushed Fair Deal and New Deal programs. In 1950 he signed a bill for a tax increase.

The president with the "average guy" image was no great friend to taxpayers. He chose to help them through federal redistribution schemes, not by increasing their liberty to use their own money as they saw fit. In any event, the hope for near-term tax relief was dashed with the advent of the Korean War.

Revenue collections are reviewed below:

Table 4.7
Tax Revenues
(In Billions of Dollars)

	Total	Income	Corp.	SS[a]	Excise	Other[b]
1941pw	$ 8.7	$ 1.3	$ 2.1	$ 2.0	$ 2.5	$ .8
1944w	43.7	19.7	14.8	3.4	4.8	1.0
1948p	41.6	19.3	9.7	3.8	7.4	1.4
1952w	66.2	27.9	21.2	6.5	8.9	1.7

p = mostly peace. w = mostly war.

a) Social Security. b) Estate and gift taxes, custom duties and fees, Federal Reserve earnings, sundry.

As a percent of average earnings, taxes went up under Truman, an obvious possible cause being the Korean War. During World War Two, the nation shifted into war mode and trimmed nonmilitary expenses. Did Truman do the same? The answer to that question will unfold as analysis continues.

Table 4.8
Revenues and Spending

Year	Federal Dollars		Per Capita Dollars			Per Capita Percentages of Average Earnings	
	Taxes	Spending	Taxes	Spending	Avg. Earnings	Taxes	Spending
1941[a]	$ 9 bil.	$ 14 bil.	$ 65	$ 102	$ 923	7.0%	11.1%
1944[a]	44 bil.	91 bil.	326	682	1148	28.4	59.4
1948	42 bil.	30 bil.	284	203	1388	20.5	14.6
1952[a]	66 bil.	68 bil.	420	430	1653	25.4	26.0

a) deficit year

As a percent of per capita earnings, taxes *allegedly* needed to support the Korean War were almost as punishing as in World War Two. *That is not reasonable.* Washington was pouring money into something other than guns during a period when, according to precedent, domestic spending should have dropped. Further analysis will identify unusual spending.

What Did It?

The purpose of these essays is to locate unrecovered costs passed from one administration to another. In 1949–1952, there was no budget deficit— no unrecovered cost. Does that excuse cost centers from further analysis? No. A financed activity is not necessarily a prudent one. Credit is due when an undertaking is paid for, but the activity itself always deserves scrutiny.

DEFENSE

Revenue in 1949–1952 was 19.4 percent higher than it was in the previous four years. On the other hand, *Defense* was 34.6 percent less. It follows that the revenue increases of 1951 and 1952 were not poured into *Defense*. The Korean War was not responsible for higher taxes.

INTEREST

The increase in *Interest* (19.1 percent) was about the same as the increase in revenue. It was fully funded.

GOVERNMENT/HUMAN RESOURCES

Government/Human Resources increased by 62.5 percent over the preceding four-year period, as opposed to a 19.4 percent increase in revenue. It follows that, *behind the mask of war*, revenues were used to expand the size of government.

GOVERNMENT

Government grew by 45.6 percent in 1949–1952, faster than any realistic forecast of revenue growth. When a major cost center of a home, a business, or a government swells in such an aggressive manner, it needs attention. What caused it? Will it continue?

Table 4.9
Government Operations, Net
(In Billions of Dollars)

	1949–52	1945–48	% Change
Energy	$ 1.5	$ .4	275.0%
Nat'l Resources/			
Environment	4.9	2.4	104.2
Commerce	4.3	- 5.1	
Transportation	4.0	7.6	- 47.4
Community development	.1	.8	- 87.5
International	17.1	14.2	20.4
Science	.2	.2	0.0
Agriculture	3.8	3.1	22.6
Justice	.8	.7	14.3
General	4.2	3.5	20.0
Total	$ 40.9	$ 27.8	47.1
Misc. Income	- 9.3	- 6.1	52.5
Net	$ 31.6	$ 21.7	45.6%

The major cause of an increase in *Government* was a budget curiosity caused by the volatility of the line item of Commerce, which is related to its high risk operations in mortgages. Over time, these aberrations tend to even out, but in a given period, they can be a distorting factor, as they were in 1949–1952.

Had the increase in *Government* been restricted to the rate of revenue growth (19.4 percent), cost would have been $25.9 billion, $5.7 billion less than actual.

HUMAN RESOURCES

The cost of *Human Resources* exploded in 1949–1952 with a growth of 76.0 percent, an unsustainable 18.8 percent per year.

Table 4.10
Human Resources
(In Billions of Dollars)

	1949–52	1945–48	% Change
Education, Training,			
Services, Employment	$ 1.0	$ .4	150.0%

Table 4.10 *(continued)*
Human Resources
(In Billions of Dollars)

	1949–52	1945–48	% Change
Health	$ 1.1	$ .8	37.5%
Income Security	14.4	8.9	63.6
Subtotal	$ 10.1	$ 10.1	65.0
Social Security[a]	$ 5.1	$ 1.6	218.8
Medicare[a]	0.0	0.0	0.0
Veterans	26.1	15.4	68.4
Subtotal	$ 31.2	$ 17.0	82.5
Grand total	$ 47.7	$ 27.1	76.0%

a) Funded by employers and employees.

The utilization of benefits by veterans of World War Two peaked in 1950 at $8.8 billion. Thereafter, although always expensive, this line item would not again show such sharp growth (over 68 percent).

Other line item increases had, however, the smell of permanence about them. In 1945–1948, *Human Resources* was 9.8 percent of GDP; in 1949–1952 it was 13.6 percent. The trend had begun. There was no deficit associated with the aggressive growth of federal programs in this cost center, but warnings were in place for those who hoped to minimize government growth and maximize personal liberty.

Had the growth in *Human Resources* been limited to the rate of revenue growth (19.4 percent), cost would have been $32.4 billion, $15.3 billion less than actual.

Conclusion

Mark it well—in 1949–1952 there was a budget surplus of $2.0 billion. Harry Truman was the only president during the period 1941–1996 to pass forward a public debt lower than the one he inherited—a drop from $216.3 billion to $214.8 billion. (Total national debt increased slightly because of off-budget Treasury sales.)

Revenues increased. The cost of *Defense* and *Interest* diminished. The magnet for increased revenue was not the cost of war but the cost of running the federal government. Analysis reveals that had such costs been controlled, a tax reduction could have been considered.

Most patriotic Americans thought higher taxes in 1949–1952 supported troops in Korea. They didn't. They financed domestic spending. Absent what seemed to be the needs of war, one wonders if taxpayers would have been so docile and compliant. Had the bill for social engineering projects been openly presented, would taxpayers have paid it?

Harry Truman. Images flit past the mind's eye at the mention of the name. In 1945, when the United States most needed a strong man at the helm, the inconspicuous Missourian stepped up to the plate. The A-bomb decision, one of the most difficult in history, was his to make and he did so with clear eyes and a sense of internal justification that allowed him to live with it. The Marshall Plan, under his supervision, created a model for the benevolent victor.

Truman faced directly the costs of his policies. He could have decided otherwise, allowing debt to increase as others had done. But he didn't. He supported a tax increase in 1950. He paid his bills, and for that, he deserves credit.

Does the credit for the budget surplus belong to Truman? Probably not, definitely not entirely.

In the Congresses of the time, whether controlled by Republicans or Democrats, there existed the same aging bloc of lawmakers who had resisted much of FDR's New Deal. Truman championed the New Deal and proposed more of the same in his own Fair Deal programs that would have expanded the arm of government even further into areas like health, education, and housing. To the extent that restraint was exercised, it came from Congress, not the presidency.

In the context of this work, Truman gets good short-term grades because he held the line on debt, but he did so kicking and screaming. Fate, not philosophy, made him a successful fiscal president. Given his way, the welfare state would have assaulted America 15 years sooner than it did.

Chapter 5

Dwight D. Eisenhower, 1953–1956

Benjamin Harrison was president when Dwight D. Eisenhower (Ike) was born in Denison, Texas, in 1890. The third of six surviving children of David and Ida Eisenhower, Ike grew up in a stable household, and in later years he remembered his parents fondly.

Father David (1863–1942) was a Pennsylvanian who moved to Abilene, Kansas, when he was 15 years old. After his marriage to Ida Stover (1885), David dropped the engineering courses he had been taking and, with a partner, opened a store in Hope, Kansas. His partner later absconded with the company's cash and left David to face creditors. David closed the store and, over time, paid them all. Thereafter he worked as a mechanic and as a manager of a gas company. Ike was on overseas assignment to General George Marshall when David died.

Mother Ida (1862–1946) was a religious pacifist who had trouble dealing with Ike's occupation. She saw his greatest days as a soldier before she died.

Ike attended grade school and high school in Abilene, Kansas. An indifferent student and an enthusiastic athlete in baseball and football, Ike did nothing consequential after graduation from high school in 1909 until he entered West Point in 1911. He had no urgent political or military ambitions but wanted a more affordable education, and at West Point it was free. Ike's grades were unimpressive—in his first year 74 percent of his class got higher marks; in his last, 64 percent. And he was not a model of good behavior; 42 percent of his classmates were better behaved.

Football was Ike's best subject. Until he hurt his knee in 1912, he was a competent halfback. Ike graduated in 1915 and was commissioned a second lieutenant. Woodrow Wilson was president, and the public debt was $3.1 billion.

During World War One, Ike was assigned to training and organizational duties in the United States and rose to the permanent rank of captain. A few years later, it was Major Eisenhower, tank commander, at Camp Dix, Fort Benning, and Camp Meade. Following a stint in the Panama Canal Zone, Ike was selected to attend the Command and General Staff School in Kansas, the first educational institution to offer him a learning program unattached to football or baseball. He blossomed intellectually and finished first in a class of 275 hand-picked officers, a result that must have amazed his West Point professors. When he completed the course in 1926, Ike was 36 years old, with his military career in full gear. Calvin Coolidge was president, and the public debt was $19.6 billion.

The next decade saw Ike circulating in the higher circles of military life. He received more education at the Army War College (1928–1929) and was assigned to the War Department (1929–1932). In 1932 he joined General Douglas MacArthur's staff. In 1935, Lieutenant Colonel Eisenhower followed MacArthur to the Philippines as his aide. He served in that capacity until 1939, when he was 49. Franklin Roosevelt was president. Public debt, after dropping from $27 billion under Woodrow Wilson (World War One) to $16 billion under Herbert Hoover, had increased again to $40 billion, thanks to the Great Depression.

Ike returned to stateside duty in 1940. At the time of Pearl Harbor, he was a brigadier general serving on the staff of General Walter Krueger. His advancement was swift thereafter.

In March 1942, Ike was made a major general. A few months later, Lt. Gen. Eisenhower was commander of America's forces in Europe and later became Allied commander for the invasions of North Africa. He became a general in February 1943, and in December of that year he was made Supreme Allied Commander.

After returning from the war as a five-star general in 1945, Ike served as chief of staff for Harry Truman until his resignation from the army in 1948. In 1950–1952, at the behest of Truman, Ike came out of retirement to serve as commander of the North Atlantic Treaty Organization forces. He was the first to command NATO's multinational troops.

Until he was ready to enter the political arena, Ike kept his attitudes toward civilian issues to himself. Headhunters dispatched from both political parties sought the hand of the individual who, arguably, was the most popular man in the world. Truman apparently thought he had a lock on Ike's loyalties, and he was livid when he learned that his hand-picked successor would run for president in 1952 as a Republican. The war hero of heroes easily defeated Adlai E. Stevenson in the race for political power.

For the first two years, Ike had Republican leadership in the House and Senate. Joe Martin of Massachusetts was Speaker of the House, and Robert A. Taft of Ohio was the Senate majority leader. When Taft resigned, he was succeeded by William F. Knowland of California. But in the 84th Congress (1955–1956), Democrats returned to power; Rayburn again became Speaker of the House, and Lyndon B. Johnson became Senate majority leader. Both were Texans.

Ike assumed office in January 1953. The Korean War was ongoing; public debt, summarized below, was $214.8 billion.

Table 5.1
Summary of Deficits/Debt, 1941–1952 (In Billions of Dollars)

Years		Total	Defense	Interest	Govt.	Human Resources
Before 1941		$ 42.8	$ 42.8[a]	$ 0.0	$ 0.0	$ 0.0
1941–44 (FDR)		127.8	127.8	0.0	0.0	0.0
1945–48 (FDR/HST)		47.6	37.4	5.4	0.0	4.8
1949–52 (HST)[b]		- 2.0	- 2.0	0.0	0.0	0.0
	Deficits	$ 216.2	$206.0	$ 5.4	$ 0.0	$ 4.8
	Adjust[c]	- 1.4				
	Debt	$ 214.8				
	Convert[d]	$ 1271.8				
	Debt 1996	$ 3732.9				
	Debt 1952					
	% of 1996	34.1%				

a) Includes cost of Great Depression (see p. 19). b) Surplus. c) Government figures come from a variety of sources and differ somewhat. This adjustment "forces" the above total to agree with the public debt amount reported by the Office of Management and Budget, Historical Tables, 7.1. d) Convert subject debt to 1996 dollars.

Truman, a feisty, partisan, confrontational president, wanted to spend more on New Deal and Fair Deal programs than a relatively conservative Congress would allow. Curiously Truman, the spender, produced a budget surplus. Ike, almost apolitical in demeanor, wanted to cut federal spending and taxes more than a spending-spoiled Congress would tolerate. Yet Ike, the conservative, produced the budget deficits.

Change in Public Debt

In 1953–1956, public debt went from $214.8 billion to $222.2 billion, as follows:

Table 5.2
Change in Public Debt, 1952–1956
(In Billions of Dollars)

Public debt, 1952	$ 214.8
Deficit, 1953–1956	6.6
Total	$ 221.4
Adjustment[a]	.8
Public debt, 1956	$ 222.2

a) See Table 5.1, note c.

The Truman regime had two defining characteristics: 1) In a break with the past, nonmilitary spending during war-time was not cut but instead increased substantially; 2) Truman's tax increase, allegedly to support the Korean War, was actually used to fund domestic cost expansion. These two factors established the budget atmosphere within which Ike had to work. He inherited a war, accelerating domestic spending, and high taxes.

A president's power is increased when he controls Congress and limited when he doesn't. In his first term, Ike was fortunate. His control of the 83d Congress set the fiscal tone of his last three years which, for all practical purposes, featured a balanced budget. The deficit during his first term ($6.6 billion) mostly took place in his first year, during which he operated under the last budget of the Truman administration.

Table 5.3
Profile of Power, 1949–1956

Cong.	House	Senate	President
81	Rayburn (D)	Lucas (D)	Truman (D)
82	Rayburn (D)	McFarland (D)	Truman (D)
83	Martin (R)	Taft[a] (R)	Eisenhower (R)
83		Knowland (R)	
84	Rayburn (D)	Johnson (D)	Eisenhower (R)

a) Resigned.

Perspectives

Ike matured in the weak military institution that existed after World War One. He dutifully accepted that weakness, happily directed its renewed strength in Europe, sorrowfully saw it diminish again under Truman, and energetically helped it back to its feet to meet the challenge of Korea. As well as any man in the world, he respected the Soviet threat, and by his actions he prepared America to face it.

When Stalin died in 1953, Malenkov became the Soviet premier. Winston Churchill and Ike were the largest World War Two personalities still operating on the world stage. A hero in Russia and Europe, as well as in the United States, Ike by his mere presence acted as a deterrent against adventurous foes. He reeked of credibility. As promised, Ike brought the Korean War to a close, thus ending one Communist threat. But the explosion of a hydrogen bomb by Russia made it clear that the days of trouble were not entirely gone.

Vietnam reached the consciousness of Americans in 1954 when the French military post in Dien Bien Phu was overrun, signaling the end of

French influence in that country. As far back as 1950, America had been quietly and modestly involved in France's attempt to maintain a colonial presence in Vietnam. Ike continued that practice but was consistently opposed to deeper involvement, a wise posture, from one trained in the logistics of warfare, that lesser-trained leaders later ignored, much to their regret and the regret of the country.

America's deadly dance with Russia moved in a different direction in 1955 when Nikolai Bulganin succeeded Malenkov as Soviet premier. Direction shifted again when the Lion of London, Winston Churchill, resigned, thus removing from the international arena one of Communism's staunchest and most able antagonists.

International nerves grew unsettled when America's own lion, Dwight Eisenhower, suffered an attack of coronary thrombosis that temporarily felled the highly respected and feared American president.

Perhaps sensing weakness, perhaps driven by events, the Soviets became bolder in 1956. Nikita Khrushchev followed in the footsteps of Bulganin and crushed the revolts against Soviet rule in Poland and Hungary. In another part of the world, disputes over the Suez Canal involving Egypt, Israel, France, and England resulted in a short war which, with the assistance of the United States, was cooled. Ike recovered his health during this frenzy and ran again for president on a record of peace and prosperity and won easily. Ike was amazingly popular with voters. His image as a man who would and could stand up to Communists was part of his attraction.

The rights of America's Afro-American citizens drew long-needed attention in Ike's first term, perhaps triggered by the Supreme Court decision (*Brown v. Board of Education*, Topeka) that banned racial segregation in public schools. Separate but equal was a dogma in disrepair. Protests followed. Martin Luther King became a prominent voice urging the elimination of segregation in schools, buses, restaurants, and wherever else the hated practice prevailed.

America was at peace, it was prosperous, and it turned its eyes inward, desiring to cleanse aspects of its national character that had been stained for too long by race issues. The wheels of confrontation were in motion, and soon the position of blacks in American society would be a preoccupying issue. This racial tension and the national mood to resolve it in 1953–1956 were major considerations when arguments were developed at a later time in support of a more active role for the federal government. Had there been no racial issue in the 1950s, would there be a welfare state in the 1990s?

After World War Two, *Defense* dropped from a high in 1945 of $83.0 billion to a low in 1948 of $9.1 billion. In 1950, the first year of Korea, Truman increased *Defense* to $13.7 billion. In 1953, the last year of the war and the first of Ike's administration, *Defense* was $52.8 billion.

Unlike Truman, the first cold war president, who abruptly dismantled

America's arsenal after the Second World War, Ike kept a strong military when its immediate justification, the Korean War, ended. He was the first president to face the Soviet threat with actions as well as words—the second cold war president, but the first to pay the piper.

Over the next three years, *Defense* ranged from $42 billion to $49 billion. Ike's defense policies and his attempts to slow the rate of growth in federal spending impressed his personal stamp on the financial profile of America.

Table 5.4
Financial Profile

	1940 (pop: 132.5 mil)[a]	**1952** (pop: 157.6 mil)	**1956** (pop: 168.9 mil)	**1996** (pop: 265.5 mil)
Federal Income and Outlay, in Billions of Dollars				
GDP[b]	$ 100.0	$ 371.4	$ 448.5	$7636.0
Taxes	6.5	66.2	74.6	1453.1
Spending	9.5	67.7	70.6	1560.5
Debt	42.8	214.8	222.2	3732.9
Interest	.9	4.7	5.1	241.1
Federal Income and Outlay—Proportional Comparisons, in Percentages				
Taxes/GDP	7%	18%	17%	19%
Spending/GDP	10	18	16	20
Debt/GDP	51	58	50	49
Taxes/Debt	15	31	34	39
Interest/Taxes	14	7	7	17
Federal Income and Outlay Per Capita, in Dollars				
Taxes	$ 49	$ 420	$ 442	$ 5473
Spending	72	430	418	5878
Debt	323	1363	1316	14060
Interest	7	30	30	908
Average Per Capita Income, in Dollars[c]				
	$ 849	$ 1653	$ 1949	$ 24231
Federal Income and Outlay as Percentage of Avg. Per Capita Income				
Taxes	6.0%	25.0%	23.0%	23.0%
Spending	8.0	26.0	21.0	24.0
Debt	38.0	82.0	68.0	58.0
Interest	.8	1.8	1.5	3.7
Misery index, in percentages[d]				
Prime interest	1.5%	3.0%	4.0%	8.3%
Unemployment	14.6	3.0	4.1	5.3
Inflation	.7	2.0	1.5	3.0

a) Population: U.S. Bureau of Census. b) GDP: 1940, 1942, 1944—Salem State College; other years—Federal Reserve Board, Chicago. c) Average income was not available for all years. Figures for missing years were estimated on a linear basis. d) Rates taken from several U.S. government sources.

A president must be lucky as well as competent if he is to escape punishing deficits. The business cycle has in the past made poor presidents look good and good presidents look bad. In 1953–1956, Ike was both good and lucky.

The business cycle was good to him. The growth in GDP that began under Harry Truman in 1949 kept going for seven months into Ike's first year. Then a down cycle set in for 10 months before the final growth cycle began in mid–1954 and continued until (and beyond) the rest of his term. Real growth in GDP for the four years was 17.7 percent, a target no peacetime president would reach or approximate until Ronald Reagan took office in the 1980s.

Table 5.5
Economic Indicators, 1953–1996

President	Year[a]	Cycle[b]	GDP[c]	CPI[d]	Rev.[e]
Eisenhower	**1956**	**79%**	**18%**	**3%**	**39%**
Eisenhower	1960	65	7	10	9
Kennedy/Johnson	1964	96	23	6	19
Johnson	1968	100	24	15	18
Nixon	1972	77	14	23	18
Nixon/Ford	1976	67	7	39	0
Carter	1980	88	7	48	14
Reagan	1984	67	9	28	15
Reagan	1988	100	14	16	16
Bush	1992	83	3	19	8
Clinton	1996	100	7	13	13
Range:					
High		97	19	33	24
Low		70	6	7	6
Average[f]		82	10	18	14

a) The final year of the term. b) Ratio of months of growth in GDP to 48 months. c) Real growth, four years. d) Inflation, four years. e) Real growth in federal revenue, four years. f) The working average of those within the range.

Ike had a better business cycle, stronger growth, lower inflation, and a healthier revenue increase than the average in all of those categories. The deficit in 1953–1956 was cost driven, with no income component.

Public debt in 1956 was slightly higher than it was in 1952, but as a percentage of GDP, it dropped from 58 percent to 50 percent. *Interest* will usually rise when debt does, so the increase in the absolute amount of debt was bad news. On the other hand, moving public debt to a lower percent of GDP is always a welcome development.

Interest increased again in 1953–1956. It would be difficult to convince any layman that prime interest rates are not directly related to the size of public debt, given their symmetrical course through history. Public debt, the father of *Interest*, is a hand in the pocket of future generations and a pickpocket of current credit-supported taxpayers who pay a bit more for every noncash purchase because of increasing interest costs related to poor public policy.

The misery index was 9.6 percent in 1956 as compared with 8.0 percent in 1952, an increase of 20 percent. *Interest* was on its expected (by now) upward course—a dangerous long-term indicator; unemployment went up as *Defense* went down, but at 4.1 percent was not considered troublesome. Of the three indicators, only inflation took a downward course.

Cold war. A new term. A new world, featuring a relatively high *Defense* during a time of peace because of the existence of a nonshooting enemy who could destroy America or impair its national interests throughout the world. In such a climate, the priorities of America continued to shift.

Table 5.6
Spending Priorities[a]

	1940	1952	1956	1996
Defense	17.9%	68.1%	60.2%	17.0%
Interest	9.5	6.9	7.2	15.5
Total	27.4	75.0	67.4	32.5
Government	29.5	7.6	9.8	6.1
Soc. Sec.	0.0	3.1	7.8	22.4
Medicare	0.0	0.0	0.0	11.2
Veterans	.6	7.8	6.9	2.4
Welfare	42.5	6.5	8.1	25.4
Total	100.0%	100.0%	100.0%	100.0%

a) See discussion following Table 2.4.

A hot war was in process in 1952; a cold one in 1956. The above table shows that as *Defense* decreased, a shift was made to *Human Resources*. Lower *Defense* during times of peace is an important source of debt reduction funds that were not used wisely during this period.

Transactions

Ike entered his first term faced with a deeply rooted set of federal programs that he had no hand in creating and with two attitudes of his own, all of which would make it more difficult to balance the budget. The federal programs were notable for exploding costs. Ike's attitudes were that taxes were too high and *Defense* should not be allowed to disintegrate when the Korean War ended.

The deficit for the period was $6.6 billion, and the reasons for it will be revealed when the following schedule is dissected.

Table 5.7
Transactions (In Billions of Dollars)

		1953–1956		1949–1952
Taxes		$ 279.4		$ 196.6
Less:				
Defense	$ 187.3		$ 96.6	
Interest	20.0		18.7	
Total		207.3		115.3
Net		$ 72.1		$ 81.3
Less:				
Government	$ 22.9		$ 31.6	
Hum. Resources	55.8		47.7	
Total		78.7		79.3
Net		-$ 6.6		$ 2.0
Debt, beg		- 214.8		- 216.3
Total		-$ 221.4		-$ 214.3
Adjustment[a]		- .8		- .5
Debt, end		-$ 222.2		-$ 214.8

a) See Table 5.1, note c.

Taxes

Harry Truman approved increases in corporate and individual tax rates in 1950. Revenues exploded in 1951 and 1952 for Truman, then stabilized during Ike's first two years. In the third year, 1955, revenue actually dropped (for only the fourth time since the 1930s). The average for the final two years was about the same as for the first two. It was essentially an era of stable revenues.

Ike started with a revenue base of $264.8 billion (1952 revenue x 4) and ended up collecting $279.4 billion—5.5 percent higher. Compared with 1949–1952, revenues were up by 42.1 percent, most of which was already in place when Ike took office.

Table 5.8
Tax Revenues (In Billions of Dollars)

	Total	Income	Corp.	SS[a]	Excise	Other[b]
1941pw	$ 8.7	$ 1.3	$ 2.1	$ 2.0	$ 2.5	$ .8
1944w	43.7	19.7	14.8	3.4	4.8	1.0
1948p	41.6	19.3	9.7	3.8	7.4	1.4
1952w	66.2	27.9	21.2	6.5	8.9	1.7
1956p	74.6	32.2	20.9	9.3	9.9	2.3

p = mostly peace. w = mostly war.

a) Social Security. b) Estate and gift taxes, custom duties and fees, Federal Reserve earnings, sundry.

Ike ended his first term with 12.7 percent higher revenue than he started with (1956 vs 1952). The average tax load on citizens was reduced under Ike.

Table 5.9
Revenues and Spending

Year	Federal Dollars		Per Capita Dollars			Per Capita Percentages of Average Earnings	
	Taxes	Spending	Taxes	Spending	Avg. Earnings	Taxes	Spending
1941[a]	$ 9 bil.	$ 14 bil.	$ 65	$ 102	$ 923	7.0%	11.1%
1944[a]	44 bil.	91 bil.	326	682	1148	28.4	59.4
1948	42 bil.	30 bil.	284	203	1388	20.5	14.6
1952[a]	66 bil.	68 bil.	420	430	1653	25.4	26.0
1956	75 bil.	71 bil.	442	418	1949	22.6	21.4

a) deficit year

What Did It?

In 1953–1956, *Interest* increased by 7.0 percent. The cost of *Government* went down; *Human Resources* went up 17.0 percent. In short, these cost centers were fully funded by the 42.1 percent increase in revenue.

By deduction, the deficit was caused by *Defense*, most especially because of the windup costs of the Korean War in 1953. Of the total deficit of $6.6 billion, $6.5 billion was experienced in 1953.

Whatever the justification or lack thereof for spending levels in *Government* and *Human Resources*, within the scope of these essays (to track unrecovered costs), they presented no problem in 1953–1956.

Conclusion

FDR faced mounting involvement in the European war and increasing tensions with Japan in 1940, yet he did little to improve America's military machine until war was declared in 1941.

After World War Two, despite Russia's antagonistic international stance, Truman disarmed the military and didn't rebuild it until 1950, when the shooting started in Korea.

In 1954, after the Korean War was finished, Ike kept a strong military in place because of continuing Soviet pressures against America and its allies. From a financial standpoint, that was perhaps the major difference in style between Ike and his immediate predecessors relative to the handling of international tensions. FDR and Truman reacted; Ike anticipated.

Domestically, FDR was an activist, and Truman was his first apostle. Although he uncharacteristically created the Health, Education and Welfare Department (HEW), Ike slowed things down.

Two characteristics of a president capture the fancy of historians and the media above all others: 1) innovation on the home front, that is, legislation dealing with rights or programs that benefit citizens; 2) strategic and diplomatic skills associated with war or significant treaties. Honors are withheld from leaders who, like Ike, through personality, skill, influence, or chance bring quiet time to their people.

Ike wanted a smaller federal government, not a larger one; fewer federal programs, not more. By and large, the media are energized by an expanding government with endless programs. Ike's reputation overseas (including in the USSR) was so huge that, standing alone, it represented a deterrent against adventurous behavior aimed at the United States.

Is it purely coincidence that less prestigious leaders supported by weaker military establishments were tested in Korea, Cuba, and Vietnam? Is a fiscally prudent president who keeps the peace of less value than social engineers or war leaders?

Would debt have dropped had Ike allowed *Defense* to deteriorate? Unlikely. Since World War Two, Washingtonocrats had become used to wartime revenues, and as fast as emergencies lessened, they found programs to which "war taxes" could be diverted. The power that such projects brought to "givers" was more useful to them than tax reductions for the people.

Given the resistance of Congress to lower spending and the needs of *Defense* in a troubled world, Ike was probably lucky to restrict budget deficits to $6.6 billion.

Table 5.10
Unrecovered Cost (In Billions of Dollars)

Defense	$ 6.6
Interest	0.0
Government	0.0
Human Resources	0.0
Total	$ 6.6

Because of a heart attack in 1955 and an ileitis operation in 1956, many wondered if Ike would retire. But the old soldier, looking fit, fooled them all and gave it another try. Would it be better the "second time around"?

Chapter 6

Dwight D. Eisenhower, 1957–1960

Dwight D. Eisenhower ran for reelection in 1956 and defeated Adlai Stevenson with a 58 percent vote, a majority greater than he had enjoyed in their first contest (55 percent).

Unfortunately, Ike's charm was not infectious. During the last two years of his first term, Sam Rayburn and Lyndon Johnson, Democrats and Texans, ruled the House and Senate. It would be the same in 1957–1960.

Now 67, Ike not only faced for the second time a violent world and a growing public debt of $222.2 billion, but he did so after suffering a stroke in 1957, his third collision with a major medical problem in as many years.

Table 6.1
Summary of Deficits/Debt, 1941–1956 (In Billions of Dollars)

Years		Total	Defense	Interest	Govt.	Human Resources
Before 1941		$ 42.8	$ 42.8[a]	$ 0.0	$ 0.0	$ 0.0
1941–44 (FDR)		127.8	127.8	0.0	0.0	0.0
1945–48 (FDR/HST)		47.6	37.4	5.4	0.0	4.8
1949–52 (HST)[b]		- 2.0	- 2.0	0.0	0.0	0.0
1953–56 (Ike)		6.6	6.6	0.0	0.0	0.0
	Deficits	$ 222.8	$ 212.6	$ 5.4	$ 0.0	$ 4.8
	Adjust[c]	- .6				
	Debt	$ 222.2				
	Convert[d]	$ 1281.7				
	Debt 1996	$ 3732.9				
	Debt 1956					
	% of 1996	34.3%				

a) Includes cost of Great Depression (see p. 19). b) Surplus. c) Government figures come from a variety of sources and differ somewhat. This adjustment "forces" the above total to agree with the public debt amount reported by the Office of Management and Budget, Historical Tables, 7.1. d) Convert subject debt to 1996 dollars.

America was at peace in 1957, a peace of the modern type, with nobody shooting at the United States but bullets whizzing over its head from all parts of the world. Korea had settled down but required on-site American firepower. In Europe the American presence served as a deterrent against Soviet aggression. Soviet technologists were adept competitors in the space race. The Middle East was in its usual bedlam, with Israel fighting for its life. Off the Florida coast, Castro succeeded Batista in 1959, and by the close of 1960, Cuba's alliance with the USSR was obvious. In such a climate, Ike maintained a healthy *Defense*.

Change in Public Debt

Ike had a surplus in 1957 and in 1960, but the two middle years showed a deficit of $15.6 billion, resulting in an overall deficit for the four years of $12.1 billion. Total public debt increased from $222.2 billion to $236.8 billion, as follows:

Table 6.2
Change in Public Debt, 1956–1960 (In Billions of Dollars)

Public debt, 1956	$ 222.2
Deficit, 1957–1960	12.1
Total	$ 234.3
Adjustment[a]	2.5
Public debt, 1960	$ 236.8

a) See Table 6.1, note c.

The president and Congress develop and approve the ideas that result in a budget surplus or a deficit. Working in harness with congressional leaders from his own party, a president can be a dynamic force. If Congress is controlled by the opposition, however, a president can be impotent, capable of little more than slowing down the programs of others. For the first two years of his two-term presidency, Ike had a chance to plant his own ideas for a smaller government. But ideological roots do not sink deeply in such a short period of time. In his second term, Ike operated under the thumb of Democrats Sam Rayburn and Lyndon Johnson, two of the most powerful congressional leaders in modern American political history.

Table 6.3
Profile of Power, 1949–1960

Cong.	House	Senate	President
81	Rayburn (D)	Lucas (D)	Truman (D)
82	Rayburn (D)	McFarland (D)	Truman (D)

Table 6.3 *(continued)*
Profile of Power, 1949–1960

Cong.	House	Senate	President
83	Martin (R)	Taft[a] (R)	Eisenhower (R)
83		Knowland (R)	
84	Rayburn (D)	Johnson (D)	Eisenhower (R)
85	Rayburn (D)	Johnson (D)	Eisenhower (R)
86	Rayburn (D)	Johnson[a] (D)	Eisenhower (R)

a) Resigned.

In terms of presidential power, Ike was in the weakest position possible—zero control over Congress.

Perspectives

Ike was the second president to preside over the cold war, a tension with the USSR that had the capacity to destroy America or any other nation. For that reason alone, Ike would keep his forces on a quasi-wartime footing. Over the four-year period, military spending ranged from $45 billion to $49 billion—a stable era for *Defense*. Ike left behind a few advisers in Vietnam (and the advice to keep it that way) and a military capability that the next two presidents would gratefully utilize.

Congress was controlled by Democrats in 1957–1960, as it had been in 1955–1956, but with an important difference. Lyndon B. Johnson solidified his position as Senate majority leader in 1957–1960, and in the waning years of the forcible Sam Rayburn, he emerged as America's most powerful politician. With his rise, the congressional bloc that had resisted New Deal/Fair Deal programs collapsed, do-gooders flooded into government, and liberals took control of the most powerful spending machine on the face of the earth.

Over the next three decades, Johnson and his followers completely changed the relationship between government and the private sector that had existed for two centuries. In fact, they drove the nation deeply into debt by rejecting the time-proven fiscal policies that had made America strong.

The civil rights debate grew in intensity during Ike's second term and was perhaps epitomized by his decision in 1957 to send federal troops to Little Rock, Arkansas, in support of attempts to integrate the schools. The publicized decision to put the weight of the federal government behind the Supreme Court decision was probably more important than the actual event. Those who wanted to perpetuate the doctrine of separate but equal were served clear notice that their cause was hopeless.

Khrushchev, fresh from brutal victories in Poland and Hungary, solidified his power base in 1957–1960. It was a good time for the USSR, which opened the space race by launching Sputnik, the first earth-orbiting satellite, in 1957. The feat gave the Soviets a public relations advantage that was little diminished when America countered with Explorer I in 1958. Internationally, a triumph over America of this character lifted the Soviet image as a power broker to the level of America's, providing all nations with animus toward the United States with a supportive Big Brother. In a technological era when Russia's brutal quest for expanded power seemed endless, the loss of superiority in technology was a national security issue in America with budget ramifications.

Since the end of World War Two, American leaders with responsibilities in foreign affairs had faced the Soviets at breakfast, lunch, and dinner. Each dawn and throughout the day the persistent question was: What are they up to now? And it was an intelligent focus because lurking behind a regional disturbance could often be found Soviet influence, urging, and support.

In Cuba, for example, Fidel Castro's revolutionary forces deposed President Batista in 1959. Castro was hailed as the great liberator. By the end of 1960, he was confiscating U.S. property, and diplomatic relations with Cuba were terminated in 1961. The USSR had a new friend off the Florida coast, an unpleasant development.

World War Two had left in its wake an America that was different. From an isolationist nation beset by the Great Depression, removed by two oceans from wars in Europe and Asia, America emerged as an international power supported by economic prosperity, ready for free-world leadership. This metamorphosis in identity, occurring in less than 20 years, shocked America into maturity.

The financial profile of the United States in 1940 was that of a prewar nation that was not involved internationally. In 1956, the United States was at peace (post–Korea) with the mightiest economy in the world; in 1960, the nation was somewhat battered from political strife but not yet torn by Vietnam and racial conflict.

Table 6.4
Financial Profile

	1940 (pop: 132.5 mil)[a]	1956 (pop: 168.9 mil)	1960 (pop: 180.7 mil)	1996 (pop: 265.5 mil)
Federal Income and Outlay, in Billions of Dollars				
GDP[b]	$ 100.0	$ 448.5	$ 523.9	$7636.0
Taxes	6.5	74.6	92.5	1453.1
Spending	9.5	70.6	92.2	1560.5
Debt	42.8	222.2	236.8	3732.9
Interest	.9	5.1	6.9	241.1
Federal Income and Outlay—Proportional Comparisons, in Percentages				
Taxes/GDP	7%	17%	18%	19%
Spending/GDP	10	16	18	20
Debt/GDP	51	50	45	49

Table 6.4 *(continued)*
Financial Profile

	1940	**1956**	**1960**	**1996**
	(pop: 132.5 mil)[a]	(pop: 168.9 mil)	(pop: 180.7 mil)	(pop: 265.5 mil)
Taxes/Debt	15%	34%	39%	39%
Interest/Taxes	14	7	7	17

Federal Income and Outlay Per Capita, in Dollars

Taxes	$ 49	$ 442	$ 512	$ 5473
Spending	72	418	510	5878
Debt	323	1316	1310	14060
Interest	7	30	38	908

Average Per Capita Income, in Dollars[c]

	$ 849	$ 1949	$ 2219	$ 24231

Federal Income and Outlay as Percentage of Avg. Per Capita Income

Taxes	6.0%	23.0%	23.0%	23.0%
Spending	8.0	21.0	23.0	24.0
Debt	38.0	68.0	59.0	58.0
Interest	.8	1.5	1.7	3.7

Misery index, in percentages[d]

Prime interest	1.5%	4.0%	5.0%	8.3%
Unemployment	14.6	4.1	5.5	5.3
Inflation	.7	1.5	1.7	3.0

a) Population: U.S. Bureau of Census. b) GDP: 1940, 1942, 1944—Salem State College; other years—Federal Reserve Board, Chicago. c) Average income was not available for all years. Figures for missing years were estimated on a linear basis. d) Rates taken from several U.S. government sources.

Ike slowed spending trends in his first term, and he did better in his second term than the numbers indicate. The business cycle in 1957–1960 was more punitive than usual, and revenue was lower than it might have been in a normal period.

Table 6.5
Economic Indicators, 1953–1996

President	Year[a]	Cycle[b]	GDP[c]	CPI[d]	Rev.[e]
Eisenhower	1956	79%	18%	3%	39%
Eisenhower	**1960**	**65**	**7**	**10**	**9**
Kennedy/Johnson	1964	96	23	6	19
Johnson	1968	100	24	15	18
Nixon	1972	77	14	23	18
Nixon/Ford	1976	67	7	39	0
Carter	1980	88	7	48	14
Reagan	1984	67	9	28	15

Table 6.5 *(continued)*
Economic Indicators, 1953–1996

President	Year[a]	Cycle[b]	GDP[c]	CPI[d]	Rev.[e]
Reagan	1988	100	14	16	16
Bush	1992	83	3	19	8
Clinton	1996	100	7	13	13
Range:					
High		97	19	33	24
Low		70	6	7	6
Average[f]		82	10	18	14

a) The final year of the term. b) Ratio of months of growth in GDP to 48 months. c) Real growth, four years. d) Inflation, four years. e) Real growth in federal revenue, four years. f) The working average of those within the range.

The above table indicates that a president with average luck relative to economic factors over which he has little control will realize an average increase in federal revenue of 14 percent. In 1957–1960, there were fewer growth months than in any other period shown, and the real increase in revenue was 9.1 percent. Had the increase reached the norm (14 percent), revenue for the period would have been $345.1 billion, or $13.8 billion more than actual, an amount that exceeds the deficit for the period. It is reasonable to assume that had the additional revenue been collected in that prewelfare era, it would have been applied to the deficit. Under that theory, the deficit for 1957–1960 was caused by a downturn in the business cycle of sufficient depth and duration to justify its addition to public debt.

GDP in 1960 was 16.8 percent higher than 1956. Adjusted for inflation (9.5 percent), real growth in GDP in 1957–1960 was 7.3 percent, well below average (10 percent).

Revenue in 1960 of $92.5 billion was 24 percent higher than the base inherited in 1956 by Ike. The 1957–1960 tax load as a percent of personal income was similar. The deficit for the period and the growth of spending (1960 vs 1956) by 31 percent warned that debt reduction was unlikely.

The misery index in 1960 was 12.2 percent, versus 9.6 percent in 1956. Inflation was under control, but prime interest rates were up and unemployment (over 5 percent) had moved into problem territory. Times were not bad in 1960, but they were better in 1956.

A warning sign: After eliminating extremes (1944, 1948, 1980), the average of end-of-term rates in 1941–1996 was 6.5 percent. In 1960 the prime rate was up to 5.0 percent, heading for 8.3 percent (see Table 6.4) in 1996. Climbing debt balances and climbing interest rates are a deadly combination that can drive *interest* through the budget roof.

The allocation of resources was different at the end of Ike's second term. The needs of *Defense* had declined after the Korean War, a situation that made a reduction in public debt thinkable. But the appearance of "fresh" money was a temptation too powerful for political leaders to resist. New ways were found to spend the peace dividend.

Table 6.6
Spending Priorities[a]

	1940	1956	1960	1996
Defense	17.9%	60.2%	52.2%	17.0%
Interest	9.5	7.2	7.5	15.5
Total	27.4	67.4	59.7	32.5
Government	29.5	9.8	11.9	6.1
Soc. Sec.	0.0	7.8	12.6	22.4
Medicare	0.0	0.0	0.0	11.2
Veterans	.6	6.9	5.9	2.4
Welfare	42.5	8.1	9.9	25.4
Total	100.0%	100.0%	100.0%	100.0%

a) See the discussion following Table 2.4.

This chart profiles a country which in 1956 and 1960 was still on military alert, with over 50 percent of its resources devoted to *Defense*. But it also depicts evolving attitudes toward the role of the federal government, attitudes that would affect public debt for the rest of the century. In a period of high *Defense*, for example, the relative slice of the budget for *Government* and *Human Resources* went from 32.6 percent in 1956 to 40.3 percent in 1960, an early sign that absolute growth in those cost centers would be formidable.

Transactions

In 1956, Ike's total spending was $70.6 billion, 4 percent higher than the spending level he inherited ($67.7 billion, 1952). In 1960, spending was $92.2 billion, a 30.5 percent increase in four years. What was the difference?

In 1957–1960, Democrats led Congress. Moving from a condition of partial support in 1953–1956 to one of total opposition was a major cause of higher spending during the latter period.

The following schedule lays out the transactions for Ike's two terms. From this raw material, the identity of troublesome cost centers will be discovered.

Table 6.7
Transactions (In Billions of Dollars)

	1957–1960	1953–1956
Taxes	$ 331.3	$ 279.4

Table 6.7 *(continued)*
Transactions (In Billions of Dollars)

	1957–1960		1953–1956
Less:			
Defense	$ 189.3		$ 187.3
Interest	23.7		20.0
Total		213.0	207.3
Net		$ 118.3	$ 72.1
Less:			
Government	$ 38.8		$ 22.9
Hum. Resources	91.6		55.8
Total		130.4	78.7
Net		-$ 12.1	-$ 6.6
Debt, beg		- 222.2	- 214.8
Total		-$ 234.3	-$ 221.4
Adjustment[a]		- 2.5	- .8
Debt, end		-$ 236.8	-$ 222.2

a) See Table 6.1, note c.

Taxes

Ike started his second term with a four-year revenue base of $298.3 billion and actually collected $331.3 billion—an 11.1 percent increase. This means that 7.5 percent of the 18.6 percent revenue increase between the 1957–1960 and 1953–1956 periods was in the pipeline when Ike's second term began, and 11.1 percent was new money related to the current economic environment. And the 18.6 percent increase melted down to 9.1 percent after inflation. Given Washington's spending proclivities, that fact alone made higher deficits probable.

Prior to World War Two, taxes were not a large part of the average American's life. World War Two justified the initial surge in tax demand. Social Security, unemployment compensation, and the GI Bill justified a permanent increase in the base tax rate that was generally acceptable to the public. The cold war and its sidebars (Korea, later Cuba, Vietnam) kept high the cost of defense. And in 1960 the federal appetite for taxes was expanding again, this time to support the development of a larger and more "caring" federal government.

Table 6.8
Tax Revenues (In Billions of Dollars)

	Total	Income	Corp.	SS[a]	Excise	Other[b]
1941pw	$ 8.7	$ 1.3	$ 2.1	$ 2.0	$ 2.5	$ .8
1944w	43.7	19.7	14.8	3.4	4.8	1.0
1948p	41.6	19.3	9.7	3.8	7.4	1.4

Table 6.8 *(continued)*
Tax Revenues (In Billions of Dollars)

	Total	Income	Corp.	SS [a]	Excise	Other [b]
1952w	$ 66.2	$ 27.9	$ 21.2	$ 6.5	$ 8.9	$ 1.7
1956p	74.6	32.2	20.9	9.3	9.9	2.3
1960p	92.5	40.7	21.5	14.7	11.7	3.9

p = mostly peace. w = mostly war.

a) Social Security. b) Estate and gift taxes, custom duties and fees, Federal Reserve earnings, sundry.

Ike started with revenue of $74.6 billion in 1956 and passed along $92.5 billion in 1960—a 24.0 percent increase.

On a per capita basis, taxes increased in 1956–1960, as follows:

Table 6.9
Revenues and Spending

Year	Federal Dollars		Per Capita Dollars			Per Capita Percentages of Average Earnings	
	Taxes	Spending	Taxes	Spending	Avg. Earnings	Taxes	Spending
1941[a]	$ 9 bil.	$ 14 bil.	$ 65	$ 102	$ 923	7.0%	11.1%
1944[a]	44 bil.	91 bil.	326	682	1148	28.4	59.4
1948	42 bil.	30 bil.	284	203	1388	20.5	14.6
1952[a]	66 bil.	68 bil.	420	430	1653	25.4	26.0
1956	75 bil.	71 bil.	442	418	1949	22.6	21.4
1960	93 bil.	92 bil.	512	510	2219	23.1	23.0

a) deficit year

The Korean War ended in 1953. Thereafter there were no shooting wars during the Eisenhower administration. Under the debt management principles that guided earlier presidents, 1954–1960 would have been a time of debt paydown or tax decreases or both. It was not to be. In a time of peace, with a well-stocked military force at the ready, taxes per capita were on the rise. *If taxes cannot be reduced, or debt paid down, in such an era, when can they be?* The same situation pertains in 1999.

What Did It?

DEFENSE

Military spending peaked at $53 billion in 1953, the final year of the Korean War, declined steadily to $42 billion by 1956, and then went up again to $48 billion in 1960. Total military spending in 1957–1960 compared to the previous four years was flat, and in no way contributed to the increase in public debt during the period.

Apart from budget impact, *Defense* in 1957–1960 (55 percent of total expenditures) was consistent with the atmosphere of the times.

Table 6.10
Defense vs GDP/Spending (In Billions of Dollars)

	1956	1960
GDP	$ 448.5	$ 523.9
Spending	$ 70.6	$ 92.2
Defense	$ 42.5	$ 48.1
Defense as a percentage of GDP	9.4%	9.2%
Defense as a percentage of total spending	60.2%	52.2%

Eisenhower, experienced in world affairs, had been personally affected during his career by Soviet attitudes and capabilities. He brought that experience to bear when he approved defense budgets. In 1956, with Korea behind him, Ike did not purge the military establishment as Harry Truman had done after World War Two. Instead, he maintained a strong defense and projected a powerful presence to the Soviets. America was at peace, but Ike, unlike Truman, kept his powder dry, a decision that benefited the nation and the presidents who had to deal with the Vietnam War.

INTEREST

Debt levels are seldom reported to the public in any meaningful way—out of sight, out of mind. One is left with the impression that many politicians prefer it that way, that many economists accept deferred payments for federal programs as examples of progressive leadership that is operating within sound economic theory.

Interest is the tattletale that by its mere presence silently draws attention to public debt. The inevitable question is *Interest* on what? Arrogantly, brusquely, or politely, depending on his disposition, the bureaucrat may admit, when pressed, that debt gives birth to *Interest* every day of every year, that with less debt it would be less costly.

In 1957–1960, *Interest* was 7 percent of federal revenues, not enough in the hurly-burly days of the cold war to get anyone but insiders excited. But as a budget item, it was larger than Energy, Natural Resources, Commerce, or Transportation, or all of them put together; about the same as International and Agriculture; 20 times larger than Justice; and more costly than many of the line items about which "cost-savers" argue so vociferously each year.

Interest went up 18.5 percent, less than the rate of revenue increase (18.6 percent). The increase was fully funded and did not add to the deficit for the period.

GOVERNMENT

Funds available for *Government/Human Resources* ($118.3 billion—See Table 6.7) were 50.3 percent higher than the expenditures in those combined cost centers in 1953–1956. Growth in *Government* below that level would not contribute to the deficit; above it, it would.

Table 6.11
Government Operations, Net (In Billions of Dollars)

	1957–60	1953–56	% Change
Energy	$ 1.4	$ 1.3	7.7%
Nat'l Resources/			
Environment	5.7	4.1	39.0
Commerce	5.8	1.3	346.2
Transportation	11.8	5.2	126.9
Community Development	.7	.4	75.0
International	12.6	8.3	51.8
Science	1.1	.3	266.7
Agriculture	11.9	11.1	7.2
Justice	1.4	1.1	27.3
General	4.2	3.9	7.7
Total	$ 56.6	$ 37.0	53.0
Misc. Income	- 17.8	- 14.1	26.2
Net	$ 38.8	$ 22.9	69.4%

The major (size) line items in *Government* that exceeded the permissible growth rate (50.3 percent) were Transportation and International. Concerning Transportation, Ike paid a price for the absence of separate budgets for capital spending (long-term investments) to which the cost of a national highway system would have been charged. Instead, 1957–1960 bore the full cost of the project. Under the policies set by earlier presidents, excess costs would have been financed by debt.

The European Economic Community Treaty was signed. The Eisenhower Doctrine calling for aid to Middle Eastern countries that resisted Communism was announced, and U.S. Marines were sent to Lebanon at the request of its besieged president. Egypt seized, then later released, the Suez Canal. Fidel Castro assumed power in Cuba. This sampling of events establishes the busy tone of the 1957–1960 period during which the costs charged to International grew by 51.8 percent.

Had the increase in *Government* been restricted to the level of permissible growth (50.3 percent), $34.4 billion would have been spent, or $4.4 billion less than actual. *To that extent* Government *added to the public debt.*

Most cost increases in *Government* did not represent an expansion of government but were related to events specific to the period, events that would end and bring about the restoration of lower cost levels.

HUMAN RESOURCES

Human Resources went up 64.1 percent in 1957–1960, more than the amount allowed (50.3 percent) for a balanced budget.

Table 6.12
Human Resources (In Billions of Dollars)

	1957–60	1953–56	% Change
Education, Training,			
Services, Employment	$ 3.0	$ 1.8	66.6%
Health	2.5	1.3	92.3
Income Security	28.5	18.0	58.3
Subtotal	$ 34.0	$ 21.1	61.1
Social Security[a]	$ 36.3	$ 16.0	126.8
Medicare[a]	0.0	0.0	0.0
Veterans	21.3	18.7	13.9
Sub total	$ 57.6	$ 34.7	66.5
Grand total	$ 91.6	$ 55.8	64.1%

a) Funded by employers and employees.

In Ike's first term, *Human Resources* was 17 percent higher than in the previous four years. But that relatively modest rate of increase (made possible by declining demand for veterans benefits), masked a 33 percent increase in Education, Health, and Income programs, and a 162 percent increase in Social Security. So, the runaway cost of *Human Resources* began in 1953–1956 and exploded in 1957–1960.

Had growth in Human Resources *been limited to 50.3 percent, the expenditure would have been $83.9 billion, $7.7 billion less than actual, its share of additional debt.*

Conclusion

The 1957–1960 administration did not have the normal amount of income to work with because of the business cycle. Under prudent fiscal discipline, the deficit for the period would be a legitimate addition to public debt. That isn't to say that lagging income excuses surging costs. More spending control would have lessened the problem.

Major cost increases in *Government* were understandable. But this wasn't the case in *Human Resources*. When *Human Resources* cannot restrict itself to a four-year growth rate of 50.3 percent, cost controls are nonexistent. Such was the case in 1957–1960, and public debt increased by $12.1 billion, as follows:

Table 6.13

Unrecovered Cost (In Billions of Dollars)

Defense	$ 0.0
Interest	0.0
Government	4.4
Human Resources	7.7
Total	$ 12.1

While it was true that spending in *Government* and *Human Resources* grew disproportionately in 1957–1960, it is also true that the business cycle denied to the period a normal amount of tax receipts (revenue lag), which places a different cast on the deficit for the period.

Table 6.14

Analysis of Deficit, 1957–1960 (In Billions of Dollars)

Total Deficit	$ 12.1
Less: Revenue Lag[a]	13.8
Net	$ 1.7

a) See p. 66.

Given average luck with the business cycle, Ike would have had a small surplus in his second term.

Even Ike succumbed to the give them-more, affordable-or not mind of Washington when he expanded Social Security to cover disabilities that had previously not been covered. It sounded like a good idea; most welfare programs do. But why the federal government? Why expand cost when revenues are weak? How much is enough?

Dwight Eisenhower produced a commendable record in his eight years. His expansion of government (HEW) was for organizational, not programmatic, purposes. His deficits were legitimate additions to public debt (Korean War, national highway system) or could be related to the business cycle. The debt problem that plagued America in 1996 cannot be laid at the feet of Dwight Eisenhower or his predecessors.

Chapter 7

John F. Kennedy/ Lyndon B. Johnson, 1961–1964

Woodrow Wilson was president when John F. Kennedy was born in 1917 in his Brookline home in the shadow of World War One. The second son of wealthy parents, Joseph and Rose, JFK had a political heritage long and deep that came from both sides of the family.

Paternal grandfather Patrick served in the Massachusetts House and Senate in the 1800s; maternal grandfather "Honey Fitz" Fitzgerald functioned in local and national politics until a few years before John's birth. And most important of all, John's father Joseph became an intimate of Franklin Roosevelt's. A career in politics for John Kennedy was almost a certainty from the day of his birth.

Joseph Kennedy (1888–1969) was a Harvard graduate at 24, the youngest bank president in Massachusetts at 25, married to Rose Fitzgerald at 26, and a millionaire at 35. He amassed a huge fortune in banking, investing, liquor, real estate, and movies, becoming in the process a colorful character and a ladies' man. His support of Roosevelt in 1932 led him into the public sector as chairman of the Securities and Exchange Commission (1934–1935) and the U.S. Maritime Commission (1937), and, finally, as ambassador to Great Britain (1937–1940). In the latter post, his relationship with Roosevelt disintegrated because of Kennedy's resistance to the involvement of America in World War Two.

Young John Kennedy led the privileged life of a rich boy. Private schools in Massachusetts, New York, and Connecticut groomed him until he entered Choate School in Wallingford, Connecticut, at the age of 14. He graduated in 1935, 64th in a class of 112. He was apparently more a prankster than a student. Most of the next year was lost due to illness (jaundice), but in 1936 he entered Harvard. He graduated cum laude in 1940. Franklin Roosevelt was

74

president. Public debt was \$42.8 billion, and the Great Depression was 11 years old.

In 1940–1941, John Kennedy took courses at Stanford Business School and toured South America before joining the navy as an ensign. In 1942 he was Lieutenant Kennedy, captain of a PT boat. In 1943 his boat was rammed and some of his crew were lost, but days later, he and other survivors were rescued. For this incident, which aggravated his bad back, he received several decorations. Kennedy returned stateside and was discharged in 1945. Harry Truman was president, and the public debt was \$235.2 billion. John Kennedy was 28 years old.

For a short time after his discharge from the service, Kennedy dabbled in journalism, but he knew that, with the death of his brother Joe, he was destined for a political career under the energetic sponsorship and direction of his father. John Kennedy's future in politics was his father's final occupation. In this effort, he was as effective as he had been at everything else.

In 1947, John F. Kennedy began his political career in the House of Representatives (1947–1952), and in 1952 he ran for the Senate seat occupied by the aristocratic Henry Cabot Lodge. The Kennedy machine went into high gear. Kennedy won impressively and moved to the Senate chambers (1953–1960). He celebrated by marrying Jacqueline Bouvier (1953), who had a background of privilege to match his own.

The ambitions of Joseph Kennedy for his son did not end with the Senate, nor did those of the son himself, a willing and able puppet in the hands of Joseph, the master manipulator. There was, for example, the vice presidential nomination that John Kennedy lost in 1956. It gained him national recognition that he put to good use in 1960. He wrested from Hubert Humphrey the nomination of the Democratic party and went on to beat Richard Nixon in one of the most controversial contests in presidential history.

Throughout his term in office, JFK had the support of Democratic leaders in Congress, Sam Rayburn of Texas and John McCormack of Massachusetts in the House; Mike Mansfield of Montana in the Senate. And his vice president, Lyndon B. Johnson, had been one of the most powerful lawmakers in the history of the Senate. During his third year in office, JFK was assassinated on a street in Dallas, Texas, in November 1963. Lyndon B. Johnson succeeded him.

The Eisenhower administration passed forward to Kennedy a public debt of \$236.8 billion, summarized as follows:

Table 7.1
Summary of Deficits/Debt, 1941–1960 (In Billions of Dollars)

Years	Total	Defense	Interest	Govt.	Human Resources
Before 1941	$ 42.8	$ 42.8[a]	$ 0.0	$ 0.0	$ 0.0
1941–44 (FDR)	127.8	127.8	0.0	0.0	0.0
1945–48 (FDR/HST)	47.6	37.4	5.4	0.0	4.8
1949–52 (HST)[b]	- 2.0	- 2.0	0.0	0.0	0.0
1953–56 (Ike)	6.6	6.6	0.0	0.0	0.0
1957–60 (Ike 2)	12.1	0.0	0.0	4.4	7.7
Deficits	$ 234.9	$212.6	$ 5.4	$ 4.4	$ 12.5
Adjust[c]	1.9				
Debt	$ 236.8				
Convert[d]	$ 1255.2				
Debt 1996	$ 3732.9				
Debt 1960					
% of 1996	33.6%				

a) Includes cost of Great Depression (see p. 19). b) Surplus. c) Government figures come from a variety of sources and differ somewhat. This adjustment "forces" the above total to agree with the public debt amount reported by the Office of Management and Budget, Historical Tables, 7.1. d) Convert subject debt to 1996 dollars.

America was at peace in 1961, but like Ike before him, JFK maintained a war-ready military force as a hedge against hot-button Cuba, slow-boiling Vietnam, and the omnipresent, always-boiling USSR.

Change in Public Debt

To most Americans, the cost of meeting international dangers explained high tax rates and ever-climbing public debt. But the experience of Ike's regime made clear that other forces, almost as powerful, imperiled America's financial stability, namely, the surging costs of federal programs. Taxpayers by and large were unaware of this, but federal politicians knew it. And in the face of such information, they watched indifferently as public debt climbed again:

Table 7.2
Change in Public Debt, 1960–1964 (In Billions of Dollars)

Public debt, 1960	$ 236.9
Deficit, 1961–1964	21.0
Total	$ 257.9
Adjustment[a]	- 1.1
Public debt, 1964	$ 256.8

a) See Table 7.1, note c.

Democratic control of both houses of Congress was deeply entrenched, an ideal power structure for JFK.

Table 7.3
Profile of Power, 1949–1964

Cong.	House	Senate	President
81	Rayburn (D)	Lucas (D)	Truman (D)
82	Rayburn (D)	McFarland (D)	Truman (D)
83	Martin (R)	Taft[a] (R)	Eisenhower (R)
83		Knowland (R)	
84	Rayburn (D)	Johnson (D)	Eisenhower (R)
85	Rayburn (D)	Johnson (D)	Eisenhower (R)
86	Rayburn (D)	Johnson[a] (D)	Eisenhower (R)
87	Rayburn (D)	Mansfield (D)	Kennedy (D)
87	Rayburn[b] (D)	Mansfield (D)	Kennedy (D)
87	McCormack (D)		
88	McCormack (D)	Mansfield (D)	Kennedy[c] (D)
88			Johnson[d] (D)

a) Resigned. b) Died in office. c) Assassinated. d) VP succession.

Keynesians in the president's Council of Economic Advisors found a willing audience in young John Kennedy, one ready to adopt the prevailing economic theory. From Kennedy's presidency on, the Keynes attitude toward debt, spending, and economic engineering would be the prevailing intellectual backdrop for politicians, despite the growing skepticism about its applicability to real-world problems and the gnawing feeling that it didn't square with common sense.

Perspectives

Fidel Castro was a major bee in the JFK bonnet. The Cuban leader fostered revolutionary movements in Central America and took every opportunity offered to smirch the reputation of the United States. His power base was a stone's throw from Florida; his patron was the USSR.

Kennedy was determined to do something about Cuba. He failed, but he did stop the Soviets' attempt to worsen the problem when he confronted them over the installation of missiles in Cuba. His blockade of Cuba led to the dismantling of the missiles. But Castro continued to be a pest in the region until he lost his sponsor in the late 1980s.

The Cuban problem had a direct budget impact. First of all, there was the military cost of dealing with the issue (Bay of Pigs, naval blockade, etc.). But more importantly, JFK's failure in Cuba may have been one of the reasons for his willingness to become more engaged in Vietnam than his predecessor,

Dwight Eisenhower, had advised. Had there been no Cuban failure, would there have been a Vietnam War?

Russia competed effectively in the space race, and JFK pledged to get America up to speed. The Soviets put the first man into orbit in April 1961 (Yuri Gagarin) and sent another man into space in August (Gherman Stepanovich). America's riposte with space flights by Alan Shepard and Virgil Grissom was not competitive. Nor was the short around-the-world orbit of John Glenn in 1962 (3 orbits vs 17 for the Russians). The space race with Russia had direct budget impact. Kennedy fought it but didn't fund it.

The Berlin Wall was erected in 1961, a monument to strained relations that represented in unresisting stone the institutionalization of the cold war. The two giants, the USSR and America, stared at each other implacably over the wall, each having little to offer the other except the power of mutual destruction that so far had kept the peace—and had kept the cost of *Defense* high.

The civil rights pot was put on the burner under Dwight Eisenhower, reached simmer under JFK, and moved to a boil with Lyndon Johnson, Kennedy's successor in office. The integration of Southern colleges continued. Huge rallies were held in Washington. Supreme Court rulings and legislation begun in the Eisenhower/Kennedy/Johnson era would establish equal rights under law that would make segregation a bad memory. The rush to solve racial problems had a direct impact on the climbing costs of *Human Resources*.

America counted 133 million people in 1941 and 192 million in 1964— 1.4 times larger. In a quarter of a century, the nation had changed significantly. There were now high taxes, an activist government, less reliance on individuals, more security, and less liberty.

Table 7.4
Financial Profile

	1940 (pop: 132.5 mil)[a]	1960 (pop: 180.7 mil)	1964 (pop: 191.9 mil)	1996 (pop: 265.5 mil)
Federal Income and Outlay, in Billions of Dollars				
GDP[b]	$ 100.0	$ 523.9	$ 675.1	$7636.0
Taxes	6.5	92.5	112.6	1453.1
Spending	9.5	92.2	118.5	1560.5
Debt	42.8	236.8	256.8	3732.9
Interest	.9	6.9	8.2	241.1
Federal Income and Outlay—Proportional Comparisons, in Percentages				
Taxes/GDP	7%	18%	17%	19%
Spending/GDP	10	18	18	20
Debt/GDP	51	45	38	49
Taxes/Debt	15	39	44	39

Table 7.4 *(continued)*
Financial Profile

	1940	**1960**	**1964**	**1996**
	(pop: 132.5 mil)[a]	(pop: 180.7 mil)	(pop: 191.9 mil)	(pop: 265.5 mil)
Interest/Taxes	14%	7%	7%	17%

Federal Income and Outlay Per Capita, in Dollars

Taxes	$ 49	$ 512	$ 587	$ 5473
Spending	72	510	618	5878
Debt	323	1310	1338	14060
Interest	7	38	43	908

Average Per Capita Income, in Dollars[c]

	$ 849	$ 2219	$ 2662	$ 24231

Federal Income and Outlay as Percentage of Avg. Per Capita Income

Taxes	6.0%	23.0%	22.0%	23.0%
Spending	8.0	23.0	23.0	24.0
Debt	38.0	59.0	50.0	58.0
Interest	.8	1.7	1.6	3.7

Misery index, in percentages[d]

Prime interest	1.5%	5.0%	4.5%	8.3%
Unemployment	14.6	5.5	5.2	5.3
Inflation	.7	1.7	1.3	3.0

a) Population: U.S. Bureau of Census. b) GDP: 1940, 1942, 1944—Salem State College; other years—Federal Reserve Board, Chicago. c) Average income was not available for all years. Figures for missing years were estimated on a linear basis. d) Rates taken from several U.S. government sources.

The business cycle had dealt Ike an uneven hand in 1957–1960, but it treated JFK tenderly. The downturn in GDP that had started in 1960 was nine months old when Kennedy took office. It lasted but two more months, after which the administration had 46 months of continual growth, no doubt assisted by America's entry into the Vietnam War in 1963. Inflation during the period was never higher than 1.4 percent and for the four years was 5.8 percent. Real growth in GDP was a robust 23.0 percent; real growth in tax revenue, 19 percent.

The administration was blessed economically with a healthy business cycle buttressed by the stimulation of wartime spending. The deficit for the period had no revenue component and was solely a matter of cost control.

The revenue base in 1964 ($112.6 billion) was 21.7 percent higher than JFK's inherited base ($92.5 billion). The average tax bite on average per capita income was roughly the same. For more than a decade, Congress had settled on a tax policy that took about 23 percent of average income per capita. As revenue increased, so did spending; for more than one day per week, Americans worked for Washington. In 1961–1964, average earnings per capita grew by about 5 percent per year.

The misery index dropped from 12.2 percent in 1960 to 11.0 percent in 1964. Each indicator improved, including a temporary drop in commercial interest rates. War was a healthy tonic for America, as it had been for Franklin Roosevelt in the 1940s.

Into World War Two under Roosevelt, out of it under Harry Truman, into Korea under Truman, out of it under Dwight Eisenhower, and back into war under Kennedy—a nasty quarter of a century, one bound to change the priorities of the United States.

Table 7.5
Spending Priorities[a]

	1940	1960	1964	1996
Defense	17.9%	52.2%	46.2%	17.0%
Interest	9.5	7.5	6.9	15.5
Total	27.4	59.7	53.1	32.5
Government	29.5	11.9	17.0	6.1
Soc. Sec.	0.0	12.6	14.0	22.4
Medicare	0.0	0.0	0.0	11.2
Veterans	.6	5.9	4.8	2.4
Welfare	42.5	9.9	11.1	25.4
Total	100.0%	100.0%	100.0%	100.0

a) See discussion following Table 2.4.

In 1960, America was at peace; in 1964, at war. Yet the slice of resources devoted to *Defense* in 1964 was less. Had the ratio established by Ike during his second term been repeated, *Defense* in 1964 would have been $61.9 billion, 13 percent higher than actual ($54.8 billion), a spending level that wasn't approximated until 1967.

On the other hand, the relative slice of expenditures allocated to *Government* and *Human Resources* during a time of war went up, a sign that the absolute level of increase in those cost centers would be prodigious, and a reminder of the changed value systems that were evolving in 1961–1964.

Transactions

A review of comparative transactions is of assistance when seeking explanations for the deficit in 1961–1964.

Table 7.6
Transactions (In Billions of Dollars)

		1961–1964		1957–1960
Taxes		$ 413.3		$ 331.3
Less:				
Defense	$ 210.1		$ 189.3	
Interest	29.5		23.7	
Total		239.6		213.0
Net		$ 173.7		$ 118.3
Less:				
Government	$ 64.5		$ 38.8	
Hum. Resources	130.2		91.6	
Total		194.7		130.4
Net		-$ 21.0		-$ 12.1
Debt, beg		- 236.8		- 222.2
Total		-$ 257.8		-$ 234.3
Adjustment[a]		1.0		- 2.5
Debt, end		-$ 256.8		-$ 236.8

a) See Table 7.1, note c.

Taxes

In 1960, federal revenue was $92.5 billion, which means that JFK began his presidency with a four-year revenue base of $370.0 billion. He actually collected $413.3 billion, 11.7 percent more than the base and 24.8 percent more than the revenue for the previous four years. About half of the increase was in place when he began his term, and half came about because of the economic environment of the times.

Federal revenues increased in every year of the JFK/LBJ administration—1961, 2.1 percent; 1962, 5.6 percent; 1963, 6.9 percent; 1964, 5.6 percent. America's economic system, its most precious material asset, poured dollars into Washington almost as fast as its politicians could find ways to spend it.

Table 7.7
Tax Revenues (In Billions of Dollars)

	Total	Income	Corp.	SS[a]	Excise	Other[b]
1941pw	$ 8.7	$ 1.3	$ 2.1	$ 2.0	$ 2.5	$ .8
1944w	43.7	19.7	14.8	3.4	4.8	1.0
1948p	41.6	19.3	9.7	3.8	7.4	1.4
1952w	66.2	27.9	21.2	6.5	8.9	1.7
1956p	74.6	32.2	20.9	9.3	9.9	2.3
1960p	92.5	40.7	21.5	14.7	11.7	3.9
1964w	112.6	48.7	23.5	22.0	13.7	4.7

p = mostly peace. w = mostly war.

a) Social Security. b) Estate and gift taxes, custom duties and fees, Federal Reserve earnings, sundry.

The percent of wages going to Washington as direct or indirect (corporate) taxes dropped, a positive development for taxpayers.

Table 7.8
Revenues and Spending

Year	Federal Dollars		Per Capita Dollars			Per Capita Percentages of Average Earnings	
	Taxes	Spending	Taxes	Spending	Avg. Earnings	Taxes	Spending
1941[a]	$ 9 bil.	$ 14 bil.	$ 65	$ 102	$ 923	7.0 %	11.1%
1944[a]	44 bil.	91 bil.	326	682	1148	28.4	59.4
1948	42 bil.	30 bil.	284	203	1388	20.5	14.6
1952[a]	66 bil.	68 bil.	420	430	1653	25.4	26.0
1956	75 bil.	71 bil.	442	418	1949	22.6	21.4
1960	93 bil.	92 bil.	512	510	2219	23.1	23.0
1964[a]	113 bil.	119 bil.	587	618	2662	22.1	23.2

a) deficit year

In 1964, taxpayers kept more of their income, but the good news was illusory. Government spending was 23.2 percent of average earnings. Savings to taxpayers represented the value of the federal government's unpaid bills.

What Did It?

Defense

In 1960, JFK inherited a $48.1 billion level of military spending—a four-year base of $192.4 billion. In 1961–1964, he actually spent $210.1 billion, only 9 percent more than the base he inherited (less, if inflation is considered).

In 1960, America had about 2,000 military advisers in Vietnam. By 1963, this was up to 15,000. And for all practical purposes, when Ngo Dinh Diem, South Vietnam's premier, was assassinated in November 1963, America was at war with North Vietnam. Before 1964 ended, the Gulf of Tonkin resolution had been passed by Congress, and Lyndon Johnson had full wartime authority over the situation.

North Vietnam was sponsored by the Soviet Union, a dangerous situation. Under these circumstances, a 9 percent increase in *Defense* over the inherited base seems, at best, modest.

Table 7.9

Defense vs GDP/Spending (In Billions of Dollars)

	1956 (Ike)	1960 (Ike)	1964 (LBJ)
GDP	$ 448.5	$ 523.9	$ 675.1
Spending	70.5	92.2	118.5
Defense	42.5	48.1	54.8
Defense as percentage of GDP	9.4%	9.2%	8.1%
Defense as percentage of total spending	60.2%	52.2%	46.2%

Note that in 1956, we were at peace, with Korea behind us; in 1960 we were at peace, with a noninvolvement policy toward Vietnam; in 1964 we were at war with North Vietnam, a Soviet ally.

Faced with lesser immediate dangers in 1956 and 1960, Dwight Eisenhower, the most respected military man in the United States, maintained a military machine that cost an average of 56.2 percent of total spending; under Johnson the amount was 46.2 percent. If the Eisenhower standard is accepted, America's strength was steadily depleted during the Vietnam War, and "savings" were transferred to federal programs.

Adequate or not, the increase in *Defense* in 1961–1964 was less than the rate of increase in revenue between the two four-year periods, and did not add to the deficit.

INTEREST

In 1961–1964, revenue was 24.8 percent higher than it was in 1957–1960. *Interest* went up 24.5 percent, a significant amount but less than the rate of revenue increase.

Interest was ignored by the public despite long-term implications because its short-term penalties were not recognized. By itself it was a symptom of a larger problem, the public debt, which was also a symptom of the primary cause of the general deficit problem: the abandonment of fiscal disciplines (pay bills and tax only when necessary) and the adoption of a code that regarded a certain percentage of GDP as federal property owed by taxpayers. Social needs as perceived by politicians, not ability to pay, determined spending levels. That policy, promoted vigorously for the first time by Lyndon Johnson, could be captured in a catchy phrase: Charge it.

Interest in 1961–1964, however large, was fully financed and played no role in the development of a deficit for the four-year period.

GOVERNMENT

Revenues in 1961–1964 were 24.8 percent higher than in the previous four years, but because growth in *Defense* and *Interest* was restrained below that level, *Government* could grow by 33.2 percent without causing a deficit problem. It was not enough, however, for the spending appetites of 1961–1964. *Government* grew by 66.2 percent.

Table 7.10
Government Operations, Net (In Billions of Dollars)

	1961–64	1957–60	% Change
Energy	$ 2.2	$ 1.4	57.1%
Nat'l Resources/ Environment	8.5	5.7	49.1
Commerce	3.1	5.8	- 46.5
Transportation	18.1	11.8	53.3
Community Development	2.3	.7	228.5
International	19.0	12.6	50.8
Science	10.6	1.1	863.6
Agriculture	15.1	11.9	25.9
Justice	1.8	1.4	28.6
General	5.1	4.2	21.4
Total	$ 85.8	$ 56.6	51.6
Misc. Income	- 21.3	- 17.8	19.7
Net	$ 64.5	$ 38.8	66.2%

Agriculture, Justice and General grew at a rate that made sense relative to revenue growth. The bookkeeping anomaly in Commerce kept the total variance of 66.2 percent from being even worse. All other line items grew unreasonably relative to the growth in federal income.

Science stands out in a group of bloated companions, higher costs being related to the attempt to match the Soviet space program. Kennedy's speeches during the presidential race were stirring, but his fiscal policy said: "Let someone else pay for it." The problem was known when he took office; costs had been estimated and a small cost reduction elsewhere would have covered the bulge. But he and Lyndon Johnson charged it. Future taxpayers will pay for their reputations as space warriors.

Had the growth in Government *been restricted to 33.2 percent, expenditures would have been $51.7 billion, $12.8 billion less than actual. To that extent it was responsible for the $21.0 billion deficit in 1961–1964.*

HUMAN RESOURCES

Human Resources was 42.1 percent higher than in 1957–1960.

Table 7.11
Human Resources (In Billions of Dollars)

	1961–64	1957–60	% Change
Education, Training, Services, Employment	$ 5.3	$ 3.0	76.7%

Table 7.11 *(continued)*
Human Resources (In Billions of Dollars)

	1961–64	1957–60	% Change
Health	$ 5.4	$ 2.5	$ 116.0
Income Security	37.8	28.5	32.7
Subtotal	$ 48.5	$ 34.0	42.6
Social Security[a]	$ 59.2	$ 36.3	63.1
Medicare[a]	0.0	0.0	0.0
Veterans	22.5	21.3	5.6
Subtotal	$ 81.7	$ 57.6	41.8
Grand total	$ 130.2	$ 91.6	42.1%

a) Funded by employers and employees. Note: Major federal programs added since the 1960s are Medicaid, 1961; Food Stamps, 1962.

"Guns and butter too" was the saying of the times, meaning that social programs could expand vigorously even during wartime. And they did. New Frontier and Great Society programs, on top of the Roosevelt/Truman legacy, flexed their muscles under the combined leadership of JFK and LBJ—Education up 77 percent; Health, 116 percent. Absolute amounts were not yet large in federal budget terms, but the signs of unstoppable growth were clear. But nobody cared, and debt grew again.

Had growth in Human Resources *been limited to 33.2 percent, it would not have contributed to the deficit. Spending at that growth rate would have produced a cost of $122.0 billion, $8.2 billion less than actual. To that extent, the cost center added to the deficit in 1961–1964.*

Conclusion

How could politicians face such spending growth and remain complacent? What information demonstrated that revenues to cover such expansion would be forthcoming? What economic theory defended ever-increasing debt caused not by heavy *Defense*, but by unrecovered costs of federal programs? If expenditures for Science, Education, or Health were valid, why didn't politicians argue for the taxes needed to support them? Did they find it easier to blame deficits on Vietnam than to explain the need to restrain spending? What made political leaders decide that the nonemergency needs of the current citizens should be borne by future taxpayers? Where were the conservative, responsible politicians in 1961–1964? Where was the press? Had America forgotten how to count?

Federal revenues are reductions in the people's income. Funds sent to Washington represent a slice of freedom given up by the taxpayer. Except for the wealthy who, whatever the tax policy, always have enough, citizens with less money because of higher taxes curtail activities that require money—vacations, movies, and a cold beer. They sent a big slice of themselves to Washington in 1961–1964, the slice that eases the burdens of life, not to defend America or to help a neighbor, but to make the world conform to some image of perfection imagined by imperfect federal politicians. Did the people know what they were paying for? Would they have paid it had they known?

In 1964 the Vietnam War, the civil rights movement, protest marches, and the power chess game with the USSR lulled Americans to sleep as the federal government moved deeper into their private lives, establishing in the process a structure of social programs that would strap average-income taxpayers to the plow with or without war, with or without the USSR.

Despite an ongoing war in Vietnam, *Defense* retreated and "savings," instead of reducing debt or taxes, went into the bottomless pit of federal programs. Those who sponsored high spending did not mention the size of new debt that was slickly passed along to the next president. This time, debt increased by $21.0 billion, as follows:

Table 7.12
Unrecovered Cost (In Billions of Dollars)

Defense	$ 0.0
Interest	0.0
Government	12.8
Human Resources	8.2
Total	$ 21.0

In 1961–1964, with a Democratic Congress and Johnson as vice president/president, liberal spenders made it clear that they would continue social legislation that would expand the role of government, war or no war. The period carries the name of John Kennedy, but its legislative successes bear the unmistakable mark of Lyndon B. Johnson, the father of the public debt we experience today.

LBJ labeled Barry Goldwater, his opponent in the presidential race of 1964, a warmonger, one not to be trusted with war-making power. LBJ was the peace candidate. While he was president, however, the Vietnam War matured into a great embarrassment for the United States.

Chapter 8

Lyndon B. Johnson, 1965–1968

Theodore Roosevelt was president when Lyndon B. Johnson was born in 1908 in a farmhouse near Stonewall, Texas, his origins as humble and unpromising as John Kennedy's were posh and auspicious. Johnson was the oldest of five children, three girls and two boys.

Lyndon Johnson had political blood in his veins. His father, Sam Johnson (1877–1937), a teacher, farmer, and trader, was an on-and-off-again member of the House of Representatives in Texas for two decades (1905–1925). During the San Francisco earthquake (1906), Sam lost significant assets, but he took the blow and resurfaced in middle-management positions with the state railroad commission.

Sam Johnson operated with natural wit supported by a high school education, but Rebekah Baines Johnson (1881–1958) was a graduate of Baylor University. She worked as a teacher and journalist before and after her marriage to Sam in 1907. Sam lived to see his son serve in the House, and Rebekah saw her son become the Senate majority leader.

Because of his mother's tutoring, Lyndon was a precocious child; he could read at age four. But he was also somewhat of a hellion. After attending local grammar schools, he went to Johnson City High School. Never prominent in sports, he became known instead as a debater and the youngest member of his 1924 graduating class. Calvin Coolidge was president, and the public debt was $21 billion.

The presidency and the public debt were far from the mind of untamed Lyndon B. Johnson. Spurning Rebekah's pleas, he ignored college until ambition reared its head in 1927. He worked his way through Texas State College, Southwest (1927–1930) and did well in some subjects like political science and poorly in others like mathematics. On campus the tall young man drew attention as a debater, writer, and politician.

After graduation, Johnson taught debate and public speaking in Pearsall and Houston, Texas. But his eyes were on the political ring. He became secretary to Representative Richard Kleberg in 1931, saw Washington, and loved it.

After his stint with Kleberg (1931–1934), Johnson waited for an opportunity to get into politics as an active player, patiently serving as director of a Texas youth program until in 1937 his chance arrived. He ran for and won a House seat. He was 29 and a firm supporter of the New Deal. Roosevelt was president, the public debt was $36 billion, and the Great Depression was in full swing.

Johnson represented Austin, Texas, in the House, except for a short stint in the navy (1941–1942), until at age 41, he won a Senate seat (1949). There he built a record (1949–1960) that made him one of the most powerful majority leaders in the history of that dignified organization.

In 1960, Johnson joined John Kennedy (much to the surprise of everybody), in the run for the presidency against Richard M. Nixon. In a controversial result (that Nixon with good reason could have contested), Kennedy won by 119,000 votes.

In November 1963, Johnson assumed the presidency after JFK was assassinated. In 1964 he won the presidency on his own and faced one of the busiest agendas in history—Vietnam, civil rights, protest marches, college riots, an exploding drug culture, the implementation of an enormously expensive social agenda, a world full of tension, and the presence of the Soviet Union.

In 1968 the tall Texan, broken by disappointments in Vietnam and embarrassed by the lack of support for his war policies, announced he would not again run for office. Five years later he died after a heart attack.

LBJ, the 36th president of the United States, ruled over the 89th and 90th Congresses headed by John McCormack of Massachusetts in the House, and Mike Mansfield of Montana in the Senate. Both congressional leaders were Democrats, and together these power brokers put into law the most intrusive social programs that America had ever experienced. From that time on, government drew closer to the private affairs of corporate and individual citizens, controlling behavior as never before through the power of the purse and the threat of recrimination.

LBJ was a full-time participant and a part-time leader (1963–1964) of the previous administration's budget deficit that featured, behind publicity surrounding dramatic world affairs, large increases in *Government* and *Human Resources.* He took office in 1965 with a public debt of $256.8 billion, summarized as follows:

Table 8.1
Summary of Deficits/Debt, 1941–1964 (In Billions of Dollars)

Years		Total	Defense	Interest	Govt.	Human Resources
Before 1941		$ 42.8	$ 42.8[a]	$ 0.0	$ 0.0	$ 0.0
1941–44 (FDR)		127.8	127.8	0.0	0.0	0.0
1945–48 (FDR/HST)		47.6	37.4	5.4	0.0	4.8
1949–52 (HST)[b]		- 2.0	- 2.0	0.0	0.0	0.0
1953–56 (Ike)		6.6	6.6	0.0	0.0	0.0
1957–60 (Ike 2)		12.1	0.0	0.0	4.4	7.7
1961–64 (JFK/LBJ)		21.0	0.0	0.0	12.8	8.2
	Deficits	$ 255.9	$ 212.6	$ 5.4	$ 17.2	$ 20.7
	Adjust[c]	.9				
	Debt	$ 256.8				
	Convert[d]	$ 1299.7				
	Debt 1996	$ 3732.9				
	Debt 1964					
	% of 1996	34.8%				

a) Includes cost of Great Depression (see p. 19). b) Surplus. c) Government figures come from a variety of sources and differ somewhat. This adjustment "forces" the above total to agree with the public debt amount reported by the Office of Management and Budget, Historical Tables, 7.1. d) Convert subject debt to 1996 dollars.

Alert readers will notice that 100 percent of new debt from the Kennedy/Johnson administration had nothing to do with external events. It is especially interesting that in 1961–1964, a time of war, there was no debt related to *Defense*.

Change in Public Debt

Under Johnson, the size of the four-year deficit increased by 85.2 percent, from $21.0 billion to $38.9 billion, and total debt increased 12.7 percent to $289.5 billion, as follows:

Table 8.2
Change in Public Debt, 1964–1968 (In Billions of Dollars)

Public debt, 1964	$ 256.9
Deficit, 1965–1968	38.9
Total	$ 295.8
Adjustment[a]	- 6.3
Public debt, 1968	$ 289.5

a) See Table 8.1, note c.

Most citizens believed that budget deficits and the increases in public debt were directly related to the war effort. Clearly an increase in debt to support war is consistent with historical practice, and if the increase in 1965–1968 were required for that understandable purpose, no criticism would be due. But the previous chapters of this review do not leave one optimistic that such was the case.

As a psychological, public relations tool, LBJ had the memory of Kennedy's administration and the mythology that was enveloping it (Camelot), plus control of both houses of Congress to support his legislation. That was power. Who could deny the president who wanted to make "Jack's" dream come true?

Table 8.3
Profile of Power, 1949–1968

Cong.	House	Senate	President
81	Rayburn (D)	Lucas (D)	Truman (D)
82	Rayburn (D)	McFarland (D)	Truman (D)
83	Martin (R)	Taft[a] (R)	Eisenhower (R)
83		Knowland (R)	
84	Rayburn (D)	Johnson (D)	Eisenhower (R)
85	Rayburn (D)	Johnson (D)	Eisenhower (R)
86	Rayburn (D)	Johnson[a] (D)	Eisenhower (R)
87	Rayburn (D)	Mansfield (D)	Kennedy (D)
87	Rayburn[b] (D)	Mansfield (D)	Kennedy (D)
87	McCormack (D)		
88	McCormack (D)	Mansfield (D)	Kennedy[c] (D)
88			Johnson[d] (D)
89	McCormack (D)	Mansfield (D)	Johnson (D)
90	McCormack (D)	Mansfield (D)	Johnson (D)

a) Resigned. b) Died in office. c) Assassinated. d) VP succession.

No president had more power, psychological and actual, than did Lyndon B. Johnson, and few knew how to use it better than he.

Perspectives

Johnson had the usual trouble with Communist nations in 1965–1968. China, for example, joined the hydrogen bomb club, which was especially notable because of China's ideological split with the Soviet Union in 1960. On the other side of the world, the USSR followed its rape of Poland and Hungary (1956) with an invasion of Czechoslovakia in 1968. The cold war was omnipresent.

But LBJ's administration will be remembered more for domestic decisions than for direct confrontations with the Soviets—for its policies in Vietnam, for the marches and mayhem that tore at the fabric of American society, and for its social and civil rights legislation.

America's involvement with Vietnam began with a trickle of advisers under Harry Truman. Dwight Eisenhower handled the situation the same way—in 1960, about 2,000 advisers were in Vietnam. John Kennedy was more aggressive; he put 15,000 men in Vietnam. Under LBJ, the civil war in Vietnam became America's war.

The Vietnam War never drew the public support that existed during World War Two. The press was negative, and the conflict had two unusual characteristics that didn't sit well with Americans: 1) America fought to contain, not win, the war, and 2) College students were exempt from the draft.

The first aspect made American troops look ineffective; the second resulted in two undesirable things: a) a military force unfairly made up of less advantaged young men, and b) a guilt-ridden student body ripe for mischief. The country seethed with discontent. Civil rights activists, always ebullient during the administration of a liberal president, were joined on the streets by student protesters.

It was a dark hour for LBJ. He had sent over a half-million men to Vietnam, and in 1968 the problem was as bad as ever. In the face of a raging populace, LBJ in effect resigned from politics at the end of his term, refusing to seek the nomination of his party.

Johnson's social legislation stands today partly as a reaction to the civil rights conflicts of the 1960s and partly as a collection of grandiose ideas that nobody yet has shaped into affordable form.

The last year of Johnson's administration (1968) was three decades away from the beginning and the ending years of this study, the midpoint between an America that was essentially uninvolved in world affairs and an America that led the free world. Such a dramatic journey was bound to change the spirit of the United States and its financial profile.

Table 8.4
Financial Profile

	1940	**1964**	**1968**	**1996**
	(pop: 132.5 mil)[a]	(pop: 191.9 mil)	(pop: 200.7 mil)	(pop: 265.5 mil)
Federal Income and Outlay, in Billions of Dollars				
GDP[b]	$ 100.0	$ 675.1	$ 936.8	$7636.0
Taxes	6.5	112.6	153.0	1453.1
Spending	9.5	118.5	178.1	1560.5
Debt	42.8	256.8	289.5	3732.9
Interest	.9	8.2	11.1	241.1

Federal Income and Outlay—Proportional Comparisons, in Percentages

Table 8.4 *(continued)*
Financial Profile

	1940 (pop: 132.5 mil)[a]	**1964** (pop: 191.9 mil)	**1968** (pop: 200.7 mil)	**1996** (pop: 265.5 mil)
Taxes/GDP	7%	17%	16%	19%
Spending/GDP	10	18	19	20
Debt/GDP	51	38	31	49
Taxes/Debt	15	44	53	39
Interest/Taxes	14	7	7	17

Federal Income and Outlay Per Capita, in Dollars

Taxes	$ 49	$ 587	$ 762	$ 5473
Spending	72	618	887	5878
Debt	313	1338	1442	14060
Interest	7	43	55	908

Average Per Capita Income, in Dollars[c]

	$ 849	$ 2662	$ 3445	$ 24231

Federal Income and Outlay as Percentage of Avg. Per Capita Income

Taxes	6.0%	22.0%	22.0%	23.0%
Spending	8.0	23.0	26.0	24.0
Debt	38.0	50.0	42.0	58.0
Interest	.8	1.6	1.6	3.7

Misery index, in percentages[d]

Prime interest	1.5%	4.5%	6.6%	8.3%
Unemployment	14.6	5.2	3.6	5.3
Inflation	.7	1.3	4.2	3.0

a) Population: U.S. Bureau of Census. b) GDP: 1940, 1942, 1944—Salem State College; other years—Federal Reserve Board, Chicago. c) Average income was not available for all years. Figures for missing years were estimated on a linear basis. d) Rates taken from several U.S. government sources.

The surge of spending related to the Vietnam War forestalled what might have been an economic downturn sometime in 1965–1968 and turned the period into a continuation of the upward swing in GDP that began in 1961. Together John Kennedy and Lyndon Johnson shared 94 straight months of growth in GDP, the longest stretch of good times enjoyed by any back-to-back presidents in the 1941–1996 era.

Table 8.5
Economic Indicators, 1953–1996

President	Year[a]	Cycle[b]	GDP[c]	CPI[d]	Rev.[e]
Eisenhower	1956	79%	18%	3%	39%
Eisenhower	1960	65	7	10	9
Kennedy/Johnson	1964	96	23	6	19

Table 8.5 *(continued)*
Economic Indicators, 1953–1996

Johnson	1968	100	24	15	18
Nixon	1972	77	14	23	18
Nixon/Ford	1976	67	7	39	0
Carter	1980	88	7	48	14
Reagan	1984	67	9	28	15
Reagan	1988	100	14	16	16
Bush	1992	83	3	19	8
Clinton	1996	100	7	13	13
Range:					
High		97	19	33	24
Low		70	6	7	6
Average[f]		82	10	18	14

a) The final year of the term. b) Ratio of months of growth in GDP to 48 months. c) Real growth, four years. d) Inflation, four years. e) Real growth in federal revenue, four years. f) The working average of those within the range.

Johnson had 48 months of economic growth, the highest rate of GDP growth (23.6 percent) since 1941–1945, above average revenue growth, and below average inflation. As under Kennedy, these were good times. Income was no problem. The deficit was strictly cost related.

The misery index increased, however, from 11.0 percent to 14.4 percent, an indicator that all was not well. Things—important things—were beginning to unravel, but they were doing so quietly behind a rate of unemployment (3.6 percent in 1968) that pleased the public. Prime interest rates moved up, adding a premium to the large purchases of the average taxpayer, and inflation was on the march. In 1961–1964, inflation, that insidious threat to the dollar, was 5.8 percent; in 1965–1968 it was 15.2 percent. The wisdom of hindsight would later identify these overheated years as the beginning of hard times for America. Future years would rarely see again an inflation rate below 4 percent.

Taxes in relation to average earnings per capita were about the same, but this was illusory. Expenditures in relation to average earnings went from 23.2 percent to 25.7 percent. Washington was not paying for what it was spending in 1965–1968. Someone, sometime would.

Debt increased, but as a percent of GDP, it dropped from 38 percent to 31 percent, a healthy sign. *Interest* was 35 percent higher in 1968 than in 1964 and prime interest rates had climbed to 6.6 percent, a sure signal that the child of debt (*Interest*) would soon become a primary budget problem in its own right.

The Vietnam War was a major, prolonged (1963–1975), expensive event, one that involved over 200,000 casualties. In World War Two, resources of the country were primarily devoted to the war, domestic spending being curtailed. In 1942, for example, 73 percent of expenditures went to *Defense*; in 1944, 87 percent. One would have expected similar emphasis in 1965–1968, but it didn't happen.

Table 8.6
Spending Priorities [a]

	1940	1964	1968	1996
Defense	17.9%	46.2%	46.0%	17.0%
Interest	9.5	6.9	6.2	15.5
Total	27.4	53.1	52.2	32.5
Government	29.5	17.0	14.5	6.1
Soc. Sec.	0.0	14.0	13.4	22.4
Medicare	0.0	0.0	2.6	11.2
Veterans	.6	4.8	3.9	2.4
Welfare	42.5	11.1	13.4	25.4
Total	100.0%	100.0%	100.0%	100.0%

a) See discussion following Table 2.4.

Despite the increasing intensity of the Vietnam War, *Defense* received a smaller slice of resources in 1968 than it did in 1964. And the relative slice of domestic spending continued to rise as the absolute amounts of higher revenue poured into Washington. Priorities were the reverse of what one might have reasonably expected.

Transactions

A statement of transactions dealing with the subject period and the previous one provides the database that makes identification of broad causes for budget deficits possible. It reveals the relationship between the flowery promises of politicians and how their ideas are actually implemented in terms of dollars and cents.

Table 8.7
Transactions (In Billions of Dollars)

	1965–1968		1961–1964	
Taxes		$ 549.4		$ 413.3
Less:				
Defense	$ 262.0		$ 210.1	
Interest	39.4		29.5	
Total		301.4		239.6
Net		$ 248.0		$ 173.7
Less:				
Government	$ 96.3		$ 64.5	
Hum. Resources	190.6		130.2	
Total		286.9		194.7
Net		-$ 38.9		-$ 21.0
Debt, beginning		- 256.8		- 236.8
Total		-$ 295.7		-$ 257.8

Table 8.7 *(continued)*
Transactions (In Billions of Dollars)

	1965–1968	1961–1964
	1965–1968	1961–1964
Adjustment[a]	6.2	1.0
Debt, end	-$ 289.5	-$ 256.8

a) See Table 8.1, note c.

Taxes

Energized, no doubt, by his economic advisers, LBJ was a dynamo of economic engineering. He produced no less than nine changes in tax policy, a level of intercession that would have made Lord Keynes proud. Since businessmen hate instability more than anything because they can't plan, it is safe to assume that such a level of interference must have been as welcome as dishwater on pancakes.

Johnson began with a four-year revenue base of $450.4 billion (1964 x four). In 1965–1968, actual revenue was $549.4 billion, 22.0 percent higher than the inherited base and 32.9 percent more than was collected in 1961–1964. About one-third of the increase (10.9 percent) was in the pipeline, the remainder related to the economic conditions and policies in play during LBJ's term.

Revenue increased in every year of Johnson's term: 3.7 percent in 1965, 12.0 percent in 1966, 13.8 percent in 1967, 2.8 percent in 1968.

Table 8.8
Tax Revenues (In Billions of Dollars)

	Total	Income	Corp.	SS[a]	Excise	Other[b]
1941pw	$ 8.7	$ 1.3	$ 2.1	$ 2.0	$ 2.5	$ .8
1944w	43.7	19.7	14.8	3.4	4.8	1.0
1948p	41.6	19.3	9.7	3.8	7.4	1.4
1952w	66.2	27.9	21.2	6.5	8.9	1.7
1956p	74.6	32.2	20.9	9.3	9.9	2.3
1960p	92.5	40.7	21.5	14.7	11.7	3.9
1964w	112.6	48.7	23.5	22.0	13.7	4.7
1968w	153.0	68.7	28.7	33.9	14.1	7.6

p = mostly peace. w = mostly war.

a) Social Security. b) Estate and gift taxes, custom duties and fees, Federal Reserve earnings, sundry.

Taxes as a relationship to earnings per capita remained steady at 22.1 percent. Was the shell game still sweeping mistakes into the federal closet labeled "Public Debt?"

Table 8.9
Revenues and Spending

Year	Federal Dollars		Per Capita Dollars			Per Capita Percentages of Average Earnings	
	Taxes	Spending	Taxes	Spending	Avg Earnings	Taxes	Spending
1941[a]	$ 9 bil.	$ 14 bil.	$ 65	$ 102	$ 923	7.0 %	11.1 %
1944[a]	44 bil.	91 bil.	326	682	1148	28.4	59.4
1948	42 bil.	30 bil.	284	203	1388	20.5	14.6
1952[a]	66 bil.	68 bil.	420	430	1653	25.4	26.0
1956	75 bil.	71 bil.	442	418	1949	22.6	21.4
1960	93 bil.	92 bil.	512	510	2219	23.1	23.0
1964[a]	113 bil.	119 bil.	587	618	2662	22.1	23.2
1968[a]	153 bil.	178 bil.	762	887	3445	22.1	25.7

a) deficit year

The shell game was alive and well under the masterly direction of LBJ. Yes, the tax bite as a percent of average income per capita was the same, but spending soared beyond available revenues. Was it caused by *Defense*?

What Did It?

DEFENSE

In 1964, LBJ had a four-year defense base of $219.2 billion. In 1965–1968, he spent $262.0 billion, 19.5 percent above the base and 24.7 percent above the *Defense* of 1961–1964.

But in 1964, America had 15,000 advisers in Vietnam; in 1968 it had 525,000 troops there. Increased dollars are not compatible with the degree of new effort. Why didn't *Defense* increase more? In the previous four years, the increase was also mild. Was Johnson surviving on the preparedness of Dwight Eisenhower? If the Soviets had provoked a second front, could America have responded?

Defense was fully financed by the revenue increase and in no way added to the deficit for the period. Thus is the notion eliminated that LBJ financed war with debt.

INTEREST

Interest has two determining components: the level of debt and the rate of interest. Since 1948, interest rates were on a steady upward course.

In 1965–1968, *Interest* was 33.6 percent higher than it was in 1961–1964. Had it grown at the same rate as revenue (32.9 percent), it would have cost

$39.2 billion, $.2 billion less than it actually did. *To that extent,* Interest *was not financed by the revenue increase and was responsible for the budget deficit.*

GOVERNMENT

Funds available for *Government* allowed 27.4 percent growth in this cost center. Actual growth was 49.3 percent, as follows:

Table 8.10
Government Operations, Net (In Billions of Dollars)

	1965–68	1961–64	% Change
Energy	$ 3.1	$ 2.2	40.9%
Nat'l Resources/			
Environment	11.1	8.5	30.6
Commerce	12.7	3.1	309.6
Transportation	23.6	18.1	30.9
Community development	4.7	2.3	104.3
International	21.8	19.0	14.7
Science	24.1	10.6	128.3
Agriculture	13.9	15.1	- 7.9
Justice	2.4	1.8	33.3
General	6.6	5.1	29.4
Total	$ 124.0	$ 85.8	44.8
Misc. Income	- 27.7	- 21.3	30.0
Net	$ 96.3	$ 64.5	49.3%

Commerce, Community Development and Science stand out in the above comparisons.

Commerce is a highly volatile line item. In 1961–1964, its cost decreased 46.5 percent from its 1957–1960 level, but in 1965–1968, it went up by 309.6 percent. The duties of the Commerce Department include mortgage credits (loans and guarantees for would-be homeowners), the Small Business Administration, and the regulation of lending institutions, including protection of depositors against bank failure (the latter responsibilities in the 1980s would result in heavy expense to the federal government). In 1965–1968, costs associated with mortgage credits were especially volatile, and the primary cause of the cost surge. Absent a full study of the Commerce budget, which is beyond the scope of this book, one must conclude that the variance reflected the current costs of its risky ventures.

Community Development went up 104.3 percent. The absolute increase was $2.4 billion, not a large amount in the terms of the federal budget. This increase was a reflection of LBJ's Great Society vision and a sign that this line item would grow in importance in years to come.

The increase in Science ($13.5 billion, 128.3 percent) was an additional investment in the reputations of John Kennedy and LBJ as space pioneers, the cost of which they passed on to future generations.

If the distortive influence of Commerce is eliminated from the above table, the growth in *Government* was 36.2 percent. A war was on. Such growth in a secondary cost center did not represent belt-tightening of the World War Two variety.

Had Government *limited itself to the allowable growth level (27.4 percent), expenditures would have been $82.2 billion, $14.1 billion less than actual. To that extent,* Government *added to the budget deficit.*

HUMAN RESOURCES

For a balanced budget to be the result, *Human Resources* could grow by 27.4 percent. Actually, it increased 46.4 percent, as follows:

Table 8.11
Human Resources (In Billions of Dollars)

	1965–68	1961–64	% Change
Education, Training, Services, Employment	$ 20.6	$ 5.3	288.7%
Health	12.1	5.4	124.1
Income Security	41.3	37.8	9.3
Subtotal	$ 74.0	$ 48.5	52.6
Social Security[a]	$ 83.8	$ 59.2	41.6
Medicare[a]	7.5	0.0	
Veterans	25.3	22.5	12.4
Subtotal	$ 116.6	$ 81.7	42.7
Grand total	$ 190.6	$ 130.2	46.4%

a) Funded by employers and employees. Note: Major federal programs since the 1960s—Medicaid, 1961; Food Stamps, 1962; Medicare, 1967; Student Aid, 1966.

Income Security and Veterans were fully financed in 1965–1968; Medicare appeared for the first time. Given the war in Vietnam and the tax load on the American people, the growth rate of Education and Health was obscene.

The cost of Education, etc., increased by 288.7 percent. All of this while America was at war. Did high taxes support the "boys over there" or the "politicians over here"?

Health increased 124.1 percent over 1961–1964 cost levels, Medicaid being the driving force. Enough facts were already in to support the projection that the cost of this line item would surely explode. Was anyone looking? Did anyone care?

In or out of war, but especially when a war was on, the imposition of such a range of social programs was, at best, bad timing or at worst, unconscionable. Moreover, the support given these programs by federal politicians was insulting because it said to the American people that they couldn't take care of themselves and their neighbors absent direct help from Washingtonocrats, a position that contravened 200 years of American history.

Had growth in Human Resources *been limited to 27.4 percent, expenditures would have been $166.0 billion, $24.6 billion less than actual. To that extent,* Human Resources *added to the deficit in 1965–1968.*

Conclusion

In 1964, LBJ ran against Barry Goldwater and won the prize with the largest popular margin (61 percent) in history. The Great Society was his program. In addition to civil rights, he sponsored aid to education, war against disease and poverty, Medicare, urban renewal, beautification and conservation, aid to depressed regions, and crime control. He also added two new federal agencies to supervise some of his sprawling interests—Housing and Urban Development, and Transportation.

The Democratic Congress signed on to the game and together with the president lifted to an art form the practice of funding domestic programs with debt. Don't raise taxes. Charge it. And the forays of Franklin Roosevelt into the private lives of Americans paled in comparison to LBJ's redistribution schemes that sought to cure the ills of the earth according to the Gospel of St. Lyndon. *This was the real beginning of the debt monster that wanders the halls of the federal government today. In four years, LBJ did more to socialize America than Franklin Roosevelt, his mentor, ever dreamt of.*

In 1965–1968, Johnson added $38.9 billion to the public debt and left behind a broad range of burgeoning social programs and entitlements that would haunt future presidents.

Table 8.12
Unrecovered Cost (In Billions of Dollars)

Defense	$ 0.0
Interest	0.2
Government	14.1
Human Resources	24.6
Total	$ 38.9

In 1965–1968, there were 48 straight months of economic growth, inflation was modest, and federal revenues grew at more than the average pace, but despite all this there was a deficit of $38.9 billion. If a president is at least partly measured by how well he managed the resources available to his administration, to that extent LBJ failed.

Perhaps the most important impact of the Johnson years was the installation of the federal government in the role of benefactor. State power was diminished, and individuals became more dependent on programs, grants, and aid. Special interest groups, no longer required to persuade 50 states to adopt favorable courses of action, gratefully trained their guns on the power brokers in the increasingly centralized federal government.

The power of Washington's politicians grew geometrically. Spawned by Roosevelt, encouraged by Truman, suffered by Eisenhower, and led to the Promised Land by Lyndon Johnson, they changed the face of America which, as it became bigger and richer, borrowed more, all of this behind the convenient curtains of World War Two, Korea, and Vietnam.

Roosevelt's excesses are legendary. His policies did not fix the Great Depression. LBJ's political excesses are legendary. His policies did not establish the Great Society. World War Two redeemed Franklin Roosevelt, but Vietnam destroyed Lyndon Johnson.

Chapter 9

Richard M. Nixon, 1969–1972

Richard M. Nixon was born in 1913 in Yorba Linda, California. The year before his birth, William H. Taft, a member of the Nixon family tree, completed his term as the 27th president of the United States. Nixon was the second of five brothers, all supervised by Quaker parents with modest resources.

In 1932, Nixon, who was 19, was attending Whittier College in California when another member of the family tree, Herbert Hoover, completed his single term in office. Presidential blood flowed through Nixon's veins.

Nixon's presence at Whittier was directly related to his outstanding high school record (first in the class of 1930), an achievement that brought scholarship opportunities for higher education. At Whittier, he majored in history and graduated in 1934 second in his class. Franklin D. Roosevelt was president.

Good grades, not personal or family wealth, fueled Nixon's academic career, this time qualifying him for Duke University Law School (1934–1937). Living off-campus in a farmhouse and working as a research assistant to cover expenses didn't deter the focused Californian from posting another personal and academic record of high achievement; he was an honor student and president of his class. He was admitted to the California bar in 1937. Roosevelt was still president.

For the next four years, Nixon experimented with a law career and a business venture. In 1942, when he was 29 years old, he had his first taste of government work in the Office of Price Administration in Washington. He didn't enjoy it and resigned to join the navy.

A member of the generation that faced military service shortly after graduation from college and before their careers had taken root, Nixon spent five years in a successful naval career that saw him rise from lieutenant junior grade to lieutenant commander. During the latter part of his service career, after a stint in the South Pacific, he returned to Washington and the Navy Department's Bureau of Aeronautics. He was discharged in 1946 when he was 33 years old. Harry Truman was president.

Aided by supporters who saw promise in the bright war veteran, Nixon began his political career in his home district with a surprise victory in 1946 over the incumbent congressman, Jerry Voorhis, with 57 percent of the vote. Four years later Nixon was a national figure because of his duties as chairman of the House Un–American Activities Committee which, among other things, uncovered the Russian spy, Alger Hiss. Friends of Hiss and their allies in the media chastised Nixon for decades for his part in that national drama but, in the 1990s, KGB information released revealed without doubt that Nixon's charges against Hiss were valid.

Capitalizing on his enlarged reputation, Nixon sought the seat of the retiring senator from California, Sheridan Downey, and defeated Helen Gahagan Douglas (wife of movie idol, Melvin Douglas) by a large margin. In this campaign his hard-hitting tactics earned him the nickname "Tricky Dick" that followed him thereafter. Now 38, Nixon was the youngest senator in the Senate chamber (1951). He served with distinction as a powerful critic of Truman until Dwight Eisenhower invited him aboard his presidential ticket in 1952.

After eight years as a well-traveled vice president, Nixon ran for the presidency in 1960 against John F. Kennedy and lost by fewer than 200,000 votes. In what may have been the finest hour of his political career, he didn't contest the result despite ample evidence that vote tampering, not Kennedy, had defeated him. His munificence spared the nation an endless quarrel over presidential succession.

Nixon retired to private pursuits after the election until he made an unsuccessful bid for the governor's seat in California in 1962. Thereafter he practiced law and limited his political activities to support appearances on behalf of Senator Barry Goldwater and other Republicans until he won his party's nomination for president in 1968.

Running against Vice President Hubert Humphrey and the war policies of Lyndon B. Johnson, Nixon won by a half-million votes. Perhaps the best-trained man ever to assume the presidential reins, with superb academic, military, and legal credentials, Nixon became the 37th president in 1969 when he was 56 years old.

Although his victory over Humphrey was clear, Nixon's popularity was not sufficient to gain control of Congress. John W. McCormack of Massachusetts (91st Congress), and Carl Albert of Oklahoma (92d Congress), both Democrats, ruled the House. Mike Mansfield, a Democrat from Montana, was majority leader in the Senate.

When Nixon assumed office, conservatives in both parties were anxious about the reach of Lyndon B. Johnson's Great Society programs. Nixon, with good conservative credentials, was expected to slow down what many thought to be a runaway train toward socialism. However else his presidency was to be evaluated, conservative followers expected him to make sense out of government spending, deficits, and the rise in public debt, and at the end of his administration he would be judged by them accordingly. He assumed a public debt of $289.5 billion, 28.4 percent of which related to unfunded federal programs and *Interest*, as follows:

Table 9.1

Summary of Deficits/Debt, 1941–1968 (In Billions of Dollars)

Years		Total	Defense	Interest	Govt.	Human Resources
Before 1941		$ 42.8	$ 42.8[a]	$ 0.0	$ 0.0	$ 0.0
1941–44 (FDR)		127.8	127.8	0.0	0.0	0.0
1945–48 (FDR/HST)		47.6	37.4	5.4	0.0	4.8
1949–52 (HST)[b]		- 2.0	- 2.0	0.0	0.0	0.0
1953–56 (Ike)		6.6	6.6	0.0	0.0	0.0
1957–60 (Ike 2)		12.1	0.0	0.0	4.4	7.7
1961–64 (JFK/LBJ)		21.0	0.0	0.0	12.8	8.2
1965–68 (LBJ)		38.9	0.0	.2	14.1	24.6
	Deficits	$294.8	$212.6	$ 5.6	$ 31.3	$ 45.3
	Adjust[c]	5.3				
	Debt	$ 289.5				
	Convert[d]	$ 1305.2				
	Debt 1996	$ 3732.9				
	Debt 1968 % of 1996	35.0%				

a) Includes cost of Great Depression (see p. 19). b) Surplus. c) Government figures come from a variety of sources and differ somewhat. This adjustment "forces" the above total to agree with the public debt amount reported by the Office of Management and Budget, Historical Tables, 7.1. d) Convert subject debt to 1996 dollars.

The changed political philosophy advocated by Lyndon Johnson is reflected in the above table. Prior to his ascension to power as majority leader in the Senate (1955), the winsome explanation of the Treasury Department for climbing public debt (see the Introduction) pertained. Thereafter it does not. Deficits beyond that point would, to the greatest extent, represent an act of free will by liberal leaders with an agenda, the result of which was a steady increase in debt with no end in view.

The second term (1957–1960) of Dwight D. Eisenhower, which was dominated by a "Johnson" Congress, saw the beginnings of a new trend that was a departure from the tried and true. Domestic programs were partially funded with debt.

Eight years later, at the end of Johnson's presidency (1968), the portion of debt related to unfunded domestic programs and excessive interest charges had risen to $82.2 billion. This huge addition was organized by liberals and tolerated by conservatives.

Would Nixon change this trend? If so, how?

Change in Public Debt

In his first year, Nixon had a budget surplus of $3.3 billion. Then everything went downhill. The deficit in the second year almost wiped out his small gain, and during the last two years, deficits were above $20 billion each. Debt increased to $322.4 billion.

Table 9.2
Change in Public Debt, 1968–1972 (In Billions of Dollars)

Public debt, 1968	$ 289.5
Deficit, 1969–1972	46.1
Total	$ 335.6
Adjustment[a]	- 13.2
Public debt, 1972	$ 322.4

a) See Table 9.1, note c.

Some pardon Nixon for his high deficits because Congress was controlled by liberals. But nobody put a muzzle on him or made it impossible for him to raise his eloquent voice in dissatisfaction with the unsound fiscal policies that were driving America into debt. Nixon did not adequately educate the public, a tool of inestimable value in the hands of a skilled rhetorician, which Nixon most certainly was.

Debt had steadily increased under all presidents since World War Two for various reasons and to varying degrees:

Table 9.3
Public Debt (In Billions of Dollars)

	Beginning	End	%
FDR	$ 42.8	$ 184.8	331.8%
FDR/HST	184.8	216.3	17.0
HST	216.3	214.8	- .7
Ike	214.8	222.2	3.4
Ike 2	222.2	236.8	6.7
JFK/LBJ	236.8	256.8	8.4
LBJ	256.8	289.5	12.7
RMN	289.5	322.4	11.4

The debt problem was not yet a major one, but the symptoms of things to come became clear in 1969–1972. The cost growth of federal programs was alarming. It was time to take another look, time to rethink decisions so hastily made during the previous administration. To do so, Nixon needed a cooperative Congress, but he didn't have one.

Table 9.4
Profile of Power, 1949–1972

Cong.	House	Senate	President
81	Rayburn (D)	Lucas (D)	Truman (D)
82	Rayburn (D)	McFarland (D)	Truman (D)
83	Martin (R)	Taft[a] (R)	Eisenhower (R)
83		Knowland (R)	
84	Rayburn (D)	Johnson (D)	Eisenhower (R)
85	Rayburn (D)	Johnson (D)	Eisenhower (R)
86	Rayburn (D)	Johnson[a] (D)	Eisenhower (R)
87	Rayburn (D)	Mansfield (D)	Kennedy (D)
87	Rayburn[b] (D)	Mansfield (D)	Kennedy (D)
87	McCormack (D)		
88	McCormack (D)	Mansfield (D)	Kennedy[c] (D)
88			Johnson[d] (D)
89	McCormack (D)	Mansfield (D)	Johnson (D)
90	McCormack (D)	Mansfield (D)	Johnson (D)
91	McCormack[a](D)	Mansfield (D)	Nixon (R)
92	Albert (D)	Mansfield (D)	Nixon (R)

a) Resigned. b) Died in office. c) Assassinated. d) VP succession.

As problem solvers, Nixon inherited two men, McCormack and Mansfield, who had helped to create his biggest headache—the Great Society.

Perspectives

If Lyndon B. Johnson weren't the busiest president in modern history, Nixon was; he had to deal with civil rights, war protesters, the cold war, foreign affairs, and the economy. Wherever he turned, there were problems, serious ones.

Except for the World War Two era and a modest blip in the 1950s, inflation had been a minor problem for Truman, Eisenhower, and Kennedy, seldom rising above 2 percent until under Johnson it rose to 4.2 percent (1968). In 1970 the rate increased to 5.7 percent and led Nixon to a decision that shocked conservatives (1971); he froze wages and prices for 90 days and imposed thereafter a system of controls that lasted to a decreasing degree until the end of 1973. Inflation dropped from a high of 5.7 percent to 3.2 percent. But the long-term impact of the controls was predictably horrid, as consumer demand, once unleashed, drove the rate up again (see Chapter Ten).

While Nixon unwisely tinkered with national controls, the unemployment rate crept from 3.6 percent in 1968 to 5.6 percent in 1972. Unemployment compensation payments in 1972 were almost $5 billion higher than in 1968 as a consequence.

These significant economic problems were faced during a time of social turbulence, the root causes being the Vietnam War, civil rights clashes, and (a new phenomenon for the United States) activists for a variety of causes. Civility took a beating in the 1970s and the budget for law enforcement increased.

The moods of the world were no better. Terrorists, feeling themselves aggrieved, engaged in an undeclared war against selected neighbors and waged it in a gruesome way against civilians. A prime example of this uncivilized behavior was the murder of eight Israeli athletes at the 1972 Olympic games by Arab terrorists.

Nixon did well in Vietnam, steadily reducing the involvement of American troops. Under Lyndon Johnson, the buildup had reached 543,000 men. The number was down to 340,000 by the end of 1970, 177,000 in 1971, and 25,000 in 1972. It was a remarkable achievement, but not good enough to impress protesters or the media.

It was a time of great international and domestic stresses which together exerted upward pressures on federal spending and took the analytical eye away from where the money was going, what the money was doing. In a time of such pressures, it was expected that the financial profile of America would change substantially, and it did.

Table 9.5
Financial Profile

	1940 (pop: 132.5 mil)[a]	1968 (pop: 200.7 mil)	1972 (pop: 209.9 mil)	1996 (pop: 265.5 mil)
Federal Income and Outlay, in Billions of Dollars				
GDP[b]	$ 100.0	$ 936.8	$1286.8	$7636.0
Taxes	6.5	153.0	207.3	1453.1
Spending	9.5	178.1	230.7	1560.5
Debt	42.8	289.5	322.4	3732.9
Interest	.9	11.1	15.5	241.1
Federal Income and Outlay—Proportional Comparisons, in Percentages				
Taxes/GDP	7%	16%	16%	19%
Spending/GDP	10	19	18	20
Debt/GDP	51	31	25	49
Taxes/Debt	15	53	64	39
Interest/Taxes	14	7	7	17
Federal Income and Outlay Per Capita, in Dollars				
Taxes	$ 49	$ 762	$ 988	$ 5473
Spending	72	887	1099	5878

Table 9.5 *(continued)*
Financial Profile

	1940 (pop: 132.5 mil)[a]	**1968** (pop: 200.7 mil)	**1972** (pop: 209.9 mil)	**1996** (pop: 265.5 mil)
Debt	313	1442	1536	14060
Interest	7	55	74	908

Average Per Capita Income, in Dollars[c]

	$ 849	$ 3445	$ 4677	$ 24231

Federal Income and Outlay as Percentage of Avg. Per Capita Income

Taxes	6.0%	22.0%	21.0%	23.0%
Spending	8.0	26.0	23.0	24.0
Debt	38.0	42.0	33.0	58.0
Interest	.8	1.6	1.6	3.7

Misery index, in percentages[d]

Prime interest	1.5%	6.6%	5.8%	8.3%
Unemployment	14.6	3.6	5.6	5.3
Inflation	.7	4.2	3.2	3.0

a) Population: U.S. Bureau of Census. b) GDP: 1940, 1942, 1944—Salem State College; other years—Federal Reserve Board, Chicago. c) Average income was not available for all years. Figures for missing years were estimated on a linear basis. d) Rates taken from several U.S. government sources.

The American economy prospers in times of war. Nixon was a beneficiary of that phenomenon, though not to the extent of his immediate predecessors. The positive business cycle that began in 1961 was 94 months old when he took office in 1969. It lasted for 12 more months at a weaker level, moved into a down cycle for 11 months, and then returned robustly for the final 25 months of Nixon's first term. Considered in terms of fiscal years, the business cycle provided Nixon with a weak first year, a bad second one, and two strong years of growth in GDP.

Table 9.6
Economic Indicators, 1953–1996

President	Year[a]	Cycle[b]	GDP[c]	CPI[d]	Rev.[e]
Eisenhower	1956	79%	18%	3%	39%
Eisenhower	1960	65	7	10	9
Kennedy/Johnson	1964	96	23	6	19
Johnson	1968	100	24	15	18
Nixon	**1972**	**77**	**14**	**23**	**18**
Nixon/Ford	1976	67	7	39	0
Carter	1980	88	7	48	14
Reagan	1984	67	9	28	15
Reagan	1988	100	14	16	16
Bush	1992	83	3	19	8

Table 9.6 *(continued)*
Economic Indicators, 1953–1996

President	Year[a]	Cycle[b]	GDP[c]	CPI[d]	Rev.[e]
Clinton	1996	100	7	13	13
Range:					
High		97	19	33	24
Low		70	6	7	6
Average[f]		82	10	18	14

a) The final year of the term. b) Ratio of months of growth in GDP to 48 months. c) Real growth, four years. d) Inflation, four years. e) Real growth in federal revenue, four years. f) The working average of those within the range.

Inflation was a disturbance in 1969–1972, but the other economic indicators were all positive for Nixon, especially the increase in tax revenue. Deficits were driven by cost, not the absence of income.

The misery index in 1972 was 14.6 percent versus 14.4 percent in 1968. Unemployment was worse, reflecting in part the hordes of troops returning stateside in search of jobs.

On Table 9.5, it appears that inflation abated in 1969–1972, and it is true that a direct comparison of the single years 1968 and 1972 is favorable. But that was a temporary downward blip, and the four-year inflation rate was 1.5 times higher than in 1965–1968.

Prime interest rates were down to 5.8 percent in 1972, but in 1969 and 1970, they approached 8 percent before they headed down. The fact that four-year growth of *Interest* was well ahead of the growth rate of public debt was a clear indication that high effective rates of interest still prevailed.

The increase in Nixon's revenue in 1969–1972 was well above average. Since military activity in Vietnam was down, one could hope for improved budget performance. The funds were there to mend some fiscal fences.

Taxes and federal expenditures in relation to income per capita dropped under Nixon, as did public debt in relation to GDP, all healthy indicators. But in absolute terms, public debt continued to rise in a period of vigorous growth, a warning that an insidious element in the budget process had a bottomless appetite that would one day, in less affluent times, extract a bitter price.

Nixon inherited a defense budget of $81.9 billion and in 1972 spent $79.2 billion; it didn't vary much during the interim years. Now two factors were in place that should have brought improved budget performance—strong revenues and stable *Defense*.

Spending priorities are expected to change when a nation moves from a wartime to a peacetime mode, and they did, but not in the direction one might have preferred.

Table 9.7
Spending Priorities[a]

	1940	1968	1972	1996
Defense	17.9%	46.0%	34.3%	17.0%
Interest	9.5	6.2	6.7	15.5
Total	27.4	52.2	41.0	32.5
Government	29.5	14.5	12.5	6.1
Soc. Sec.	0.0	13.4	17.4	22.4
Medicare	0.0	2.6	3.3	11.2
Veterans	.6	3.9	4.6	2.4
Welfare	42.5	13.4	21.2	25.4
Total	100.0%	100.0%	100.0%	100.0%

a) See discussion following Table 2.4

By the end of Nixon's first term, programs related to the New Deal, the Fair Deal, and the Great Society were fixtures in the federal budget. Nixon wasn't particularly inclined to rock the boat. Hopes of conservatives sagged as their champion buckled under the spending momentum in place. They feared that to be responsible was politically suicidal. At the same time, unfortunately, Americans who enjoyed the welfare state went up in numbers and down in literacy. Fears of conservative politicians became serious. To give was popular; to conserve was not. To feel was popular; to think was not. Group responsibility was in; personal responsibility was out. The "What-can-I-give-you?" politics emanating from Washington was dangerously popular to an increasing number of citizens.

Transactions

Despite the availability of higher income (40.9 percent), Nixon ran larger deficits than Johnson during a period when *Defense* had a relatively smaller claim on resources. Why? Comparing primary transactions of both administrations provides clues to that riddle.

Table 9.8
Transactions (In Billions of Dollars)

		1969–1972		1965–1968
Taxes		$ 774.1		$ 549.4
Less:				
Defense	$ 322.3		$ 262.0	
Interest	57.4		39.4	
Total		379.7		301.4
Net		$ 394.4		$ 248.0
Less:				
Government	$ 99.7		$ 96.3	

Table 9.8 *(continued)*
Transactions (In Billions of Dollars)

	1969–1972		1965–1968
Hum. Resources	340.8		190.6
Total		440.5	286.9
Net		-$ 46.1	-$ 38.9
Debt, beginning		- 289.5	- 256.8
Total		-$ 335.6	-$ 295.7
Adjustment[a]		13.2	6.2
Debt, end		-$.322.4	-$ 289.5

a) See Table 9.1, note c.

Taxes

Lyndon Johnson left behind a four-year revenue base of $612.0 billion (1968 revenue x four). Actual revenues in 1969–1972 amounted to $774.1 billion, a 26.5 percent increase related to the policy and economic environment during Nixon's years. The total increase in revenue in 1969–1972 over the previous four years was 40.9 percent, 14.4 percent of which was in the pipelines when Nixon took office.

Revenues increased in each of the four years of Nixon's first term except for 1971: 22 percent in 1969; 3.2 percent in 1970; -3.0 percent in 1971; and 11.8 percent in 1972. A decrease was not without precedent. Revenue dropped once in the 1930s (1939), three times in the 1940s (1946, 1948, 1949), and three times in the 1950s (1955, 1958, 1959).

Table 9.10
Tax Revenues (In Billions of Dollars)

	Total	Income	Corp.	SS[a]	Excise	Other[b]
1941pw	$ 8.7	$ 1.3	$ 2.1	$ 2.0	$ 2.5	$ .8
1944w	43.7	19.7	14.8	3.4	4.8	1.0
1948p	41.6	19.3	9.7	3.8	7.4	1.4
1952w	66.2	27.9	21.2	6.5	8.9	1.7
1956p	74.6	32.2	20.9	9.3	9.9	2.3
1960p	92.5	40.7	21.5	14.7	11.7	3.9
1964w	112.6	48.7	23.5	22.0	13.7	4.7
1968w	153.0	68.7	28.7	33.9	14.1	7.6
1972w	207.3	94.7	32.2	52.6	15.5	12.4

p = mostly peace. w = mostly war.

a) Social Security. b) Estate and gift taxes, custom duties and fees, Federal Reserve earnings, sundry.

Taxes in 1972, as a percent of average earnings per capita, were down by a full point (see below), good news from the standpoint of short-term benefit to taxpayers. But as an indicator of healthy fiscal policy, the change was illusory.

Total federal spending in 1972 was 23.5 percent of average income per capita. Had the government fully funded its programs, taxes would have been 23.5 percent of income, better than the record posted by Johnson in 1968 (25.7 percent), but it was also a continuation of the philosophy that had been in place for better than a decade: Never pay today what someone else can pay tomorrow. Conservatives had hoped that Nixon would change that policy, but he did not.

Table 9.11
Revenues and Spending

Year	Federal Dollars		Per Capita Dollars			Per Capita Percentages of Average Earnings	
	Taxes	Spending	Taxes	Spending	Avg. Earnings	Taxes	Spending
1941[a]	$ 9 bil.	$ 14 bil.	$ 65	$ 102	$ 923	7.0%	11.1%
1944[a]	44 bil.	91 bil.	326	682	1148	28.4	59.4
1948	42 bil.	30 bil.	284	203	1388	20.5	14.6
1952[a]	66 bil.	68 bil.	420	430	1653	25.4	26.0
1956	75 bil.	71 bil.	442	418	1949	22.6	21.4
1960	93 bil.	92 bil.	512	510	2219	23.1	23.0
1964[a]	113 bil.	119 bil.	587	618	2662	22.1	23.2
1968[a]	153 bil.	178 bil.	762	887	3445	22.1	25.7
1972[a]	207 bil.	231 bil.	988	1099	4677	21.1	23.5

a) deficit year

Three straight administrations had approved spending beyond the limits of revenue and had watched cost centers grow at rates recognizable as hazardous by a mathematical zombie. Accidental? Maybe. Or was it a deliberate attempt by a powerful group to change the role of government, using as a cover tax funds that citizens believed were needed for *Defense*? Perhaps.

But the practice of financing current operating costs with debt, whatever the motivation, had been institutionalized by 1972, and the political culture in Washington changed to accommodate it. "Charge it" was the slogan boldly proclaimed by liberals and sheepishly accepted by conservatives.

The silent agreement between the political parties to limit debt financing (for rare, huge, and wartime causes) that had controlled the behavior of American presidents and Congresses for almost 200 years had been trashed.

The race was on. Who could be the most compassionate, the kindest, the most sensitive? Who could spend the most, thereby becoming the darling of the establishment, defeat-proof at the voting booth?

What Did It?

DEFENSE

In 1956, Eisenhower maintained a military budget that took 60.2 percent of all spending. The times were relatively peaceful. Vietnam was a far-off war that Eisenhower wanted no part of. Peace reigned, or what passed for it in the hurly-burly world of that time. But the cold war with the USSR and the irritants that accompanied it mandated that the president maintain well-prepared American forces. *Defense* in 1960 was still dominant in the budget (52.2 percent of spending).

At the near peak of America's largest commitment to the war in Vietnam (1968), Johnson kept *Defense* at 46.0 percent of all spending, lower than Dwight Eisenhower's peacetime share. With the Soviet Union arguably more intransigent than ever, military spending dipped to 34.3 percent under Nixon in 1972. What magic bullet had Johnson and Nixon discovered? Was "adequate" defense cheaper in 1968? in 1972? Or was America less prepared?

Whatever the answers to those questions, it is clear that those who constantly blamed *Defense* for taking too large a slice of the revenue pie had no historical basis for their claims.

Defense increased 23.0 percent in 1969–1972, well below the rate of revenue increase (40.9 percent). The increase was fully financed and in no way added to the deficit for the period.

The conclusion was the same under Kennedy and Johnson. *Since all but the final days of the Vietnam War took place during the regimes of Kennedy, Johnson, and Nixon (first term), it follows that the total cost of it was financed with current revenues. Generally speaking, the same holds true of the Korean War. Only $6.6 billion of its total cost was funded with debt.*

Citizens who believed that the high taxes of the 1950s and 1960s were needed to support troops overseas will be dismayed to learn that instead they paid for the largest expansion of federal power in American history, one that brought the arms of Washington into their states, towns, churches, schools, living rooms, and bedrooms to a degree not even imagined by the Founding Fathers.

INTEREST

In 1969–1972, public debt increased from $289.5 billion to 322.4 billion—11.4 percent. *Interest*, on the other hand, went up by 45.7 percent. An increase in debt size and higher interest rates were the reason.

Had the increase been limited to the rate of revenue increase (40.9 percent), spending would have been $55.5 billion, or $1.9 billion less. Interest *added to the deficit in 1969–1972 to that limited extent.*

Was unfunded *Interest* a reasonable addition to public debt? Yes. Commercial interest rates dropped from 6.6 percent to 5.8 percent during the period, but they rose as high as 8.5 percent before dropping to the lower level. The effective rate during the period (6.7 percent) was above average for all presidents (extremes eliminated, 6.5 percent). The unfunded amount was part of a heavy, inflationary cost.

Interest was 7.4 percent of revenue. Commercial enterprises could not long exist with such an interest charge. Only in government is a line item of that size ignored. Given the spending philosophies in place, *Interest* will grow even more until it will finally reach a level that inconveniences politicians. Maybe then they will investigate the cause.

GOVERNMENT

Government increased by 3.5 percent in 1969–1972, well under the rate of revenue increase. For that reason, it did not contribute to the deficit for the period. It is prudent, however, to glance at the line items to maintain contact with the impact of policy decisions.

Table 9.12
Government Operations, Net (In Billions of Dollars)

	1969–72	1965–68	% Change
Energy	$ 4.3	$ 3.1	38.7%
Nat'l Resources/ Environment	14.1	11.1	27.0
Commerce	6.6	12.7	- 48.0
Transportation	30.0	23.6	27.1
Community Development	10.3	4.7	119.1
International	17.9	21.8	- 17.9
Science	17.9	24.1	- 25.8
Agriculture	20.6	13.9	48.2
Justice	4.8	2.4	100.0
General	9.6	6.6	45.4
Total	$ 136.1	$124.0	9.8
Misc. Income	- 36.4	- 27.7	31.4
Net	$ 99.7	$ 96.3	3.5%

Using the rate of revenue increase (40.6 percent) as the yardstick of acceptability, Community Development and Justice draw the eye from a cost control standpoint.

In 1957–1960, Community Development was less than $1 billion. Part of the Johnson heritage, it was over $10 billion and climbing under Nixon. The increase in Justice represented the attention that Republicans usually give to law and order. The footprints of budget cutters trying to slow spending in the few areas that do not unduly antagonize entrenched interests can be sensed in the cutbacks reflected in some line items.

HUMAN RESOURCES

The 1969–1972 budget of the Nixon administration was not entirely without restraints. Cost growth in *Defense* and *Government* was modest, and only a small portion of the growth in *Interest* ($1.9 billion) was unfunded. But in *Human Resources* one searches in vain for any signs that Richard Nixon had imposed restraints on Lyndon Johnson's newly created, and chronically unfunded, welfare state.

Despite the outpouring of the nation's resources into Vietnam, and the gnawing costs, social and financial, of inflation, Richard Nixon, leader of the political party that preached balanced budgets and fiscal restraint, stood idly by while the public debt and its corrosive partner, interest expense, climbed ever upward. If ever there was any doubt about the costs attached to the utopian dreams of the Great Society, it disappeared in the cost explosions of 1969–1972.

Table 9.13
Human Resources (In Billions of Dollars)

	1969–72	1965–68	% Change
Education, Training, Services, Employment	$ 38.4	$ 20.6	86.4%
Health	26.6	12.1	119.8
Income Security	79.2	41.3	91.8
Subtotal	$ 144.2	$ 74.0	94.9
Social Security[a]	$ 133.8	$ 83.8	59.7
Medicare[a]	26.0	7.5	246.7
Veterans	36.8	25.3	45.5
Subtotal	$ 196.6	$ 116.6	68.7
Grand total	$ 340.8	$ 190.6	78.8%

a) Funded by employers and employees. Note: Major federal programs since the 1960s—Medicaid, 1961; Food Stamps, 1962; Medicare, 1967; Student Aid, 1966; Coal Miners Benefits, 1970.

All line items except Veterans in *Human Resources* grew at a rate far beyond the allowable rate (55.6 percent).

Education, Training, Employment, and Social Services grew by 86.4 percent, but that only tells part of the sad tale. The cost of that line item in the single year 1972 ($12.5 billion) was 7.5 times higher than it was in 1964 ($1.6 billion) under Johnson. At zero growth, projected cost in 1973–1976 was $50.0 billion.

Health grew by 119.8 percent. But the single year 1972 compared with 1964 shows that the line item grew 5.1 times in eight years.

Income Security grew by 91.8 percent. This line item was the home of many favored programs (food, housing, etc.), and its growth was completely out of control.

Inflation as an answer? Forget it. As an explanation for spending growth, it's not worth the time it would take to calculate comparable dollars. No inflation rate can explain a four-year cost increase of 78.8 percent.

Payments to and in behalf of veterans vary from era to era depending upon the use of the military.

Social Security and Medicare programs continued the commitment made in the Roosevelt era to provide a safety net for the elderly of the nation. These were popular programs which, under the old system of federal priorities, would have been financed with little difficulty. During Nixon's term, if not sooner, however, it became apparent that their growth was faster and bigger than anticipated. They needed reexamination. If revisions had been made in those years, subsequent problems would have been avoided.

Few people have available to them more data dealing with demographics than federal politicians, and they have easy access to those who can interpret statistical data and extrapolate probabilities from it. How many of them, faced with such hearty early-warning signals, took the time to estimate where these popular program were headed?

The numbers in the *Human Resources* table speak for themselves. Reading them elicits the shock one *should feel* when faced with such eagerness to spend the mountains of dollars made available by American taxpayers.

The 1969–1972 deficit was $46.1 billion. Cost increases in *Defense* and *Government* were fully funded; only $1.9 billion of *Interest* was unfunded. *The balance of the deficit, $44.2 billion, relates to the cost eruption in* Human Resources.

Conclusion

Whatever presidential evaluation panels have to say about Nixon, he was popular with the voters in 1972. In the presidential race of that year, he whipped Democrat George McGovern by 18 million votes—about 61 percent of the vote. Ordinarily this would mean that conclusive remarks related to his performance in office would be withheld until the eight-year record was complete. But Nixon was not to have an eight-year record. In August 1974 he resigned in disgrace following the Watergate scandal that has been voluminously reported elsewhere. For that reason his 1969–1972 record, relative to control of the public debt, will be treated as complete.

Nixon became president in 1969 supported by 44 percent of the voters. The effective presence of George C. Wallace in that presidential race, as leader of the American Independent party (he drew almost 10 million votes), drew away the votes that might have gone to a majority winner. Vice President Hubert Humphrey came within a half-million votes of keeping Nixon from the presidency.

When these two elections are viewed with the wisdom of hindsight, it becomes clear that the media and the mob do not speak for the American people. Humphrey, representing the most controversial war policies in the recent history of the United States, almost won. Four years later, vilified from all quarters for his Vietnam policy, Nixon coasted to a big win over the peace advocate Senator George McGovern.

Debt increased under Nixon by $46.1 billion, as follows:

Table 9.14
Unrecovered Cost (In Billions of Dollars)

Defense	$ 0.0
Interest	1.9
Government	0.0
Human Resources	44.2
Total	$ 46.1

Within the analysis of *Interest*, it was concluded that the unfunded amount represented an unusual cost of inflation that could with reason be added to public debt, which fact reduces the above "fiscal mistake" ($46.1 billion) from 100.0 percent to 95.9 percent.

The destructive cost potential of *Human Resources* should have pulled from Nixon a rhetorical barrage of protest, but it didn't. At this crucial stage in the development of the welfare state, conservatives could see the dangerous potential of the Great Society and, given a stronger backbone, might have redirected its course. They didn't, and an opportunity was lost.

The Council of Economic Advisors became influential in 1946 under Harry Truman and was increasingly staffed with men trained in the theories of John Maynard Keynes, the economist who was undisturbed by deficits and debt. There is some evidence that Nixon had accepted the Keynesian view himself, although how seriously one cannot say. But given the fact that ideas usually precede action, it is important to be aware of the intellectual atmosphere within the ranks of those who advise presidents. Those who are afraid of deficits are less likely to create them than those who are not.During the Nixon years, conservatives worried about Lyndon Johnson's policies that were now the law of the land. How did they square with ideas like justice, order, and freedom? Had they not been tried before under different names and in different places (like the Soviet Union) and found wanting?

Many Americans voted for Nixon in 1968 to bring order to this rush to perfection. They hoped he would slow the train to heaven and replant the country's feet in its heritage.

He didn't. And no effective cries from conservative members of Congress were heard to admonish him for not making a better effort.

History had placed Nixon in a position to articulate a new direction for

America, taking the good from New Deal, Fair Deal, and Great Society programs and rejecting the bad; reshaping the survivors in forms that would permit sensible and affordable growth. Nixon owed the American people an honest explanation of how their taxes had been used for the last three decades and how they would be used in the future if needed reforms were ignored.

Nixon did not recognize the once-in-a-lifetime chance that he had in 1969–1972 to reshape America, so intent was he on foreign affairs. In the end, his first term ended with the liberal agenda intact and debt soaring. The best-trained man ever to assume the presidency, the ex-naval officer, had missed the boat.

Chapter 10

Richard M. Nixon/
Gerald R. Ford 1973–1976

Richard M. Nixon won handily his presidential race in 1972 over Senator George McGovern. Despite criticism from the press and protesters that kept the Vietnam War issue burning, citizens believed Nixon had retreated from the war with all possible speed, or so they voted. They sent him back to the White House.

Ironically, Nixon's enemies assisted in his reelection by assuming that the public believed what the press and the TV-heads endlessly repeated—that Nixon's war policies were unpopular throughout the country. Led by McGovern's left-wing supporters, they attacked Nixon's measured retreat from Vietnam, which was his strong suit with voters, and soft-pedaled criticism of his weak suit—continued deficits and growing debt. Had McGovern focused voter attention on the economy instead of a war that was yesterday's news, he might have done better. By muting economic issues, McGovern protected Nixon's weakest flank.

No sooner was Nixon sworn in for the second time than the scandal known as the Watergate affair surfaced and gained steady momentum. And if that weren't enough, Vice President Spiro Agnew was forced to resign in 1973 because of alleged financial misdealings.

Pressures associated with Watergate drew closer to Nixon in 1973 even as he dealt with foreign affairs and other major matters of state. His original advisers were gone by 1974, and he was surrounded by assistants he hardly knew. The congressional investigation of Watergate reached its apex when he refused to release tapes of presidential meetings, claiming executive privilege. The case went to the Supreme Court, and there Nixon lost his final and determining battle. The tapes were released, his lies revealed, and in August 1974, he resigned. Gerald R. Ford, who had succeeded Agnew as vice president, assumed the presidency.

When Gerald R. Ford was born in Omaha, Nebraska, in 1913, he was named Leslie L. King, Jr. His parents divorced when he was two years old, and his mother moved to Grand Rapids, Michigan, where she in due course married a local businessman, Gerald Ford. Ford adopted the boy and named him Gerald R. Ford. Woodrow Wilson was president.

Twenty years later Ford was a football star at the University of Michigan, where he graduated in 1935. Despite an active athletic schedule, he had maintained a B average.

Ford turned his back on a professional football career (he had contract offers from the Detroit Lions and the Green Bay Packers) and went to Yale as its head boxing coach and assistant football coach. He also studied law part-time and in 1938 became a full-time student. He graduated in 1941 in the top 25 percent of his class. Ford returned to Michigan, passed the bar, and joined a law firm in Grand Rapids. It was the first year of Roosevelt's third term as president.

Like Richard Nixon (they were the same age), Ford was a member of the generation that spent many years in uniform during World War Two. In 1942 he locked the doors of his law office and joined the navy as an ensign. He was eventually assigned to the USS *Monterey*, a light aircraft carrier in the fleet of Admiral Bull Halsey. Serving as a gunnery officer, Ford took part in several great battles in the South Pacific, including Wake Island, Okinawa, and the recapture of the Philippines. He earned 10 battle stars and in 1946 was discharged as a lieutenant commander. Ford was a bright and brave man, two characteristics that would later be ignored by the Washington press, which seemed to delight in portraying him as a slow-witted, clumsy buffoon.

After the war, Ford joined a law firm in Grand Rapids until in 1948 he defeated the incumbent congressman, Bartell Junkman, a Republican, in the primaries and then went on to win the general election. His political career was launched. Harry Truman was president.

Ford brought the toughness and intelligence to the House that he had shown in football, the navy, and his law career. He was one of two House members on the Warren Commission that investigated the assassination of President Kennedy, he was a critic of Lyndon Johnson's War on Poverty ("a lot of washed-up old programs"), and by 1965 he was at age 52 the minority leader and potential Speaker of the House. But fate decided otherwise. Vice President Spiro Agnew resigned because of a financial scandal, and in 1973 Ford replaced him.

Richard Nixon resigned in August 1974, and in September 1974 President Ford granted him a "full, free and absolute pardon," a brave and wise act of a man with a job to do. It was brave because it jeopardized his political future and wise because it took Nixonmania off the front pages (where it otherwise would have remained for years) and permitted the political process to move forward.

Nixon won big in 1972 (over 60 percent of the vote) but his coattails were short and Congress remained in the hands of the same two liberal Democrats—Carl Albert, House Speaker, and Mike Mansfield, Senate majority leader—bad news for any president who hoped to reverse spending trends.

The public debt inherited by Nixon was now Ford's to deal with. It had grown to $322.4 billion in 1969–1972, and $128.3 billion of it (29.4 percent) was related to interest charges and unfunded federal programs, as follows:

Table 10.1
Summary of Deficits/Debt, 1941–1972 (In Billions of Dollars)

Years		Total	Defense	Interest	Govt.	Human Resources
Before 1941		$ 42.8	$ 42.8[a]	$ 0.0	$ 0.0	$ 0.0
1941–44 (FDR)		127.8	127.8	0.0	0.0	0.0
1945–48 (FDR/HST)		47.6	37.4	5.4	0.0	4.8
1949–52 (HST)[b]		-2.0	2.0	0.0	0.0	0.0
1953–56 (Ike)		6.6	6.6	0.0	0.0	0.0
1957–60 (Ike 2)		12.1	0.0	0.0	4.4	7.7
1961–64 (JFK/LBJ)		21.0	0.0	0.0	12.8	8.2
1965–68 (LBJ)		38.9	0.0	.2	14.1	24.6
1969–72 (RMN)		46.1	0.0	1.9	0.0	44.2
	Deficits	$ 340.9	$212.6	$ 7.5	$ 31.3	$ 89.5
	Adjust[c]	18.5				
	Debt	$ 322.4				
	Convert[d]	$ 1210.2				
	Debt 1996	$ 3732.9				
	Debt 1972					
	% of 1996	32.4%				

a) Includes cost of Great Depression (see p. 19). b) Surplus. c) Government figures come from a variety of sources and differ somewhat. This adjustment "forces" the above total to agree with the public debt amount reported by the Office of Management and Budget, Historical Tables, 7.1. d) Convert subject debt to 1996 dollars.

When Nixon assumed office in 1969, the portion of debt represented by unfunded *Interest, Government,* and *Human Resources* was $82.2 billion. His first job, relative to the budget, was to slow the spending in those cost centers. And that responsibility was passed on when Ford assumed control. Congressional resistance was formidable.

The inability of Nixon/Ford to control the growth of the welfare state went beyond political resistance. The cost of entitlements is not subject to the same kind of scrutiny as are expenditures for, say, battleships. Once launched, welfare programs tend to sail unmolested. Otherwise, outgo is limited only by eligibility criteria. And there is no overall spending cap. (Attempts to establish one have always failed.)

No president can halt the spending of an undisciplined Congress under such a system. Overhaul is the only way to stop it or lighten it.

Such is the legacy of Lyndon B. Johnson.

Change in Public Debt

The first year of Nixon's second term was promising only in the sense that the deficit ($14.9 billion) was lower than the previous year ($23.4 billion). Ford saw the same occurrence in 1974—the deficit dropped to $6.6 billion. But the improvement was illusory. Spending, not revenue, had always been the core of the deficit issue, and it was apparent in 1974 that the major problem persisted. It showed itself with a large growl in the next two years when spending soared. In Ford's final two years, total deficits were $126.9 billion; for the four years, they were $148.0 billion.

Table 10.2
Change in Public Debt, 1972–1976 (In Billions of Dollars)

Public debt, 1972	$ 322.4
Deficit, 1973–1976	148.0
Total	$ 470.4
Adjustment[a]	7.0
Public debt, 1976	$ 477.4

a) See Table 10.1, note c.

Public debt increased by 48.1 percent in 1973–1976. At that rate it would double in 100 months. The situation that had been worsening for a decade was hitting its full stride.

Table 10.3
Public Debt (In Billions of Dollars)

	Beginning	End	Percent
FDR	$ 42.8	$ 184.8	331.8%
FDR/HST	184.8	216.3	17.0
HST	216.3	214.8	- .7
Ike	214.8	222.2	3.4
Ike 2	222.2	236.8	6.7
JFK/LBJ	236.8	256.8	8.4
LBJ	256.8	289.5	12.7
RMN	289.5	322.4	11.4
RMN/GRF	322.4	477.4	48.1

"A fool and his money are soon parted," some wise man once said. American politicians, as the above chart shows, seem determined to prove the wisdom of that observation.

Presidents alone do not create debt. It takes teamwork, the type at which

Washingtonocrats excel. Congressional allies or opponents are equal partners in the fiscal affairs of Washington.

Table 10.4
Profile of Power, 1949–1976

Cong.	House	Senate	President
81	Rayburn (D)	Lucas (D)	Truman (D)
82	Rayburn (D)	McFarland (D)	Truman (D)
83	Martin (R)	Taft[a] (R)	Eisenhower (R)
83		Knowland (R)	
84	Rayburn (D)	Johnson (D)	Eisenhower (R)
85	Rayburn (D)	Johnson (D)	Eisenhower (R)
86	Rayburn (D)	Johnson[a] (D)	Eisenhower (R)
87	Rayburn (D)	Mansfield (D)	Kennedy (D)
87	Rayburn[b] (D)	Mansfield (D)	Kennedy (D)
87	McCormack (D)		
88	McCormack (D)	Mansfield (D)	Kennedy[c] (D)
88			Johnson[d] (D)
89	McCormack (D)	Mansfield (D)	Johnson (D)
90	McCormack (D)	Mansfield (D)	Johnson (D)
91	McCormack[a](D)	Mansfield (D)	Nixon (R)
92	Albert (D)	Mansfield (D)	Nixon (R)
93	Albert (D)	Mansfield (D)	Nixon[a] (R)
94	Albert[a] (D)	Mansfield (D)	Ford[d] (R)

a) Resigned. b) Died in office. c) Assassinated. d) VP succession.

At a time when a president badly needed ideological allies, Nixon and Ford had none.

Perspectives

The shooting war in Vietnam was over for the United States when Ford assumed command, but tensions persisted at home, albeit at a subdued level, and one more major embarrassment remained to the international image of America.

In an attempt to defuse local tempers, Ford offered clemency in September 1974 (the same month he pardoned Nixon) to draft evaders and deserters. The idea met with mixed reviews. The American Legion thought the terms too liberal, some malefactors considered them too tough, others accepted the opportunity to get square with the law. Cynics regarded Ford's offer as blatant politics, an attempt to blunt attacks from the media relative to the pardon of Nixon. Trying to heal America's bruises, however, was probably worthwhile as a signal, if nothing else, that the federal government heard the voices in the streets.

The final major embarrassment related to Vietnam took place in the spring of 1975. Saigon, the capital city of South Vietnam, was taken by the Communists, the American Embassy was ravaged, and television cameras worldwide were treated to a final view of Americans turning tail and running to safety. Vietnam was unified soon after as the Socialist Republic of Vietnam. The capital city, Saigon, was renamed Ho Chi Mihn City after the esteemed leader of North Vietnam.

It was over. Whatever America's objective had been in Vietnam, which was never clear, it was thwarted. The war America never fought to win was lost. The grim experience affected the use of America's military power from that day until today.

The presidential plate of Ford was not as full or as varied as that faced by Johnson or Nixon, but it was far from being empty of considerable challenges. This was a time when hijackers changed forever the casual serenity of airports. Pro-Palestinian forces, for example, took an Air France plane and held over 100 hostages until Israeli commandos freed them in a raid on Uganda's Entebbe airport.

And domestic turbulence continued despite the cutback in Vietnam, the civil rights legislation, and the flood of Great Society money that poured into federal programs, all of it designed by Washington's politicians to cure the nation's ills. As an example of the idiocy at large, in 1974 the 19-year-old daughter of William Randolph Hearst was kidnapped by the Symbionese Liberation Army.

And this was a time that effluence from the Watergate affair continued to irritate the political process. John Mitchell, John Ehrlichman and H. R. Haldeman, who were insiders with Nixon, were found guilty of cover-up activity and jailed. The mood in Congress toward the president and between the political parties was antagonistic, which partly explains why Ford exercised his veto power 61 times in 27 months. His need to do so was not lessened by the defensive position that he, the post-Watergate Republican president, had inherited.

The cost of Watergate in terms of the power of the presidency cannot be overestimated. Seeing Nixon on the ropes, Democratic opponents seized the moment to increase their power in the budget process. A month before he resigned, a subdued Nixon signed the Budget Control Act. In so doing, he established the Congressional Budget Office (CBO) and eliminated the presidential power to impound (to hold back on the payment of approved expenditures), putting into place as a substitute the toothless power of recision.

CBO is a bureau that does for Congress what the Office of Management and Budget (OMB) does for the executive. Its creation put two fact-finding groups into competition, guaranteeing that the basic information, especially revenue projections upon which decisions are based, would thereafter be politicized. This competition lessened the power of the presidential office, the only one responsible to all of the people, and it increased the power of Congress. The de facto elimination of the power of the president to impound took away one of the few controls over spending that remained.

And three other factors that lessened control were now fixed elements of the budget process:

> 1) Attitude—Conservative fiscal policies of Adam Smith, once shared by both parties, had been replaced by or were at least challenged by those of John Maynard Keynes. High spending and growing debt were supported by respected economic theory.
> 2) Entitlements—Lyndon Johnson introduced a plethora of entitlement programs. Once approved, entitlements escape the regular approval process; spending is automatic.
> 3) Seniority—The seniority system in the House was a force against radical, hasty change. It was all but destroyed, and the result is an endless group of ungovernable committees and chairpersons.

Such things destroyed the ability of government to control spending and made it unlikely that Ford or any future president would make inroads on the problem.

Another sign of the changing times was the two attempts to assassinate Ford in September 1975. The shooters were young women. The New Age had arrived. Modern women, it was demonstrated, could be just as bad as old-fashioned men, an aspect of the Great Society that many could live without.

Ford could dodge bullets, but he could not get away from economic problems that began with Johnson, accelerated under Nixon, and exploded in 1975–1976. The Grim Reaper had arrived to claim his price. The financial profile of America, ever evolving, showed signs of strain brought on by a 12-year spending orgy.

Table 10.5
Financial Profile

	1960 (pop: 180.7 mil)[a]	1972 (pop: 209.9 mil)	1976 (pop: 218.1 mil)	1996 (pop: 265.5 mil)
Federal Income and Outlay, in Billions of Dollars				
GDP[b]	$ 523.9	$1286.8	$1880.3	$7636.0
Taxes	92.5	207.3	298.1	1453.1
Spending	92.2	230.7	371.8	1560.5
Debt	236.8	322.4	477.5	3732.9
Interest	6.9	15.5	26.7	241.1
Federal Income and Outlay—Proportional Comparisons, in Percentages				
Taxes/GDP	18%	16%	16%	19%
Spending/GDP	18	18	20	20

Table 10.5 *(continued)*
Financial Profile

	1960 (pop: 180.7 mil)[a]	1972 (pop: 209.9 mil)	1976 (pop: 218.1 mil)	1996 (pop: 265.5 mil)
Debt/GDP	45	25	25	49
Taxes/Debt	39	64	62	39
Interest/Taxes	7	7	9	17

Federal Income and Outlay Per Capita, in Dollars

Taxes	$ 512	$ 988	$ 1367	$ 5473
Spending	510	1099	1705	5878
Debt	1310	1536	2189	14060
Interest	38	74	122	908

Average Per Capita Income, in Dollars[c]

	$ 2219	$ 4677	$ 6548	$ 24231

Federal Income and Outlay as Percentage of Avg. Per Capita Income

Taxes	23.0%	21.0%	21.0%	23.0%
Spending	23.0	23.0	26.0	24.0
Debt	59.0	33.0	33.0	58.0
Interest	1.7	1.6	1.9	3.7

Misery index, in percentages[d]

Prime interest	5.0%	5.8%	6.4%	8.3%
Unemployment	5.5	5.6	7.7	5.3
Inflation	1.7	3.2	5.8	3.0

a) Population: U.S. Bureau of Census. b) GDP: 1940, 1942, 1944—Salem State College; other years—Federal Reserve Board, Chicago. c) Average income was not available for all years. Figures for missing years were estimated on a linear basis. d) Rates taken from several U.S. government sources.

A string of growth months for GDP began in 1970 and was 25 months old when Nixon's second term began. The positive trend continued for 11 more months, sunk into a downturn for 16, but then turned positive for the final 21 months of the Nixon/Ford administration. In terms of fiscal years, the first and last ones were good; the middle years were poor.

Table 10.6
Economic Indicators, 1953–1996

President	Year[a]	Cycle[b]	GDP[c]	CPI[d]	Rev.[e]
Eisenhower	1956	79%	18%	3%	39%
Eisenhower	1960	65	7	10	9
Kennedy/Johnson	1964	96	23	6	19
Johnson	1968	100	24	15	18
Nixon	1972	77	14	23	18
Nixon/Ford	**1976**	**67**	**7**	**39**	**0**
Carter	1980	88	7	48	14

Table 10.6 *(continued)*
Economic Indicators, 1953–1996

President	Year[a]	Cycle[b]	GDP[c]	CPI[d]	Rev.[e]
Reagan	1984	67	9	28	15
Reagan	1988	100	14	16	16
Bush	1992	83	3	19	8
Clinton	1996	100	7	13	13
Range:					
High		97	19	33	24
Low		70	6	7	6
Average[f]		82	10	18	14

a) The final year of the term. b) Ratio of months of growth in GDP to 48 months. c) Real growth, four years. d) Inflation, four years. e) Real growth in federal revenue, four years. f) The working average of those within the range.

Eisenhower, Kennedy, Johnson, and Nixon (first term) all had an increase in federal income higher than the inflation rate by a comfortable margin. The Nixon/Ford administration was the first in that line to suffer the opposite situation.

The number of growth months enjoyed by Nixon/Ford was among the lowest, the four-year growth of GDP was below average, inflation went through the roof, and the real growth in federal revenue was negative, nonexistent. All luck during the period was bad luck.

Had normal growth occurred (14 percent), revenue in 1973–1976 would have been $1182.8 billion, or $111.6 billion more than actual ($1071.2 billion). To that extent, on the revenue side, the deficit for the period was driven by recession, and was a proper addition to public debt.

America had a real growth rate of almost 6 percent per year when the full scope of Great Society programs first hit the budget under Johnson. But by the time Ford left office, the growth rate had sunk below 2 percent per year.

The unemployment rate went from 5.6 percent in 1972 to 7.7 percent in 1976. But that tells only part of the unemployment story. Johnson had an average unemployment rate of 3.9 percent; Nixon, 4.9 percent; Ford, 6.7 percent, and climbing. The economy was in trouble and headed for more.

Compared to 1972, revenue in 1976 was up 43.8 percent; spending, 61.1 percent. That simple comparison serves as a quiet, effective, and accurate description of the debt problem.

Interest in 1976 was 72.2 percent higher than 1972; the prime rate was up to 6.4 percent, two more facts to worry those who took comfort from the fact that debt as a relationship to GDP remained relatively stable. The circumstances that brought that relationship into line were changing rapidly under the weight of the welfare state.

Table 10.7
Percentage Growth

	1972 vs. 1960	1976 vs. 1972
GDP	145.6%	46.1%
Debt	36.1	48.1
Spending	150.2	61.1

The comparison of 1972 with 1960 measures the Kennedy/Johnson/ Nixon administrations when the seeds of the welfare state were being planted but had not yet shown themselves as major cost factors in the budget. Spending and GDP were in line. The increase in public debt was much lower than that of GDP.

The comparison of 1976 with 1972 demonstrates that the Great Society was costs as well as dreams. The welfare seeds sprouted. Spending and GDP were out of line. The increase in spending exceeded the rate of growth; debt grew faster than GDP.

The misery index in 1976 reached 19.9 percent versus 14.6 percent in 1972, a significant increase that symbolized the hardship many Americans were experiencing. All indicators were up. Economic news was bad news.

A philosophy that supported an activist role for a federal government gained favor in the 1960s and was still in vogue in 1972. Under the guidance of liberals, budget priorities changed.

Table 10.8
Spending Priorities[a]

	1960	1972	1976	1996
Defense	52.2%	34.3%	24.1%	17.0%
Interest	7.5	6.7	7.2	15.5
Total	59.7	41.0	31.3	32.5
Government	11.9	12.5	14.0	6.1
Soc. Sec.	12.6	17.4	19.9	22.4
Medicare	0.0	3.3	4.2	11.2
Veterans	5.9	4.6	4.9	2.4
Welfare	9.9	21.2	25.7	25.4
Total	100.0%	100.0%	100.0%	100.0%

a) See discussion following Table 2.4.

Pre-Eisenhower Americans looked to Washington for unemployment compensation when times were tough, education support when they fought for their country, pension and medical support for the aged. General education and welfare were local concerns. The only other federal expenditures of consequence were defense, interest, and management expenses (*Government*).

Table 10.9
Summary of Federal Spending—Base vs. Other
(In Billions of Dollars)

	1960	1972	1976	1996
Defense	$48.1	$ 79.2	$ 89.6	$ 265.7
Interest	6.9	15.5	26.7	241.1
Soc. Sec.	11.6	40.2	73.9	349.7
Medicare	0.0	7.5	15.8	174.2
Unemployment	2.9	7.1	19.5	24.9
Veterans	5.4	10.7	18.4	37.0
Government	11.0	28.8	51.9	95.4
Base	$85.9	$ 189.0	$ 295.8	$1188.0
Other	6.3	41.7	76.0	372.5
Total	$92.2	$ 230.7	$ 371.8	$1560.5

Base as percentage of total

	93.2%	81.9%	79.6%	76.1%

Eventually political philosophy is expressed in budget numbers. Liberals claim to be prudent money managers but deficits related to their decisions give a more informative reading of their true beliefs and goals. Conservatives may bellow during heated election campaigns about tax-and-spend liberals, but their lack of effective, noisy, postelection resistance to unwise legislation uncovers the hypocrisy of their rhetoric. The antics of both groups reveal a fundamental comradeship they enjoy as they run their hands through the wealth that brings them security in office and power. This backstage alliance between major political parties, not the esoteric arguments over economic theory, is responsible for the shift in priorities shown in the previous two exhibits. As a percent of total spending, the Base dropped from 93.2 percent under Dwight Eisenhower to 79.6 percent under Ford. Expenditures which as a group were hardly noticeable in 1960 were about 20 percent under Ford and growing.

Substantially improved social conditions at the expense of temporary economic troubles might be a salable formula to many Americans. But information herein displayed suggests that economic problems may not be temporary, and the table below shows that federal action and social behavior are not as closely allied as liberals think; more money does not necessarily bring fewer problems.

Table 10.10
American Social Statistics

	1965	1970	1975	1994
Murders	8773	16848	18641	22084
Rapes		37990		102100
Prisoners		196429	240593	1016760

Table 10.10 *(continued)*
American Social Statistics

	1965	1970	1975	1994
Divorces	479000	708000	1036000	1191000
Abortions			1034000	1529000[a]
Population (millions)	194.3	205.1	216.0	260.7

a) 1992 figure.

These data do not neatly synchronize with presidential eras, but the information is adequate to support the dictum that Lyndon Johnson's legacy, the Great Society, has not yet been realized.

In 1975 the number of murders was 113 percent higher than in 1965 and divorce was up 116 percent, while population grew only 11 percent. In 1975 there were a million abortions. This is progress? For this America goes into debt?

It is easy but unwise to overlook the fact that Washington became a different place as the mix of spending changed. The number of lobbyists approaching an Eisenhower administration that concentrated on management, defense, interest, veterans, and unemployment assistance was limited. But as Washington retained wartime taxes and opened its purse, special interest groups poured into the richest city on earth in search of their slice of the pie. In the 1960s fewer than 20,000 lobbyists operated in Washington; in the 1990s, there were over 60,000.

America's politicians swelled in self-importance as the mighty representatives of industry, unions, churches, charities, genetic, and ethnic groups groveled at their feet for favors. Heady wine and a dangerous brew. Even the most casual knowledge of human nature reveals the dangerous and certain consequence of such encounters—corruption.

Transactions

From charts already examined, it is clear that the deficit reached new heights under Ford. Remaining questions deal with where, how much and, to the extent that the data and logic allow, why deficits grew so robustly. Examining the major transactions of the Ford administration in comparison with those of the previous one yields insights on such questions.

Table 10.11
Transactions (In Billions of Dollars)

		1973 1976		1969–1972
Taxes		$1071.2		$ 774.1
Less:				
Defense	$ 332.1		$ 322.3	
Interest	88.6		57.4	
Total		420.7		379.4
Net		$ 650.5		$ 394.4

Table 10.11 *(continued)*
Transactions (In Billions of Dollars)

	1973–1976		1969–1972
Less:			
Government	$ 166.3		$ 99.7
Hum. Resources	632.2		340.8
Total		798.5	440.5
Net		-$ 148.0	-$ 46.1
Debt, beginning		- 322.4	- 289.5
Total		-$ 470.4	-$ 335.6
Adjustment[a]		- 7.0	13.2
Debt, end		-$ 477.4	-$ 322.4

a) See Table 10.1, note c.

Taxes

Tax income in 1973–1976 was 38.4 percent higher than in 1969–1972. In the single year 1972, income was $207.3 billion. Nixon/Ford, therefore, had a start-up revenue base of $829.2 billion which, within the economic environment of 1973–1976, grew to $1071.2 billion—29.2 percent larger than the start-up base. The remaining income growth (9.2 percent) was in the pipelines when Nixon began his second term.

The revenue increase in 1973–1976, a time of stability in *Defense*, was more than canceled out by the inflation rate, a recipe for disaster given the spending history of the recent past. To stay healthy, a reduction in the cost of government was called for. Knowing nothing else, one could safely predict that deficits would zoom and the misery index would become painful. *And, of great significance, deficits were now systemic—unavoidable in any long term until the very structure of the welfare state was changed. Cost reduction would no longer suffice; cost elimination was the requirement.*

It has been the fortunate history of the United States that the inherent strength of its economic system has always overcome the tamperings of lawmakers who annually do their best to destroy its job-making growth, the characteristic of the system that feeds more mouths and warms more bodies than all federal programs that ever were or ever will be. In nine administrations examined to this point, no president had back-to-back years as bad as Nixon/Ford's 1974 and 1975. Fiscal year 1974 began with a GDP of $3225.9 billion; fiscal 1975 ended with a GDP of $3173.4 billion—a negative growth in GDP of 1.6 percent before inflation of about 10.0 percent. From a budgetary standpoint, those were back-breaking years from which the administration could not recover.

The brakes were on.

The seemingly inexhaustible flow of increased revenues that year after year poured into the Golden City had slowed down. Spending, always at the outer edge of the revenue curve, hurtled past like a runaway horse. Would deficits that resulted frighten the liberals? Would a sense of reality return to Washington?

Economists and politicians will provide endless reasons for the economic mess born in the 1960s. But laymen must be excused for believing that people did it. Adult politicians saw and accepted the year-by-year deterioration of America's financial strength and allowed it to happen.

Why? To make themselves popular.

Table 10.12
Tax Revenues (In Billions of Dollars)

	Total	Income	Corp.	SS[a]	Excise	Other[b]
1941pw	$ 8.7	$ 1.3	$ 2.1	$ 2.0	$ 2.5	$ .8
1944w	43.7	19.7	14.8	3.4	4.8	1.0
1948p	41.6	19.3	9.7	3.8	7.4	1.4
1952w	66.2	27.9	21.2	6.5	8.9	1.7
1956p	74.6	32.2	20.9	9.3	9.9	2.3
1960p	92.5	40.7	21.5	14.7	11.7	3.9
1964w	112.6	48.7	23.5	22.0	13.7	4.7
1968w	153.0	68.7	28.7	33.9	14.1	7.6
1972w	207.3	94.7	32.2	52.6	15.5	12.4
1976p	298.1	131.6	41.4	90.8	17.0	17.3

p = mostly peace. w = mostly war.

a) Social Security. b) Estate and gift taxes, custom duties and fees, Federal Reserve earnings, sundry.

To spend outrageously is one thing—it captures votes. To tax outrageously is another—it costs votes. Harry Truman spent and taxed. One can admire him for that. He fought for the tax base needed to support his ideas. But emotions other than admiration are evoked toward those who spend beyond the limits of revenue but refuse to take the heat for the taxes needed to support their spending habits. That would be dangerous, too forthright. Spending on the cuff is safer. Voters feel and dislike taxes. Taxes are unpopular and dangerous to the job security of professional politicians. And taxpayers hardly notice increases in debt. The choice to new-breed politicians is obvious.

Charge it.

Table 10.13
Revenues and Spending

Year	Federal Dollars		Per Capita Dollars			Per Capita Percentages of Average Earnings	
	Taxes	Spending	Taxes	Spending	Avg. Earnings	Taxes	Spending
1941[a]	$ 9 bil.	$ 14 bil.	$ 65	$ 102	$ 923	7.0%	11.1%
1944[a]	44 bil.	91 bil.	326	682	1148	28.4	59.4
1948	42 bil.	30 bil.	284	203	1388	20.5	14.6
1952[a]	66 bil.	68 bil.	420	430	1653	25.4	26.0
1956	75 bil.	71 bil.	442	418	1949	22.6	21.4
1960	93 bil.	92 bil.	512	510	2219	23.1	23.0
1964[a]	113 bil.	119 bil.	587	618	2662	22.1	23.2
1968[a]	153 bil.	178 bil.	762	887	3445	22.1	25.7
1972[a]	207 bil.	231 bil.	988	1099	4677	21.1	23.5
1976[a]	298 bil.	372 bil.	1367	1705	6548	20.9	26.0

a) deficit year

Elected officials can and do use data like this to persuade people that taxes on American citizens are steady or dropping. And on the surface, they are being truthful. Taxes per capita on the above chart do show a controlled or downward trend. But if debts incurred must someday be paid, the relationship of federal spending to average earnings is more revealing than the one between taxes and earnings.

Four consecutive administrations hid from taxpayers the real cost of federal spending, and at the end of that era they left in their wake a slow-moving, debt-ridden economy.

What Did It?

DEFENSE

The Vietnam affair was history by 1976, but the increase in terrorism kept the world on edge and the Soviets were as bellicose as ever. The sense of priorities emanating from Washington indicated, however, that policymakers were more concerned with the expansion of federal programs than they were with national defense.

Table 10.14
Defense as a Share of GDP and Spending (In Billions of Dollars)

	Defense	GDP	Spending	Percent of GDP		Spending
1960p	$ 48.1	$ 523.9	$ 92.2	9.2%		52.2%

Table 10.14

Defense as a Share of GDP and Spending (In Billions of Dollars)

	Defense	GDP	Spending	Percent of GDP	Spending
1964w	54.8	675.1	118.5	8.1	46.2
1968w	81.9	936.8	178.1	8.7	46.0
1972w	79.2	1286.8	230.7	6.2	34.3
1976p	89.6	1880.3	371.8	4.8	24.1

p = mostly peace; w = mostly war

For a lifetime, Americans have heard vocal spenders demanding that *Defense* be cut so that favored programs could be added to the budget. So constant has been this clamor that it has been by and large accepted that military spending was too high. It wasn't. In fact the numbers lead one to wonder if leaders of the time valued the expansion of federal power more highly than national defense. Was America as prepared for international emergencies as it should have been? Would the need for military buildup in the 1980s have been as great had politicians of the 1970s been more responsible?

Whatever the answer to that question, *Defense* had nothing to do with the budget deficits of 1973–1976 because revenue increased by 38.4 percent, more than enough to finance the 3.0 percent increase in *Defense* (less than the rate of inflation).

INTEREST

Interest was 54.4 percent higher under Nixon/Ford than it was under Nixon. *Had its growth been limited to the growth in revenue (38.4 percent) in 1973–1976, the expenditure would have been $79.4 billion, or $9.2 billion less than actual. To that extent it added to the 1973–1976 deficit.*

Was unfunded *Interest* a reasonable addition to public debt? No. Had income in 1973–1976 been normal (14 percent real increase), it would have funded the increased *Interest*. That it didn't is the fault of the recession. But the cost of the recession has already been calculated in revenue terms on page 126. To recognize unfunded *Interest* separately would be to "double count."

GOVERNMENT

In 1973–1976, $650.5 billion was available to *Government/Human Resources* in the context of a balanced budget (see page 130). But had *Interest* been fully funded, that amount would have been $9.2 billion higher, or $659.7 billion—49.8 percent above the spending level of *Government/Human Resources* in 1969–1972. To the extent that the rate of increase in *Government* exceeded 49.8 percent during the subject period, that cost center was a contributor to the deficit of 1973–1976.

Government increased by 66.8 percent during the Nixon/Ford administration. This cost explosion was a major element of the total deficit for reasons that will become clearer when the important line items of its budget are examined.

Table 10.15
Government Operations, Net (In Billions of Dollars)

	1973–76	1969–72	% Change
Energy	$ 9.6	$ 4.3	123.3%
Nat'l Resources/ Environment	26.0	14.1	84.4
Commerce	23.1	6.6	250.0
Transportation	43.0	30.0	43.3
Community Development	18.6	10.3	80.6
International	23.3	17.9	30.2
Science	16.4	17.9	- 8.4
Agriculture	13.4	20.6	- 35.0
Justice	11.0	4.8	129.2
General	40.0	9.6	316.7
Total	$224.4	$136.1	64.9
Misc. Income	- 58.1	- 36.4	59.6
Net	$166.3	$ 99.7	66.8%

It was previously established that the vagaries of risk associated with the normal duties of Commerce result in cost distortions from period to period. It was no different in 1973–1976. And it isn't surprising to find that the costs associated with mortgage credits skyrocketed, a cost that is related to the increasingly difficult time that Americans and their institutions were having in the inflation-plagued economic environment of those years.

Absent the distortion of Commerce, *Government* cost was $143.2 billion and $93.1 billion, respectively, an increase of all other line items of 53.8 percent. Energy, Justice, General were out of line. Natural Resources/Transportation were the most expensive increases.

Four factors were primarily responsible for the major cost variance in these line items. 1) The embargo imposed on shipments of oil from OPEC nations added to the costs. 2) Under "Perspectives" a table is shown that depicts the disintegration of a civil society in America. This is a major topic that will not be probed except to say that a poorly behaved society is expensive. The costs of containing bad behavior appeared in Justice in 1973–1976. 3) Attached to Great Society programs was an increasing awareness of the condition of the environment. A lobby grew up around such issues. Increased sensitivity of the federal government was the essential reason for the cost distortions in Natural Resources. 4) One element of General is a line item called "General purpose fiscal assistance." My research did not extend beyond the title itself, but one smells a corner of the Great Society being tucked away in an innocent-appearing place. Prior to the subject period, the four-year cost of the line item was about $2 billion; in 1973–1976 it was $28.7 billion and climbing. In such a way did Congress add overhead during a time when it couldn't pay for programs of the previous year.

Together Energy and Transportation cost $34.3 billion in 1969–1972. Had they increased in 1973–1976 at the full rate of inflation (38.8 percent), their cost would have been $47.6 billion. Actual cost was $52.6 billion, $5.0 billion higher. Some make the case that the large increase in *Government* was fundamentally caused by the oil embargo and higher energy costs attached to it. Facts do not support that position, but a claim for $5.0 billion of extraordinary energy costs would have a ring of validity to it.

Had the increase in Government *in 1973–1976 been limited to 49.8 percent, the cost would have been $149.3 billion, $17.0 billion less than actual. To that extent,* Government *added to the deficit during the period.* Of that total, $5.0 billion of excessive energy costs would have been reasonable additions to public debt.

HUMAN RESOURCES

Similar to *Government, Human Resources* in the context of a balanced budget could grow by 49.8 percent in 1973–1976. Growth beyond that amount would make the cost center a contributor to the deficit. *Human Resources* grew by 85.5 percent, a rate of increase in a major cost center that even fools would recognize as dangerous and unsustainable.

Table 10.16
Human Resources (In Billions of Dollars)

	1973–76	1969–72	% Change
Education, Training, Services, Employment	$ 60.1	$ 38.4	56.5%
Health	48.7	26.6	83.1
Income Security[a]	128.5	60.0	114.2
Subtotal	$ 237.3	$ 125.0	89.8
Social Security[b]	$ 243.6	$ 133.8	82.1
Medicare[b]	46.4	26.0	78.5
Unemployment	44.5	19.2	131.7
Veterans	60.4	36.8	64.1
Subtotal	$ 394.9	$ 215.8	82.9
Grand total	$ 632.2	$ 340.8	85.5%

a) Minus unemployment compensation. b) Funded by employers and employees. Note: Major federal programs since the 1960s—Medicaid, 1961; Food Stamps, 1962; Medicare, 1967; Student Aid, 1966; Coal Miners Benefits, 1970; Commodity Donations, 1973; Supplemental Security Income, 1974; Supplemental Feeding, 1976; Earned Income Tax Credit, 1976; Legal Services, 1976.

It is always interesting and sometimes rewarding to find new cost items or trends that reflect the real views, as opposed to the announced views, of political leaders. A rewarding discovery of this type is found in the bowels of the 1973–1976 spending schedules.

Nixon and Ford, Republicans, were supposedly different in attitude from Democrats, the big spenders of Washington politics. But the following chart identifies programs that first appeared in the budget under Nixon, or Nixon/Ford.

Table 10.17
New Social Programs (In Billions of Dollars)

Program	Year	1st Year Cost	1976	1996
Coal Miners Benefits	1970	$ .0	$ 1.0	$ 1.2
Commodity Donations	1972	.6	.3	1.0
Supplemental Security Income (SSI)	1974	2.0	4.6	23.5
Supplemental Feeding	1976	.1	.1	3.7
Earned Income Tax Credit	1976	.8	.8	18.1
Legal Services	1976	.1	.1	.3
Total		$3.6	$ 6.9	$47.8

The above numbers are not adjusted for inflation, nor do they have to be to make a few simple and useful points:

- Some, but not many, federal programs serve a modest purpose at a modest cost.
- Within five years, lawmakers know whether a new program has budget-busting characteristics.
- In any age, $47.8 billion is a lot of money.

It is fair to recognize that Nixon and Ford were forced to work with a Congress ruled by the philosophical brothers and sisters of Lyndon Johnson. But yelps of pain and anguish from the two presidents or from conservative congressmen of the day were not loud enough to be believable, and news of heroic struggles since the 1970s by valiant politicians dedicated to the theory that wise generosity is limited to the ability to pay have yet to be noticed by tax-weary Americans. In short, Nixon and Ford were not as distressed by additions to welfare menus as they wanted conservative backers to think, and the suspicion that more modern Republican leaders are no less hypocritical is reasonable.

Education, etc., increased beyond the allowable rate (49.8 percent). Troublesome elements within this line item dealt with aid to higher education and research and also training and employment, the latter no doubt tied in part to the poor economy.

Health costs increased 83.1 percent in 1973–1976 over the 1969–1972 level, the growth in Medicaid being responsible for most of it. Nothing in view offered hope that health costs would moderate.

Income Security grew faster than the other line items. Once the doors were opened to the federal treasury, there seemed to be no pain that couldn't be eased with a few more federal dollars.

Social Security and Medicare programs are separately funded through payroll taxes and direct payments, but the proceeds are merged with general funds. For that reason they are examined as normal line items. Spending growth was well beyond the allowable level. Unadjusted, these programs will continue on a fast, unsustainable growth path.

Unemployment costs, harshly imposed on Ford, increased more than any other line item, a reflection of an economy in trouble. Had they increased at the rate of inflation, cost would have been fully funded at $26.6 billion. Had they increased at the full rate allowed to *Human Resources* (49.8 percent), cost would have been $28.8 billion, or $15.7 billion less than actual. To that extent, the deficit was punished by the extraordinary cost of unfunded Unemployment.

In the aftermath of the Vietnam War, the Veterans line item unsurprisingly increased by more than the allowable rate. Had it increased at the full allowable rate (49.8 percent), cost would have been $55.1 billion, or $5.3 billion less than actual. To that extent the extraordinary cost of Veterans bloated the deficit.

Had Human Resources limited itself to a growth rate of 49.8 percent, its expenditures in 1973–1976 would have been $510.4 billion, or $121.8 billion less than actual. To that extent it added to the 1973–1976 deficit. Of that total, $15.7 billion of excessive unemployment costs and $5.3 billion of costs associated with Veterans would have been reasonable additions to public debt.

Conclusion

Before appraising the impact that Nixon/Ford had on the public debt, one must deal, however perfunctorily, with the two major issues that commanded headlines of the day: Vietnam and Watergate.

Vietnam preceded Watergate.

To begin with, it was a popular cause. Congress passed with overwhelming support, for example, the Gulf of Tonkin Resolution in 1964, an agreement that gave President Johnson full wartime powers.

By the time Richard Nixon became president, the war was unpopular. It was at that time politically proper to be anti-Vietnam. Ex-supporters of Johnson scurried away from him and pointed the finger at Nixon. Vietnam became, presto, Nixon's war.

The Vietnam War is important in the context of this book because it attached to Nixon an unpopular cause. And despite Nixon's successful withdrawal from Vietnam, he was attacked until the end of his first term as if he had been the one who started it in the first place. All of this made him an easy target when Watergate became front-page news.

Watergate was many things to many people. How did it relate to the topic of this book, the public debt? Not at all, in any direct sense. But indirectly it resulted in a weaker presidency at a time when presidential power was one of the few remaining controls over spending.

Nixon had, and used (as had presidents before him), the power to impound—the power to delay expenditures. The threat of it was more powerful than the fact of it in the eyes of Congress, which wanted to eliminate it. A weakened Nixon gave them their chance. The Budget Control Act of 1974 was the result. The meaning? The presidency Ford inherited was weaker. Ford had fewer budget controls at his disposal, which made it less probable that he would have a positive influence on the deficit and debt problems of America.

The debt went up again in 1973–1976, this time by $148.0 billion, as follows:

Table 10.18
Unrecovered Cost (In Billions of Dollars)

Defense	$ 0.0
Interest	9.2
Government	17.0
Human Resources	121.8
Total	$ 148.0

Until this point, deficits had been essentially cost driven. Revenue had been adequate to support sensible expenditures, except for the slowdown in Eisenhower's second term. Not so with Nixon/Ford. They got whipsawed. Given the recession and the energy crisis, they didn't have a chance to avoid a deficit.

The chart below is meaningful because, for the first time since World War Two, the cost of external events was as important to the development of a deficit as the inability to control costs, as follows:

Table 10.19
Analysis of Deficit, 1973–1976 (In Billions of Dollars)

Total deficit		$148.0
Adjusted:		
Revenue[a]	$ 111.6	
Unemployment[b]	5.0	

Table 10.19 *(continued)*
Analysis of Deficit, 1973–1976 (In Billions of Dollars)

Veterans	5.3	
Energy[c]	15.7	$137.6
Net		$ 10.4

a) See *Perspectives* section, pp. 122–129. b) See *Human Resources* section, pp. 135–137. c) See *Government* section, pp. 135–137.

What is the meaning of the above table? Given a fair break with the business cycle and normal energy costs, the Nixon/Ford administration would have had, theoretically, a small deficit of $10.4 billion.

Interest was a modest entry ($1.9 billion) in the table of Unrecovered Cost in 1969–1972. In this table there is a sturdiness about it that promises its continued presence on future schedules. The child of debt, *Interest*, in 1973–1976 became on its own a cost center of concern—9.0 percent of tax revenue.

Added to the costs of *Government* in 1973–1976 were new law enforcement expenses related to increased crime in a deteriorating society and new costs undertaken in response to environmental lobbies. In *Human Resources*, cost control was a phrase that had no meaning.

A welfare state is expensive. To fund it, high taxes are required and, most importantly, the underlying economy must be strong and reasonably stable. No example comes quickly to the untrained historical eye of a welfare state that has had a strong, stable economy. History seems to suggest that the two ideas are incompatible. If that is true, the drift of America toward socialism will damage the growth of GDP.

Table 10.20
Gross Domestic Product/Net Growth

	GDP (In Billions of Dollars)		Adjusted GDP (In Billions of Dollars)[a]		Percent Real Growth
	Beginning	End	Beginning	End	4 Yrs
Ike	$ 371	$449	$1402	$1649	17.7%
Ike 2	449	524	1649	1770	7.3
JFK/LBJ	524	675	1770	2178	23.0
LBJ	675	937	2178	2692	23.6
RMN	937	1287	2692	3079	14.4
RMN/GRF	1287	1880	3079	3305	7.3

a) Expressed in 1983 dollars.

So far, the pursuit of the Great Society has not been a good tonic for the GDP.

Richard Nixon was the most controversial president of the twentieth century. Somehow it is fitting that Nixon's second term, shared with Gerald Ford, produced one of the weakest economic records of the last half-century. But at the end of it, a new president of sterling character was assuming office, the economy was growing again, and hope for America was alive and well.

Chapter 11

Jimmy Carter, 1977–1980

The first president born in a hospital was Jimmy Carter, the man destined to be America's 39th president. He arrived on October 1, 1924, in Wise Hospital, Plains, Georgia. The president of the United States was Calvin Coolidge. Public debt was $21 billion.

Little in Carter's demeanor hints of his colorful family background. Great-grandfather Littleberry and paternal grandfather William were killed because of disputes related to business. More contemporaneously, Carter's father James would leave the house whenever wife Lillian, a midwife to black women, entertained a black guest.

Carter's parents were not philosophical twins, but they were hard working, conscientious people. Between the father and his peanut farm and the mother working as a registered nurse, the couple prospered according to standards of Plains, Georgia. They provided a stable home environment for their four children, two boys and two girls.

James Earl Carter, Jr. (he later changed his official name to Jimmy) was the oldest of the Carter children. His early education took place in the local school system, where he is remembered as a well-behaved, bright student. Carter graduated from Plains High School in 1941 and attended Georgia Southwestern College. But his heart, even at such an early age, was set on a naval career, an ambition stimulated by admiration for his maternal uncle, Thomas Gordy, a navy radioman. Accordingly, Carter applied to the U.S. Naval Academy in 1941, studied hard at Georgia Institute of Technology in 1942, and in 1943 realized the first step in his career dream by entering Annapolis. Franklin Roosevelt was president, and public debt was $128 billion.

In June 1946, Carter's seven-year (1946–1953) naval career began; in July he married Eleanor Rosalynn Smith. Known by classmates as a casually bright student who got high grades (top 10 percent) with little effort, Carter had a career as an officer that was unremarkable until in 1951 the celebrated Admiral Hyman Rickover selected him to serve on one of the first atomic submarines, the *Sea Wolf.* This adventure was cut short in 1953, however, when the death of his father caused Carter to resign his commission (lieutenant senior grade) and return home to manage the family farm. Dwight Eisenhower was president, and debt was $218 billion.

Carter was about 30 when he returned to the family farm. Ten years later, after upgrading methods and expanding the market for his peanut business, he was a millionaire seeking a challenge. Politics provided the outlet. He ran for a seat in the state senate in 1962, and after a squabble over voter fraud, he won the race and began a new career as a lawmaker.

In 1966 the quiet man from Plains made an unsuccessful run for governor. Lessons learned, he tried again four years later and won. He served as the state's chief executive for four years (1971–1975).

Carter was a man with clear and large ambitions. When he entered state politics at the senate level, he cocked a speculating eye on the top job in the state. Eight years later he was governor. When he grew comfortable in that position, he looked above the issues of his state, appraised the performance of President Gerald Ford, and concluded that he could do better. Four years later Carter was president of the United States.

To win the Democratic nomination in 1976 was a major coup for Carter on his road to the presidency. Men with large reputations fought for the opportunity to run against Gerald Ford, the man who had pardoned Richard Nixon. Governor George Wallace of Alabama, Senator Henry Jackson of Washington, Jerry Brown, governor of California, and Representative Mo Udall of Arizona were the principal competitors; they were men of parts, men with credentials.

One by one, Carter eliminated them and earned his spot at the starting line pitted against Gerald Ford—an unknown, versus a president with a poor economic record and the legacy of Nixon's scandal on his back.

With Senator Walter Mondale at his side, Carter won a slim victory over the Republican ticket of Ford and Robert Dole. Many pundits credit the victory to the debates (Carter did well) and the burden of the Nixon pardon which they say Ford could not overcome. Few mention as major contributing factors the deficits during Ford's years.

Carter's presidential mandate was not strong. He walked into the same power structure that had controlled Washington since Lyndon Johnson became Senate majority leader in 1955. Thomas O'Neill of Massachusetts was Speaker of the House, and Robert Byrd of West Virginia was majority leader in the Senate; both were Democrats. Nixon and Ford were ineffective at curbing the high-spending Democratic Congress, but to the extent that a split power structure in those years acted as a brake on spending proclivities, that discipline would be removed, with Democrats ruling the executive and the legislative branches of government. From a public debt viewpoint, the outlook was not positive when Carter was elected.

The public debt assumed by Carter had grown by 44.3 percent to $477.4 billion under Nixon/Ford, and the deficits during the final two years of that administration were huge. Would Carter break the mold and turn America back to fiscal sanity?

Table 11.1
Summary of Deficits/Debt, 1941–1976 (In Billions of Dollars)

Years		Total	Defense	Interest	Govt.	Human Resources
Before 1941		$ 42.8	$ 42.8[a]	$ 0.0	$ 0.0	$ 0.0
1941–44 (FDR)		127.8	127.8	0.0	0.0	0.0
1945–48 (FDR/HST)		47.6	37.4	5.4	0.0	4.8
1949–52 (HST)[b]		- 2.0	- 2.0	0.0	0.0	0.0
1953–56 (Ike)		6.6	6.6	0.0	0.0	0.0
1957–60 (Ike 2)		12.1	0.0	0.0	4.4	7.7
1961–64 (JFK/LBJ)		21.0	0.0	0.0	12.8	8.2
1965–68 (LBJ)		38.9	0.0	.2	14.1	24.6
1969–72 (RMN)		46.1	0.0	1.9	0.0	44.2
1973–76 (RMN/GRF)		148.0	0.0	9.2	17.0	121.8
	Deficits	$ 488.9	$212.6	$ 16.7	$ 48.3	$ 211.3
	Adjust[c]	- 18.5				
	Debt	$ 477.4				
	Convert[d]	$ 1316.4				
	Debt 1996	$ 3732.9				
	Debt 1976					
	% of 1996	35.3%				

a) Includes cost of Great Depression (see p. 19). b) Surplus. c) Government figures come from a variety of sources and differ somewhat. This adjustment "forces" the above total to agree with the public debt amount reported by the Office of Management and Budget, Historical Tables, 7.1. d) Convert subject debt to 1996 dollars.

Unlike pre–Eisenhower years when debt increased because of wars or great emergencies, modern debt was rising because Washingtonocrats had more ideas on how to spend than they had money to spend. Managing the affairs of government as that role had been historically understood didn't satisfy the New Age politicians. Managing the behavior of the people of the United States became their preoccupation.

The across-the-aisle unspoken agreement to avoid deficits was history, a quaint practice favored by lawmakers of the pre–Kennedy era, men who did not have the inclination to engineer the American lifestyle. And it did not seem likely that Carter, the new Democrat in the White House, would reignite the disciplines of politicians from both political parties under whose guidance the United States had become the preeminent financial and military power in the world.

Change in Public Debt

Before getting into the details of Carter's handling of the problem of annual deficits and soaring debt or the economic environment in which he operated, let us pose the question, Did things get better? The answer is clearly, no.

Table 11.2
Change in Public Debt, 1976–1980 (In Billions of Dollars)

Public debt, 1976	$ 477.4
Deficit, 1977–1980	227.2
Total	$ 704.6
Adjustment[a]	14.8
Total	$ 719.4
Adjustment[b]	9.5
Public debt, 1980	$ 709.8

a) The fiscal year was changed in 1976 from July to October. In the process, one fiscal quarter was left hanging. The deficit associated with it was handled as a single figure to preserve comparability between presidential periods. b) See Table 11.1, note c.

Control of the presidency and both houses of Congress is the dream of any political party. If one is forced to choose, control of Congress is better than control of the presidency. Control of the presidency and one house of Congress is about equal in power to control of both houses of Congress. Control of the presidency is more valuable than control over one house of Congress. These appraisals of value are general but volatile, depending upon the popularity and personality of a president. People respond to people, and a bright, articulate, and popular president is a powerful figure in the United States of America.

Table 11.3
Profile of Power, 1949–1980

Cong.	House	Senate	President
81	Rayburn (D)	Lucas (D)	Truman (D)
82	Rayburn (D)	McFarland (D)	Truman (D)
83	Martin (R)	Taft[a] (R)	Eisenhower (R)
83		Knowland (R)	
84	Rayburn (D)	Johnson (D)	Eisenhower (R)
85	Rayburn (D)	Johnson (D)	Eisenhower (R)
86	Rayburn (D)	Johnson[a] (D)	Eisenhower (R)
87	Rayburn (D)	Mansfield (D)	Kennedy (D)
87	Rayburn[b] (D)	Mansfield (D)	Kennedy (D)
87	McCormack (D)		
88	McCormack (D)	Mansfield (D)	Kennedy[c] (D)
88			Johnson[d] (D)

Table 11.3 *(continued)*
Profile of Power, 1949–1980

Cong.	House	Senate	President
89	McCormack (D)	Mansfield (D)	Johnson (D)
90	McCormack (D)	Mansfield (D)	Johnson (D)
91	McCormack[a] (D)	Mansfield (D)	Nixon (R)
92	Albert (D)	Mansfield (D)	Nixon (R)
93	Albert (D)	Mansfield (D)	Nixon[a] (R)
94	Albert[a] (D)	Mansfield (D)	Ford[d] (R)
95	O'Neill (D)	Mansfield[a] (D)	Carter (D)
95		Byrd (D)	
96	O'Neill (D)	Byrd (D)	Carter (D)

a) Resigned. b) Died in office. c) Assassinated. d) VP succession.

From Harry Truman through Jimmy Carter, there were eight presidencies and 16 Congresses. How did the two parties fare in the power game?

Table 11.4
Power Summary

Power	Democrat	Republican
President +2C	8	1
2C	7	0
President +0C	0	7

If responsibility follows power, there is little doubt who created America's fiscal policy prior to Carter, or who would control it while he was in office. *And the debt grew and grew.*

Table 11.5
Public Debt (In Billions of Dollars)

	Beginning	End	Percent
FDR	$ 42.8	$ 184.8	331.8%
FDR/HST	184.8	216.3	17.0
HST	216.3	214.8	- .7
Ike	214.8	222.2	3.4
Ike 2	222.2	236.8	6.7
JFK/LBJ	236.8	256.8	8.4
LBJ	256.8	289.5	12.7
RMN	289.5	322.4	11.4
RMN/GRF	322.4	477.4	48.1
JEC	477.4	709.8	48.7

In the analysis of Nixon/Ford, it was found that external events beyond the control of presidents were responsible for the deficits of that time and

that the addition to public debt caused by them was reasonable. Did those
conditions (recession/unemployment/energy crisis) continue into 1977–1980?

Perspectives

Once America retired ingloriously from Vietnam in 1975 the guns of
the nation were returned to their holsters and what constituted peace in
1977–1980 became the order of the day, namely, nations snarling at one
another but, for the most part, limiting aggression to barks, not bites.

Carter did not have to confront the variety of flaming issues that Lyndon Johnson and Richard Nixon had had to face, but those that drew his maximum attention would have tested the mettle of any president. Not all of
them had a clear relationship to the public debt.

The cold war with the Soviets, negotiations between Israel and Egypt,
the Soviet invasion of Afghanistan, the Iran/Iraq War, and the hostage situation in Iran were all events that helped to define the Carter presidency, but
except to point to the continuing need for a strong defense, they had nothing to do with the public debt. But one event did. The oil embargo by OPEC
(Organization of Petroleum Exporting Countries).

OPEC discovered that what it had levied as a punitive tax against nations
that supported Israel had in fact become a golden spigot through which wealth
of the West poured to the East in staggering amounts, an enrichment not
easy to turn aside even when emotions attached to the Arab/Israeli War
(1973) subsided. The tendency was to milk the golden calf for as long as possible. Energy costs zoomed in the United States.

At home, Carter brought his own style to Washington. On the social
side, he offered amnesty to draft evaders (Vietnam), who, during World War
Two, would have earned harsh punishment. America was changing. The world
was changing, and with it, America's financial profile.

Table 11.6
Financial Profile

	1960 (pop: 180.7 mil)[a]	1976 (pop: 218.1 mil)	1980 (pop: 227.7 mil)	1996 (pop: 265.5 mil)
Federal Income and Outlay, in Billions of Dollars				
GDP[b]	$ 523.9	$1880.3	$2911.8	$7636.0
Taxes	92.5	298.1	517.1	1453.1
Spending	92.2	371.8	590.9	1560.5
Debt	236.8	477.4	709.8	3732.9
Interest	6.9	26.7	52.5	241.1

Table 11.6 *(continued)*
Financial Profile

	1960	1976	1980	1996
	(pop: 180.7 mil)[a]	(pop: 218.1 mil)	(pop: 227.7 mil)	(pop: 265.5 mil)

Federal Income and Outlay—Proportional Comparisons, in Percentages

	1960	1976	1980	1996
Taxes/GDP	18%	16%	18%	19%
Spending/GDP	18	20	20	20
Debt/GDP	45	25	24	49
Taxes/Debt	39	62	73	39
Interest/Taxes	7	9	10	17

Federal Income and Outlay Per Capita, in Dollars

	1960	1976	1980	1996
Taxes	$ 512	$ 1367	$ 2271	$ 5473
Spending	510	1705	2595	5878
Debt	1310	2189	3117	14060
Interest	38	122	231	908

Average Per Capita Income, in Dollars[c]

	1960	1976	1980	1996
	$ 2219	$ 6548	$ 9910	$ 24231

Federal Income and Outlay as Percentage of Avg. Per Capita Income

	1960	1976	1980	1996
Taxes	23.0%	21.0%	23.0%	23.0%
Spending	23.0	26.0	26.0	24.0
Debt	59.0	33.0	31.0	58.0
Interest	1.7	1.9	2.3	3.7

Misery index, in percentages[d]

	1960	1976	1980	1996
Prime interest	5.0%	6.4%	20.4%	8.3%
Unemployment	5.5	7.7	7.1	5.3
Inflation	1.7	5.8	13.1	3.0

a) Population: U.S. Bureau of Census. b) GDP: 1940, 1942, 1944—Salem State College; other years—Federal Reserve Board, Chicago. c) Average income was not available for all years. Figures for missing years were estimated on a linear basis. d) Rates taken from several U.S. government sources.

Carter inherited a 21-month growth cycle from Gerald Ford and was no doubt delighted to see it continue for 37 more months. But toward the end of the streak, the trend was down. Measured in fiscal years, his first two were good; his last two, bad.

Table 11.7
Economic Indicators, 1953–1996

President	Year[a]	Cycle[b]	GDP[c]	CPI[d]	Rev.[e]
Eisenhower	1956	79%	18%	3%	39%
Eisenhower	1960	65	7	10	9
Kennedy/Johnson	1964	96	23	6	19
Johnson	1968	100	24	15	18

Table 11.7 *(continued)*
Economic Indicators, 1953–1996

President	Year[a]	Cycle[b]	GDP[c]	CPI[d]	Rev.[e]
Nixon	1972	77	14	23	18
Nixon/Ford	1976	67	7	39	0
Carter	**1980**	88	7	48	14
Reagan	1984	67	9	28	15
Reagan	1988	100	14	16	16
Bush	1992	83	3	19	8
Clinton	1996	100	7	13	13
Range:					
High		97	19	33	24
Low		70	6	7	6
Average[f]		82	10	18	14

a) The final year of the term. b) Ratio of months of growth in GDP to 48 months. c) Real growth, four years. d) Inflation, four years. e) Real growth in federal revenue, four years. f) The working average of those within the range.

Carter had good luck in the number of consecutive growth months that he had, but the overall rate of growth was not good—6.9 percent, weaker than normal. Inflation was rampant and lifted the real increase in tax revenues to 14.1 percent, which was about average. The deficit for the four-year period was a cost problem, not a revenue problem—more affected by inflation than recession.

Growth in GDP is the fundamental answer to the deficit and debt problems of America, supported by cost controls. But it all begins with growth. GDP faltered again under Carter.

Table 11.8
Inflation; Debt/GDP; Real Growth

President	Inflation			Debt/ GDP[a]	Real[b] Growth
	Peak Year	Peak Rate	4 Yr. Rate		
Ike	1956	1.5%	3.1%	50%	17.7%
Ike 2	1957	3.3	9.5	45	7.3
JFK/LBJ	1963	1.4	5.8	38	23.0
LBJ	1968	4.4	15.2	31	23.6
RMN	1970	5.7	23.0	25	14.4
RMN/GRF	1974	10.7	38.8	25	7.3
JEC	1980	13.1	47.9	24	6.9

a) Debt to GDP ratio at the end of the term. b) GDP growth adjusted for inflation.

Inflation went through the roof. The oil crisis was the cause usually offered for the condition. The Arabs did it. But a glance at the above table shows that inflation had been increasing ever since Lyndon Johnson moved into power. Fiscal policies were a causative agent as well.

Criticisms of spending are often deflected by pointing to the inflation rate. And indeed it's true that spending bloats in times of high inflation like the Carter years. What is often ignored, however, is that inflation affects federal revenues as well as expenditures and that on the revenue side in pre–Reagan years the government got an additional below-the-table boost as inflated earnings slid into higher tax brackets, a phenomenon that had the same impact as an over-the-table increase in tax rates.

In 1980, tax revenues were 73.5 percent higher than in 1976; spending, 58.9 percent. The combination, attractive though it was, caused debt to rise. The same formula for destruction was at work—no matter how high the revenue, it was never high enough to eliminate deficits.

Interest in 1980 was almost double the 1976 level. The question persisted: How high must it be before influential critics howl? When Carter left office, more than 10 percent of all tax revenues were needed to cover *Interest*.

The misery index in 1980 was particularly painful—40.6 percent versus 19.9 percent four years earlier. These statistics reflected economic conditions which, if they had not changed, could have destroyed the wealthiest nation on earth. Unemployment was not as excruciatingly painful as before, but interest and inflation rates had in sum become as painful as tax rates.

Carter's priorities were not significantly different from those he inherited from Gerald Ford, but the comparison of both to Eisenhower (1960) is dramatic, America was not at war in those years. All three faced the same principal enemy, the Soviet Union. Yet, Carter and Ford used less than 25.0 percent of their resources for *Defense*, while Eisenhower used 52.2 percent.

But welfare's portion more than doubled under Carter.

Table 11.9
Spending Priorities[a]

	1960	1976	1980	1996
Defense	52.2%	24.1%	22.7%	17.0%
Interest	7.5	7.2	8.9	15.5
Total	59.7	31.3	31.6	32.5
Government	11.9	14.0	15.4	6.1
Soc. Sec.	12.6	19.9	20.1	22.4
Medicare	0.0	4.2	5.4	11.2
Veterans	5.9	4.9	3.6	2.4
Welfare	9.9	25.7	23.9	25.4
Total	100.0%	100.0%	100.0%	100.0%

a) See discussion following Table 2.4.

Prior to Kennedy/Johnson, there was an understanding in America that the role of federal government was primarily to defend the country, defend the dollar, manage the government and protect the veterans, the unemployed, the disabled and the aged. This is not a statement of opinion, but rather one of fact supported by the actual spending of the federal government in 1960. These duties of the federal government took 93.2 percent of spending in 1960 and 79.1 percent in 1980; both were peacetime years. Local governments, generous citizens, churches, and charitable organizations took care of the other social problems in the country.

Table 11.10
Summary of Federal Spending—Base vs. Other
(In Billions of Dollars)

	1960	1976	1980	1996
Defense	$48.1	$ 89.6	$ 134.0	$ 265.7
Interest	6.9	26.7	52.5	241.1
Soc. Sec.	11.6	73.9	118.5	349.7
Medicare	0.0	15.8	32.1	174.2
Unemployment	2.9	19.5	18.1	24.9
Veterans	5.4	18.4	21.2	37.0
Government	11.0	51.9	91.1	95.4
Base	$85.9	$ 295.8	$ 467.5	$1188.0
Other	6.3	76.0	123.4	372.5
Total	$92.2	$ 371.8	$ 590.9	$1560.5
Base as percentage of total	93.2%	79.6%	79.1%	76.1%

A statement of actual government spending presents an unbiased view of what America's leaders are really doing, a welcome relief from the agenda-laced comments of TV heads, because changes in numbers represent more than variances in an accountant's column. The numbers, the mathematics, are vehicles that make clear in nonpolitical terms changes in political philosophy. For example: no longer was debt paid down in peacetime; no longer was spending limited to revenue, nor was the reach of government limited to a few unintrusive duties. No longer were high taxes and high debt reserved for years of great stress and war.

When one intrudes into activity areas once reserved to others with claims that great improvements will justify the intrusion, it is reasonable to audit the results of the new approach to see if the gains are worth the sacrifice.

Table 11.11
American Social Statistics

	1965	1970	1980	1994
Murders	8773	16848	21860	22084
Rapes		37990	82990	102100

Table 11.11 *(continued)*
American Social Statistics

	1965	1970	1980	1994
Prisoners		196429	315974	1016760
Divorces	479000	708000	1189000	1191000
Abortions			1554000	1529000[a]
Population (millions)	194.3	205.1	227.7	260.7

a) 1992 figure.

Population in 1980 was 17.2 percent higher than 1965. Murders were up 149 percent; divorce, 148 percent. In a decade, rapes more than doubled. Abortion in 1980 was a national disgrace, a silent indication of a society dislodged from its moral roots that regarded the inception of new life as a phenomenon over which it had autonomous control. Johnson's Great Society had more warts than the one he started to fix.

Businessmen who permitted the continuation of a failed program like the federal welfare state would be hanged on Wall Street with the approval of everyone with ten fingers, ten toes, and the capacity to count.

Transactions

Deficits during the Carter years were constant and large. The pattern he inherited had not changed. Spenders and those without the courage to resist were in control of Congress. Nixon and Ford tolerated them. Carter joined them. At the bottom end of the prevailing power structure, Americans yearned for a leader who would resist.

Within the numbers of the Transactions table, hard-edged political truths are found.

Table 11.12
Transactions (In Billions of Dollars)

	1977–1980		1973–1976	
Taxes		$1735.6		$1071.2
Less:				
Defense	$ 452.0		$ 332.1	
Interest	160.5		88.6	
Total		612.5		420.7
Net		$1123.1		$ 650.5
Less:				
Government	$ 305.1		$ 166.3	
Hum. Resources	1045.2		632.2	
Total		1350.3		798.5

Table 11.12 *(continued)*
Transactions (In Billions of Dollars)

	1977–1980	1973–1976
Net	-$ 227.2	-$ 148.0
Debt, beginning	- 477.4	- 322.4
Total	-$ 704.6	-$ 470.4
Adjustment[a]	14.8	
Total[b]	- 719.4	
Adjustment[b]	9.6	- 7.0
Debt, end	-$ 709.8	-$ 477.4

a) Table 11.2, note a. b) See Table 11.1, note c.

Taxes

Tax receipts during Carter's years were 62.0 percent higher than those of the Nixon/Ford administration, a demonstration of a truth generally neglected by liberals who prefer to blame bloated costs and resultant deficits on inflation, while failing to note that revenues are inflated as well. After inflation, revenues were 14.1 percent higher than those available to Nixon/Ford. Yes, inflation was a problem for Carter, but it does not explain the size of his deficits.

In 1976, the revenue base that Carter inherited was $298.1 billion— $1192.4 billion in four years. Actual revenue in 1977–1980 was $1735.6 billion, 45.4 percent higher than the base, representing the portion of the increase between the two four-year periods (62.0 percent) that was the result of the tax and economic environment of the times. The remaining increase, 16.6 percent, came from the tax system that Carter inherited.

Sophisticated Washingtonocrats' contempt for balanced budgets and for concern over the size of debt are, to the extent that they have intellectual roots, based on the theories of John Maynard Keynes, plus the assumption that revenues will always grow in America to the extent of, and beyond, the needs of social engineers. No time is given to those who point out that the fiscal expansion required by wars and great calamities is possible only when tax rates, debt levels, or both are low before the demand for expansion arrives.

One cannot expand an elastic beyond its limits. In 1977–1980, spenders and their supporters caught a glimpse of what happens when the rosy scenario of unending good times does not transpire. In a very short time, a very wealthy nation can become very wobbly.

The march of increased taxes continued during the Carter administration. Average income per capita rose from $6,548 in 1976 to $9,910 in 1980, an increase of 51.3 percent. Taxes per capita went up 66.1 percent. That formula hurts taxpayers. A schedule of tax revenues by source follows.

Table 11.13
Tax Revenues (In Billions of Dollars)

	Total	Income	Corp.	SS[a]	Excise	Other[b]
1941pw	$ 8.7	$ 1.3	$ 2.1	$ 2.0	$ 2.5	$ .8
1944w	43.7	19.7	14.8	3.4	4.8	1.0
1948p	41.6	19.3	9.7	3.8	7.4	1.4
1952w	66.2	27.9	21.2	6.5	8.9	1.7
1956p	74.6	32.2	20.9	9.3	9.9	2.3
1960p	92.5	40.7	21.5	14.7	11.7	3.9
1964w	112.6	48.7	23.5	22.0	13.7	4.7
1968w	153.0	68.7	28.7	33.9	14.1	7.6
1972w	207.3	94.7	32.2	52.6	15.5	12.4
1976p	298.1	131.6	41.4	90.8	17.0	17.3
1980p	517.1	244.1	64.6	157.8	24.3	26.3

p = mostly peace. w = mostly war.

a) Social Security. b) Estate and gift taxes, custom duties and fees, Federal Reserve earnings, sundry.

Payroll taxes finance the Social Security and Medicare programs. Everybody pays, including those with the lowest earnings. The Social Security portion of the tax cuts out at one income level ($68,400 in 1998); the Medicare portion continues for all income levels.

Payroll taxes are, in terms of impact, worse than a sales tax (one doesn't have to buy) for low-income earners. Payroll taxes are the kind of taxes that hit hardest the low- and middle-income taxpayers.

Most people have seen a magician rap a table with one hand to draw attention while with the other he prepares a new trick—now you see it now you don't. The American tax system operates the same way. Annually, politicians with furrowed brows argue vociferously over amendments to the personal income tax code while with little fanfare the payroll tax pokes its nose deeper into America's wallet.

In 1960, payroll taxes were 15.9 percent of all tax revenue; 36.1 percent of personal income tax; 68.4 percent of corporate taxes. In 1980, they were 30.5 percent of all taxes; 64.6 percent of personal income taxes; 144.3 percent of corporate income taxes—a sea change in tax policy (pressure for lowered pay checks is borne by the employer, not the taxing authority).

Given the inflation and interest rates during the Carter years, this persistent movement by the federal government to dependence on payroll tax revenue was especially burdensome in 1977–1980.

If it walks like a dog, wags its tail like a dog, and barks like a dog, it's a dog. The popular myth is that the revenue from Social Security taxes is kept separate from general revenues, invested in safe federal securities, and used to pay benefits as needed. That isn't the case. This revenue is mixed with all other federal income to form the pool from which the costs of government

154   The National Debt

are paid. It looks like general revenue, it's mixed with general revenue, and it's spent like general revenue. Social Security taxes are just another way for Washington to collect money.

By the time Carter left office, all federal taxes as a percent of average income per capita were the highest in 20 years, and spending per capita in 1980 was the highest since World War Two.

Table 11.14
Revenues and Spending

Year	Federal Dollars		Per Capita Dollars			Per Capita Percentages of Average Earnings	
	Taxes	Spending	Taxes	Spending	Avg. Earnings	Taxes	Spending
1941[a]	$ 9 bil.	$ 14 bil.	$ 65	$ 102	$ 923	7.0%	11.1%
1944[a]	44 bil.	91 bil.	326	682	1148	28.4	59.4
1948	42 bil.	30 bil.	284	203	1388	20.5	14.6
1952[a]	66 bil.	68 bil.	420	430	1653	25.4	26.0
1956	75 bil.	71 bil.	442	418	1949	22.6	21.4
1960	93 bil.	92 bil.	512	510	2219	23.1	23.0
1964[a]	113 bil.	119 bil.	587	618	2662	22.1	23.2
1968[a]	153 bil.	178 bil.	762	887	3445	22.1	25.7
1972[a]	207 bil.	231 bil.	988	1099	4677	21.1	23.5
1976[a]	298 bil.	372 bil.	1367	1705	6548	20.9	26.0
1980[a]	517 bil.	591 bil.	2271	2595	9910	22.9	26.2

a) deficit year

What Did It?

DEFENSE

The world was its rambunctious self in 1977–1980 as the USSR's expansionist ambitions were further implemented and as the Middle East, especially Iran, issued economic and military challenges. But Carter was not involved in a shooting war. His defense problem was to stay on guard, watchful for threats to America's national interests.

Table 11.15
Defense as a Share of GDP and Spending (In Billions of Dollars)

	Defense	GDP	Spending	GDP	Spending
1960p	$ 48.1	$ 523.9	$ 92.2	9.2%	52.2%
1964w	54.8	675.1	118.5	8.1	46.2
1968w	81.9	936.8	178.1	8.7	46.0
1972w	79.2	1286.8	230.7	6.2	34.3

Table 11.15 *(continued)*
Defense as a Share of GDP and Spending (In Billions of Dollars)

	Defense	GDP	Spending	GDP	Spending
1976p	89.6	1880.3	371.8	4.8	24.1
1980p	134.0	2911.8	590.9	4.6	22.7

p = mostly peace; w = mostly war

It might appear that Carter engaged in a powerful buildup of the military during his term. But the truth is that Carter spent less than Gerald Ford and much less than Dwight Eisenhower, when measured as a percent of either GDP or total spending.

Defense was 36.1 percent higher than it was in 1973–1976. But revenue for the same period increased by 62.0 percent. Accordingly, the growth was fully financed and the cost center did not add to the deficit of 1977–1980.

INTEREST

The fact of inflation had been a matter of growing concern since it passed 4 percent under Lyndon Johnson; it reached as high as 11 percent under Nixon/Ford. Inflation, of course, affects the cost of money as well as everything else. The following table tracks the movement of the prime interest rate in effect at the end of each presidential period (see Financial Profiles tables).

Table 11.16
Prime Interest Rates[a]

President	Yr.	Rate
HST	1952	3.0%
Ike 1	1956	4.0
Ike 2	1960	5.0
JFK/LBJ	1964	4.5
LBJ	1968	6.6
RMN	1972	5.8
RMN/GRF	1976	6.4
JEC	1980	20.4

a) Commercial rates.

If the extremes are eliminated, an average rate of 6.5 percent emerges. When the prime rate exceeds 6.5 percent, it may be fairly said that *Interest* is, compared to other periods, unusually high.

Interest paid by Carter, and all presidents that followed Lyndon Johnson, was mostly related to the debt inherited, but partly to the deficits that couldn't be avoided because of automatic payment demands of entitlement programs. Until the welfare state is unwound, obscene interest payments will continue.

Under Carter, *Interest* was 81.2 percent higher than it was in 1973–1976. *Had its growth been limited to the rate of revenue growth (62.0 percent), the expense would have been $143.5 billion, or $17.0 billion less than actual. To that extent, this cost center added to the deficit in 1977–1980.*

Was the unfunded *Interest* for the period a reasonable addition to public debt? Yes. The period began with a 6.4 percent rate and ended with 20.4 percent. Excess cost was obviously the consequence of unbelievable inflation rates. It is exactly for such aberrational periods that the national ability to borrow should be used—*and it is because such events will occur that the national ability to borrow should be kept free of unnecessary encumbrances.*

Government/Human Resources

After deducting priority expenditures *(Defense* and *Interest)*, $1,123.1 billion (see p. 151) was available to *Government/Human Resources* in the context of a balanced budget. *Interest*, however, had grown beyond allowable limits by $17.0 billion, the portion of the period's deficit assigned to that cost center. This, in effect, lifted the allowable growth figure for *Government/Human Resources* to $1140.1 billion, or 42.8 percent higher than 1973–1976 spending.

Government

The inflation rate in 1977–1980 was 47.9 percent. This being the case, a growth allowance of 42.8 percent demanded a cost cutback, but the deficit had become institutionalized in the sense that it wouldn't go away until the cost base itself was modified—until the size of *Government* was cut. Given the spending history since the 1960s, this was not an attractive position for a president to be in.

Table 11.17
Government Operations, Net (In Billions of Dollars)

	1977–80	1973–76	% Change
Energy	$ 33.2	$ 9.6	245.8%
Nat'l Resources/ Environment	47.0	26.0	80.8
Commerce	23.5	23.1	1.7
Transportation	69.7	43.0	62.1
Community Development	40.7	18.6	118.8
International	34.1	23.3	46.4
Science	20.6	16.4	25.6
Agriculture	38.2	13.4	185.1
Justice	16.2	11.0	47.3
General	50.1	40.0	25.3
Total	$373.3	$224.4	66.4
Misc. Income	- 68.2	- 58.1	17.4
Net	$305.1	$166.3	83.5%

Washingtonocrats responded to the clarion call for cost reduction with typical cooperation—spending increased by 83.5 percent, 1.7 times higher than the inflation rate.

The Commerce, Science, and General line items were comparatively well controlled in 1977–1980. Energy, Transportation, Community Development, Agriculture, and Natural Resources were not. The percent increase in Justice was large but below the inflation rate for the period (47.9 percent).

Energy supply reflected the cost of the oil crisis that hit Gerald Ford's administration hard and Carter's harder. Had the cost of Energy in 1973–1976 ($9.6 billion) increased at the rate of inflation (47.9 percent), total cost in 1977–1980 would have been $14.2 billion, or $20.1 billion lower. This excess cost was a proper addition to debt, to be repaid when normal times returned.

The Transportation cost variance stemmed from the same source—higher energy costs related to OPEC. Had the total of Transportation increased at the inflation rate, cost would have been $63.6 billion in 1977–1980, or $9.5 billion less. This excess cost also qualified for debt financing under routines followed by earlier presidents.

Energy costs were of course a headline concern in America in 1977–1980. Carter's response to the problem was typically bureaucratic; he established the Department of Energy. In this way he assured himself that the cost trend would continue—up, up, and up again.

Carter was a peanut farmer. Somehow it wasn't surprising to find that under his administration the Farm Income Stabilization program drove the cost of Agriculture up (185.1 percent). And realizing Carter's interest in Community Development (118.8 percent) before, during, and after his administration, it wasn't a shock to find that it cost more than twice what it did in 1976.

Natural Resources and Environment increased 80.8 percent in 1977–1980. The projects that required these funds may have been worthwhile, but the time to spend this money was not in 1977–1980. This variance is partly a reflection of the cost to citizens of efficient lobbies.

An acceptable budget system denies approval to projects that cost more than current revenues can bear. Absent such a shutoff mechanism, human nature remains as the only deterrent to overspending, a weak twig upon which to hang the fiscal sanity of a nation.

The American budget system is undisciplined. A complete overhaul is indicated.

Had spending in Government *been limited to the growth rate allowed by a balanced budget (42.8 percent), its cost in 1977–1980 would have been $237.4 billion, or $67.7 billion less than actual.* To that extent the cost center added to the deficit for the period. Of that total, $29.6 billion was the unfunded cost of the oil crisis and thus was a legitimate addition to public debt.

HUMAN RESOURCES

Human Resources grew by 65.3 percent over the expenditure level of
1973–1976, well beyond the allowable amount in the context of a balanced
budget (42.8 percent).

Table 11.18
Human Resources (In Billions of Dollars)

	1977–80	1973–76	% Change
Education, Training, Services, Employment	$ 109.8	$ 60.1	82.7%
Health	79.5	48.7	63.2
Income Security[a]	219.5	128.5	70.8
Subtotal	$ 408.8	$ 237.3	72.3
Social Security[b]	$ 401.6	$ 243.6	64.9
Medicare[b]	100.7	46.4	117.0
Unemployment	56.0	44.5	25.8
Veterans	78.1	60.4	29.3
Subtotal	$ 636.4	$ 394.9	61.1
Grand total	$1045.2	$ 632.2	65.3%

a) Minus unemployment compensation. b) Funded by employers and employees. Note:
Major federal programs since the 1960s—Medicaid, 1961; Food Stamps, 1962;
Medicare, 1967; Student Aid, 1966; Coal Miners Benefits, 1970; Commodity Dona-
tions, 1973; Supplemental Security Income, 1974; Supplemental Feeding, 1976; Earned
Income Tax Credit, 1976; Legal Services, 1976; Energy Assistance, 1977.

The impact of percentage increases on total spending depends on the
size of the base amount. A 74 percent rise in the cost of a small line item will
catch the eye of an alert analyst but might have little impact on a total picture. But when the largest cost center in the budget, like *Human Resources*,
grows at levels beyond revenue growth, trouble becomes a distinct possibility.

Every line item in *Human Resources* but Veterans and Unemployment
grew faster than revenue; all increases were huge and beyond the predictable
ability of income to cover for any prolonged period.

Education, Training, Employment, and Services increased robustly across
the board. The increase in Education, etc. (82.7 percent), is not an example
of inflation bloating the budget; it is an example of bad management.

Under Gerald Ford, Health increased 83.1 percent; under Carter, 63.2
percent. How many Americans would like to have their paychecks increased
by such amounts? Medicaid, of course, is the primary problem.

Income Security increased 114.2 percent under Gerald Ford, 70.8 percent more under Carter. This catch-all title covers federal pensions, hous-
ing/food/nutrition assistance, etc. Growth in such programs has been constant
and strong since the 1960s.

If one proceeds under the myth that Social Security and Medicare programs are not in trouble as long as payroll taxes for these programs exceed obligations and are deposited in the "trust fund," then the programs were fully financed in 1977–1980. If one proceeds on the basis that Social Security taxes deducted from the payroll are just another form of taxation, that the funds are general funds and the "trust fund" is a charade supported by a ledger entry, then the programs stand at the welfare trough along with the others. In such a light, they are growing too fast. Under either proposition, programs must be modified because the concept of supporting payments to the old, solely by deductions from the young, is no longer viable.

Carter subtracted nothing from the welfare menu. His major influence on the budget was organizational, the Departments of Education and Energy, which characteristically loaded up with costs to prove they were needed.

Had the growth of Human Resources been limited to the allowable 42.8 percent, actual cost in 1977–1980 would have been $902.7 billion, $142.5 billion less than actual. To that extent, this cost center is charged with responsibility for the four-year deficit.

Conclusion

Jimmy Carter arrived at the White House in a determined frame of mind. The first man from the Deep South since Zachary Taylor to be elected president, a deacon in his Baptist Church in Georgia, Carter hoped to restore the dignity of the wounded presidency and to bring to Washington some of the unadorned virtue and civility that was an inherent part of his nature. He cultivated his image as an "outsider" in Washington, one determined to set things right for the people. As a symbol of his determination to deflate the idea of a regal, unapproachable presidency, he disposed of the presidential yacht.

The Washington establishment is deeply entrenched. All newcomers are greeted tentatively and appraised for how they might react to the game of you-support-my-bill-and-I'll-support-yours. Especially watched are reformers who brag about "outsider" status, an implied insult to "insiders." Carter was such a man.

Carter surrounded himself with trusted lieutenants from the South who served him well but who did not play kneesy with Congress. As a result, he faced more resistance from a Democratic Congress than one would have expected. His energy bill was a notable exception.

Perhaps the American people were the beneficiaries of this tension between the White House and the Hill. As bad as things worked out, they might have been even worse if a love match had existed between the spenders and a liberal president.

Carter inherited a nasty economic situation that was born under Kennedy/Johnson, matured with Nixon, and worsened under Nixon/Ford. Under Kennedy/Johnson, the days of relatively low costs and high expectations, Great Society programs were hailed as noble acts of a benevolent government, the modern description of the wolf in sheep's clothing.

Under Richard Nixon, reality replaced expectations and the presidency was weakened. Under Nixon/Ford, entitlements took hold. Nothing improved on Carter's watch. Everything got worse. The deficit for the four years was $227.2 billion;

Table 11.19
Unrecovered Cost (In Billions of Dollars)

Defense	$ 0.0
Interest	17.0
Government	67.7
Human Resources	142.5
Total	$ 227.2

Deficits encountered have mostly represented the excess cost of current projects over current revenue. The condition repeated under Carter, but not to the degree shown above.

Table 11.20
Analysis of Deficit, 1977–1980 (In Billions of Dollars)

Total Deficit		$ 227.2
Adjusted:		
Interest[a]	$ 17.0	
Energy[b]	29.6	46.6
Net		$ 180.6

a) See *Interest* section, pp. 155–156. b) See *Government* section, pp. 156–157.

About 21 percent of the deficit was a legitimate addition to the public debt. The balance represents a flaw in the fiscal system that permitted no restraints on spending.

Interest was more expensive than any two line items combined in *Government*; America spent eight times more on *Interest* than on its space program; it was more costly than Education, Health, Medicare, Unemployment, or Veterans.

And it was ignored.

The ability of Washingtonocrats to ignore penalties associated with this expensive, nonproductive line item is awe-inspiring.

It is difficult to assign unfunded *Interest* to any post–Johnson president. Carter, like Richard Nixon and Gerald Ford before him, was burdened by debt that was primarily the child of Lyndon Johnson.

Carter, a card-carrying, certified liberal, can be held accountable for unfunded *Government* except as it relates to extraordinary energy costs (above).

Human Resources is supersensitive to inflation, but its growth rate in 1977–1980 defied logic. More than enough time had passed for politicians, including Carter, to get the message that the Great Society had gone too far, that the federal government could not solve America's problems with cash.

Many factors support a healthy economy. The condition of supply and demand are two; two others are confidence and capital.

When the federal government increases debt because of poor management practices, it does not add confidence in the private sector. When it borrows heavily, it siphons off capital that might have otherwise gone to the job-making private sector.

Table 11.20

Gross Domestic Product/Net Growth

	GDP (In Billions of Dollars)		Adjusted GDP (In Billions of Dollars)[a]		Percent Real Growth
	Beginning	End	Beginning	End	4 Yrs
Ike	$ 371	$ 449	$ 1402	$ 1649	17.7%
Ike 2	449	524	1649	1770	7.3
JFK/LBJ	524	675	1770	2178	23.0
LBJ	675	937	2178	2692	23.6
RMN	937	1287	2692	3079	14.4
RMN/GRF	1287	1880	3079	3305	7.3
JEC	1880	2912	3305	3534	6.9

a) Expressed in 1983 dollars.

Downturns in the growth of GDP are not solely the consequence of government borrowing. But the above chart shows that, except when stimulated by war, the adjusted GDP of the American economy has been going down as public debt increased. Pure coincidence?

When one political party controls both legislative bodies and the White House, there isn't much the minority party can do except to stall legislation or make lots of noise about its disagreements with public policy. In 1977–1980, Republicans were in that position. To what extent can they be held responsible for surging debt?

Conservatives should have made more noise.

Since the 1960s, the philosophy of government had changed. Tax policy had changed. Attitudes toward debt and spending had changed. The mix of power between states and the federal government had changed. Lobbyists, moving in hordes to the center of power, changed the political system. There was much to talk about, much to yell about.

The silence was deafening. Conservatives, Republicans, are afraid to yell.

Jimmy Carter did not have a successful presidency. In foreign policy he had some high moments (peace talks between Israel and Egypt), but the overriding memory of his regime will be the hostage crisis in Iran and his inability to free the American captives. Domestically, Carter did nothing to scale down Great Society programs, and he enlarged the role of government by adding the Departments of Energy and Education, a sure way of increasing the cost of it.

Jimmy Carter ran again for the presidency in 1980 against Ronald Reagan, a figure from Western politics who had almost wrested the nomination from Gerald Ford in 1976. Reagan spoke a language that Washingtonocrats failed to realize was modern, up-to-date. He talked about bloated government, runaway federal programs, and the like.

Carter, with Walter Mondale repeating as his running mate, lost by seven million popular votes. He retired to Plains, Georgia, and has since lived a productive life which, on a humanitarian scale, is more impressive than that of any modern president—these are possibly his best years.

When the year 1980 closed, liberals were not repentant, and they were in charge. A bad combination.

Chapter 12

Ronald W. Reagan, 1981–1984

Ronald Wilson Reagan, the oldest president in American history, was born February 6, 1911, in Tampico, Illinois, in a five-room flat over a bakery. Destined to be the 40th president of the United States, the second child of Jack (1883–1941) and Nelle (1883–1962) immediately inherited the nickname "Dutch," thanks to his father. William Taft was president at the time, and the public debt was $2.8 billion.

Jack Reagan, with a sixth-grade education, was one of many who were battered by the Great Depression. He made a living as a shoe salesman until he was 50. During the last ten years of his life, he was an active supporter of Franklin Roosevelt and caught on as a director of New Deal projects in Dixon, Illinois.

Jack Reagan's occupational and parental objectives were compromised by alcoholism, a condition that Nelle Reagan described to the children as a sickness. She supplemented her husband's income with wages earned at a local dress shop. Whatever their personal and economic problems, Jack and Nelle Reagan provided a home life that Ronald Reagan later placed among his happiest days.

Education for Reagan was always in a state of tension with his other activities. In grade school, with few diversions to distract him, he was a high-level student. In Dixon High School (1925–1928), sports entered his life along with politics (he was president of the student body), acting, and writing, and his grades dropped to average.

What he lost in grades because of extra-curricular duties, Reagan gained in opportunity. Eureka College (1928–1932) offered him a partial football scholarship. There he maintained his typical athletic schedule. He was a campus leader, his interest in drama and writing surfaced, and he joined the debating team. Reagan worked as a dishwasher to pay his bills. He majored in economics and sociology and got by with below-average grades. He graduated in 1932. Herbert Hoover was president; debt was $19.5 billion.

The Great Depression hovered over the land. It was a world of no jobs in 1932, and the chances of new graduates in the job market were dim. But personality and leadership traits that Reagan exhibited throughout his academic career continued to serve him well. He caught on with a radio station in Davenport, Iowa, as a sportscaster. He rose rapidly in his new profession.

Six years later he was well known in the sports world of the Midwest, the voice of Big Ten Football and the clever broadcaster of telegraphed major league baseball games. But he constantly probed for a break into the acting profession. It came in 1937. A screen test resulted in a contract with Warner Brothers and a guaranteed wage that permitted him to leave broadcasting.

In 1941, when he was 30 years old and had four years behind him as an actor in films, Reagan was getting more fan mail than anyone working for Warner Brothers, except for Errol Flynn. The world was a rosy place for him and his bride of one year, actress Jane Wyman. The president of the United States was Franklin Roosevelt. Public debt had risen to $48.2 billion because of the Great Depression.

The years 1941 and 1942 were pivotal in Reagan's life. In 1941 he reached the zenith of his acting career, a feat that pleased his father, who died in the same year. In 1942 he traded Hollywood for army life. Poor eyesight kept Second Lieutenant Reagan on stateside duty from which Captain Reagan emerged three years later (1945), a middle-aged actor in Hollywood terms, with a questionable future. But his wife's career soared during the war; in 1948 Jane Wyman won the Oscar for best actress.

From his 20th to his 30th birthdays, Reagan's life took a magic turn. From the small-town college football player who was recognized only within ten miles of Eureka, he became a film star recognized anywhere in America. The next decade was quite different.

Reagan's marriage to Jane Wyman ended in 1949. In 1951 he renewed political interests and reenergized the talents that had made him a campus leader. As his 40th birthday approached, he was president of the Screen Actors Guild, a loyal Democrat, and a supporter of Helen Douglas in her race against Richard M. Nixon for a Senate seat. Harry Truman was president. The Korean War was in process; public debt was $214.3 billion.

The transformation of the 40-year-old actor to the 50-year-old politician, and from unhappy bachelor to happily married man, began for Reagan in 1952. In that year he married actress Nancy Davis, which decision—he would later say—was the best he ever made. Also, he supported Dwight Eisenhower for president in 1952, a clear signal that the early influences of Rooseveltian charm had cooled.

In 1954, his film career on the wane, Reagan signed with General Electric as television host of *GE Theater*. In this role he traveled the country as GE's spokesman and cultivated his speaking abilities. He also did another hitch as president of the Screen Actors Guild (1959–1960) and backed Richard Nixon in his unsuccessful presidential race against John Kennedy.

Reagan was 50 in 1961, happily married and already more politician than actor. John Kennedy was in his first year as president. Public debt had increased from its post–Korean War low of $219.3 billion under Eisenhower (1957) to $238.4 billion.

Retirement to the farm enters the minds of some men when they reach the half-century mark. Not so with Reagan. When his television program phased out, he signed on for another (*Death Valley Days*). In 1964 he was active as a supporter for Barry Goldwater, Republican candidate for president (defeated by Lyndon Johnson). During the campaign he gave a nationally televised speech that drew more contributions than any political speech in history.

The stage was set. The potential candidate had been tested on the campaign trails. In 1967, Reagan entered his first political race and became governor of California with a 58 percent voter mandate.

In 1971, Reagan was in the first year of his second term as governor. Richard Nixon was president. Public debt had entered the path that proclaimed the arrival of a new era, one in which deficit spending was touted as an absolute good. Paying bills was discarded as a quaint, antediluvian philosophy. After Eisenhower, public debt never went down. When Reagan glanced across the fruited plains to the Golden City, he saw a public debt of $303.0 billion supported by a political philosophy that was destined to drive it ever upward.

The rocking chair beckons to many when the 60th birthday is passed. But Reagan wasn't ready for retirement. In a life filled with momentous decades, the 1970s was one of his most exciting.

Reagan was urged to run again at the end of his second term as governor, but exposure to presidential politics in 1968 whetted his appetite for greater things. Biding his time, he polished his national reputation with a newspaper column, radio broadcasts, and speeches on the lecture circuit. In 1976, Reagan made his move and came within 60 votes of beating Gerald Ford for the Republican nomination. Four years later he was not to be denied. The nomination was his by a landslide. He went on to a big victory over Carter in the general election and, as president, was greeted with a public debt of $709.8 billion, as follows:

Table 12.1
Summary of Deficits/Debt, 1941–1980 (In Billions of Dollars)

Years	Total	Defense	Interest	Govt.	Human Resources
Before 1941	$ 42.8	$ 42.8[a]	$ 0.0	$ 0.0	$ 0.0
1941–44 (FDR)	127.8	127.8	0.0	0.0	0.0

Table 12.1
Summary of Deficits/Debt, 1941–1980 (In Billions of Dollars)

Years		Total	Defense	Interest	Govt.	Human Resources
1945–48 (FDR/HST)		47.6	37.4	5.4	0.0	4.8
1949–52 (HST)[b]		- 2.0	2.0	0.0	0.0	0.0
1953–56 (Ike)		6.6	6.6	0.0	0.0	0.0
1957–60 (Ike 2)		12.1	0.0	0.0	4.4	7.7
1961–64 (JFK/LBJ)		21.0	0.0	0.0	12.8	8.2
1965–68 (LBJ)		38.9	0.0	.2	14.1	24.6
1969–72 (RMN)		46.1	0.0	1.9	0.0	44.2
1973–76 (RMN/GRF)		148.0	0.0	9.2	17.0	121.8
1977–80 (JEC)		227.2	0.0	17.0	67.7	142.5
	Deficits	$ 716.1	$ 212.6	$ 33.7	$ 116.0	$ 353.8
	Adjust[c]	14.8				
	Total	730.9				
	Adjust[d]	- 21.1				
	Debt	$ 709.8				
	Convert[e]	$ 1351.5				
	Debt 1996	$ 3732.9				
	Debt 1980 % of 1996	36.2%				

a) Includes cost of Great Depression (see p. 19). b) Surplus. c) See Table 11.2, note a. d) Government figures come from a variety of sources and differ somewhat. This adjustment "forces" the above total to agree with the public debt amount reported by the Office of Management and Budget, Historical Tables, 7.1. e) Convert subject debt to 1996 dollars.

The Treasury Department's explanation for the increase in public debt was presented in the Introduction: "a legacy of war, economic recession and inflation." That explanation correctly describes the deficits of all presidents through Eisenhower. The Nixon/Ford regime's deficit also fits it. Otherwise, it does not apply to substantive aspects of the deficit problem.

Nine administrations have been analyzed to this point, and it has been demonstrated that external events, fundamentally causative to the expansion of debt through 1960, thereafter retreated in importance. People caused the rest of it—the biggest part of it—with their eyes wide open.

The Treasury explanation fails to headline the fundamental reason for the expansion of debt—the cost of the welfare state. One is inclined to suspect that Treasury's statement is but one more example of the pabulum that is too often released to taxpayers to keep them unaware of what they are paying for as the expanding ship of state converts itself from the American Republic established by the Founding Fathers into the American Welfare State established by Lyndon Johnson.

Change in Public Debt

Candidate Reagan had pledged to rebuild America's military might. The Iranian crisis drew attention to the fact that the Vietnam War had depleted the powerful force created and maintained by Dwight Eisenhower. Nixon, Ford, and Carter, besieged by cost increases in domestic spending, did nothing to restore America's power on land, sea, and in the air. America had ships without sailors, planes without mechanics, guns without soldiers, and a mission without morale. All of this Reagan promised to fix.

Reagan also aimed for a balanced budget but, unlike the three previous presidents, not at the price of *Defense*. The battle lines were drawn between himself and the liberal establishment.

Table 12.2
Profile of Power, 1949–1984

Cong.	House	Senate	President
81	Rayburn (D)	Lucas (D)	Truman (D)
82	Rayburn (D)	McFarland (D)	Truman (D)
83	Martin (R)	Taft[a] (R)	Eisenhower (R)
83		Knowland (R)	
84	Rayburn (D)	Johnson (D)	Eisenhower (R)
85	Rayburn (D)	Johnson (D)	Eisenhower (R)
86	Rayburn (D)	Johnson[a] (D)	Eisenhower (R)
87	Rayburn (D)	Mansfield (D)	Kennedy (D)
87	Rayburn[b] (D)	Mansfield (D)	Kennedy (D)
87	McCormack (D)		
88	McCormack (D)	Mansfield (D)	Kennedy[c] (D)
88			Johnson[d] (D)
89	McCormack (D)	Mansfield (D)	Johnson (D)
90	McCormack (D)	Mansfield (D)	Johnson (D)
91	McCormack[a] (D)	Mansfield (D)	Nixon (R)
92	Albert (D)	Mansfield (D)	Nixon (R)
93	Albert (D)	Mansfield (D)	Nixon[a] (R)
94	Albert[a] (D)	Mansfield (D)	Ford[d] (R)
95	O'Neil (D)	Mansfield[a] (D)	Carter (D)
95		Byrd (D)	
96	O'Neil (D)	Byrd (D)	Carter (D)
97	O'Neil (D)	Baker (R)	Reagan (R)
98	O'Neil (D)	Baker (R)	Reagan (R)

a) Resigned. b) Died in office. c) Assassinated. d) VP succession.

In the 97th Congress, Reagan, and his man in the senate, Howard Baker, operated mostly under the last Carter budget; they operated under their own in 1982. In 1983–1984, Reagan and Baker did what they could against an entrenched liberal establishment. It turned out to be a standoff. Reagan made cost-cutting headway, but liberals dug in on favored social programs. On the other hand, Reagan made his case for *Defense*. In 1984 he spent 70 percent more than Carter had in 1980.

Parting with past presidents who operated under the MAD doctrine (Mutually Assured Destruction—you blow me up; I blow you up), Reagan aimed to end the cold war with America as the victor. To that end, he rebuilt the military. Congress refused to cut back on domestic spending (a repetition of its behavior during the Korean and Vietnam wars) as the cost of *Defense* rose. Indeed, faced with the entitlement monster they had created, members of Congress were unable to do so without at the same time unwinding their precious creation, the welfare state.

So, a full agenda of social spending continued, as if the USSR didn't exist, and the consequences of 25 years of fiscal madness stood out for anyone to see: *America could no longer mount an adequate military machine without causing massive deficits* which in 1981–1984 amounted to $600.0 billion and drove total debt to $1300.5 billion, as follows:

Table 12.3
Change in Public Debt, 1980–1984 (In Billions of Dollars)

Public debt, 1980	$ 709.8
Deficit, 1981–1984	600.0
Total	$1309.8
Adjustment[a]	- 9.3
Public debt, 1984	$1300.5

a) See Table 12.1, note d.

As historians of the future look back on the twentieth century, they may well regard Roosevelt, Johnson, and Reagan as its most significant presidents.

Roosevelt changed the way that government dealt with people, but he did so in a way that didn't fundamentally change the form of government itself. Except for federal programs protecting the old, the unemployed, and the war veterans, the America of 1957 was much like the America of 1937.

Johnson took the principles established by Roosevelt and expanded upon them beyond belief, tearing down in the process "the Republic for which it stands" and substituting the American Welfare State. The America of 1997 is nothing like the America of 1937.

Reagan stopped the welfare train. He did not fix it or send it back to its beginnings, but he did make apparent to the nation the cost of the journey to the Great Society and the price it was paying for the mismanagement of its "credit line."

Reagan opposed big government and put *Defense* above welfare. He believed in balanced budgets and roared his disapproval of the public debt. Because of his popularity, tenacity, and bellowing, for the first time in decades the concept of a balanced budget—paying the bills—could be discussed in polite society. Reagan changed the agenda in Washington.

Increased spending for *Defense* during the Vietnam War was not as high as one might have expected. But taxes were kept high for expanding social needs, and debt went up vigorously. It hasn't stopped since.

Table 12.4
Public Debt (In Billions of Dollars)

	Beginning	End	Percent
FDR	$ 42.8	$ 184.8	331.8%
FDR/HST	184.8	216.3	17.0
HST	216.3	214.8	- .7
Ike	214.8	222.2	3.4
Ike 2	222.2	236.8	6.7
JFK/LBJ	236.8	256.8	8.4
LBJ	256.8	289.5	12.7
RMN	289.5	322.4	11.4
RMN/GRF	322.4	477.4	48.1
JEC	477.4	709.8	48.7
RWR	709.8	1300.5	83.2

Public debt increased at an ugly pace after Lyndon Johnson left office, well beyond the average growth rate of GDP which has been established at 10% for a four-year term. Under the 91st through the 98th Congresses debt grew much faster.

Mushrooming debt caused by financing of wars, unusual and non-recurring events, or great tragedies is acceptable. But the same condition caused by the uncontrolled costs related to Lyndon Johnson's Great Society is not. During Reagan's first term, this fact was gaining wider acceptance. Some rare and brave souls even dared to mention the idea of a "balanced budget."

Perspectives

When Reagan took office, the hostage crisis in Iran was the headline news. For reasons known to Iranians alone, their decision to release hostages was withheld while Jimmy Carter was in office. The mood changed when Reagan was elected, and the hostages were released. Graciously, Reagan invited Carter to welcome them home, thus closing a difficult chapter in the life of America's 39th president.

In March 1981, Reagan was shot, the bullet narrowly missing his heart (he was 70 at the time). He was discharged from the hospital 12 days later and within a few weeks was working a full schedule, his reputation even larger than before.

And before the year was over, Reagan established his image to Americans in other ways, an image that endured throughout his presidency. Two events stand out: 1) Congress enacted the largest tax cut in history. 2) Air traffic controllers went out on strike, refused to obey Reagan's order to return to work, and were fired. These actions, controversial at the least with liberals, advanced Reagan's popularity. Love him or hate him, like Franklin Roosevelt and Lyndon Johnson, he was a man who stood for something. Americans respond to that; they expect to see strength in their presidents.

The space program, a budget item of growing importance since the 1950s, received a meaningful lift in 1983 when Sally Ride, the first female astronaut, became part of the crew on the space shuttle, *Challenger*. And in a different field, Reagan's appointment of the first female to the Supreme Court, Sandra O'Connor, also drew attention. Women were to be found in high positions throughout government and the private sector in ever increasing numbers in the 1980s, a welcome sign in a world starved for leaders of quality.

As the relationship between Winston Churchill and Franklin Roosevelt became famous during World War Two, so did the relationship between Reagan and Margaret Thatcher. It seemed to solidify in 1982 when Reagan backed Great Britain and Thatcher in the war with Argentina over the Falklands.

Reagan would use America's might, given a just cause. He authorized the deployment of missiles in Europe, approved the use of U.S. Marines in Lebanon (over two hundred were killed by terrorists), and he invaded Grenada to rescue Americans and to thwart plans to make it a base for the Soviets. Such events didn't have an impact on the budget with the force of a major war, but their enumeration is needed to set the tone of the world in which Reagan operated.

The major external force, of course, was the Soviet Union. Reagan was relatively quiet on the diplomatic front during his first term in the sense that he avoided face to face confrontations with the USSR. But the American public was ever aware of his appraisal of the Soviet threat, and it was kept abreast of Reagan's plan to rebuild the military and to negotiate from a position of strength. The chill between the two superpowers remained, and Reagan, with an increasingly powerful military presence behind him, watched and waited while the Soviet leadership changed from Brezhnev to Andropov (1982) to Chernenko (1984).

The deficit and the debt were influenced, however, far more by the clash between Reagan, who wanted to win the cold war, cut spending, and reduce debt, and liberals—who were satisfied with the status quo in the cold war (they thought it unwinnable; and they thought it was unacceptably dangerous to try). They were determined to protect and expand the welfare state.

Events would prove Reagan right about the war, the cost of which (improved *Defense*) was piddling compared with the unrecovered costs of the welfare state and the countless billions that would have been spent in the future had not America prevailed in the cold war.

Domestic and international events of such a character had a powerful impact on the budget and the financial profile of America.

Table 12.5
Financial Profile

	1960 (pop: 180.7 mil)[a]	**1980** (pop: 227.7 mil)	**1984** (pop: 236.3 mil)	**1996** (pop: 265.5 mil)
Federal Income and Outlay, in Billions of Dollars				
GDP[b]	$ 523.9	$2911.8	$3996.7	$7636.0
Taxes	92.5	517.1	666.5	1453.1
Spending	92.2	590.9	851.8	1560.5
Debt	236.8	709.8	1300.5	3732.9
Interest	6.9	52.5	111.1	241.1
Federal Income and Outlay—Proportional Comparisons, in Percentages				
Taxes/GDP	18%	18%	17%	19%
Spending/GDP	18	20	21	20
Debt/GDP	45	24	33	49
Taxes/Debt	39	73	51	39
Interest/Taxes	7	10	17	17
Federal Income and Outlay Per Capita, in Dollars				
Taxes	512	2271	2821	$ 5473
Spending	510	2595	3605	5878
Debt	1310	3117	5504	14060
Interest	38	231	470	908
Average Per Capita Income, in Dollars[c]				
	$ 2219	$ 9910	$ 13114	$ 24231
Federal Income and Outlay as Percentage of Avg. Per Capita Income				
Taxes	23.0%	23.0%	22.0%	23.0%
Spending	23.0	26.0	27.0	24.0
Debt	59.0	31.0	41.0	58.0
Interest	1.7	2.3	3.6	3.7
Misery index, in percentages[d]				
Prime interest	5.0%	20.4%	11.1%	8.3%
Unemployment	5.5	7.1	7.5	5.3
Inflation	1.7	13.1	4.5	3.0

a) Population: U.S. Bureau of Census. b) GDP: 1940, 1942, 1944—Salem State College; other years—Federal Reserve Board, Chicago. c) Average income was not available for all years. Figures for missing years were estimated on a linear basis. d) Rates taken from several U.S. government sources.

Carter left behind five months of pallid growth and an overheated economy (1981 inflation rate, 13.1 percent). The mild upswing continued for seven months into Reagan's first year and then dropped into a 16-month trough that resulted in two fiscal years of negative growth (1981/1982).

To the horror of liberals, Reagan ignored pleas to raise taxes and backed instead a tax cut. In December 1982 the American economy roared back with 25 consecutive months of growth that lifted the four-year growth of the GDP to 8.9 percent, the best peacetime performance since Dwight Eisenhower's first term.

Table 12.6
Economic Indicators, 1953–1996

President	Year[a]	Cycle[b]	GDP[c]	CPI[d]	Rev.[e]
Eisenhower	1956	79%	18%	3%	39%
Eisenhower	1960	65	7	10	9
Kennedy/Johnson	1964	96	23	6	19
Johnson	1968	100	24	15	18
Nixon	1972	77	14	23	18
Nixon/Ford	1976	67	7	39	0
Carter	1980	88	7	48	14
Reagan	**1984**	**67**	**9**	**28**	**15**
Reagan	1988	100	14	16	16
Bush	1992	83	3	19	8
Clinton	1996	100	7	13	13
Range:					
High		97	19	33	24
Low		70	6	7	6
Average[f]		82	10	18	14

a) The final year of the term. b) Ratio of months of growth in GDP to 48 months. c) Real growth, four years. d) Inflation, four years. e) Real growth in federal revenue, four years. f) The working average of those within the range.

Reagan had fewer growth months than most presidents. Inflation in 1981–1984 was much higher than usual. But overall growth in GDP, thanks to the strong comeback in 1983–1984, was only slightly below normal, and the increase in tax collections over the four years was erratic, but satisfactory.

The deficit of 1981–1984 was not revenue driven. Cost control and inflation were the triggering factors.

Relative to debt reduction, the prime importance of a growing economy cannot be stressed too much. The complete turnaround in 1981–1984 was impressive, but beyond that, it is what had to happen if America was to survive as a major financial power. To this day, Americans do not appreciate how close they were in 1977–1980 to calamity, how valuable were the cures imposed on a reluctant Congress in 1981–1984. America's money-making engine was purring again. For the first time in a decade, the rate of economic growth was increasing.

Table 12.7
Inflation; Debt/GDP; Real Growth

President	Inflation Peak Year	Inflation Peak Rate	4 Yr. Rate	Debt/ GDP[a]	Real Growth[b]
Ike	1956	1.5%	3.1%	50%	17.7%
Ike 2	1957	3.3	9.5	45	7.3
JFK/LBJ	1963	1.4	5.8	38	23.0
LBJ	1968	4.4	15.2	31	23.6
RMN	1970	5.7	23.0	25	14.4
RMN/GRF	1974	10.7	38.8	25	7.3
JEC	1980	13.1	47.9	24	6.9
RWR	1981	10.2	28.4	33	8.9

a) Debt to GDP relationship at the end of the term. b) GDP growth adjusted for inflation.

Reduced inflation went along with growth in the GDP. From a startup point of 13.1 percent, the rate reached 4.5 percent in 1984, a benefit to taxpayers even more valuable than the reduction in tax rates.

In 1981, Reagan passed the largest tax reduction package in history. Liberals criticized his irresponsible behavior of cutting revenues during a period of high deficits. And they pointed to the low tax receipts in 1982 and the drop in tax revenues in 1983 as proof for their position.

Reagan believed the economy would grow under a lower tax load. In 1983, GDP grew 7.6 percent, but tax revenues lagged; in 1984, it all came together: a growing economy and strong growth in tax receipts (at lower tax rates).

Spending in 1984 was 28 percent above revenues, a reflection of the struggle between Reagan and those who were determined to protect the social spending programs they had developed since the 1960s. Reagan had a cold war to win, a government to trim. Liberals bucked him every step of the way.

Public debt increased 83.2 percent in 1981–1984; *Interest* more than doubled; the automatic cost penalty attached to loan growth was aggravated by abnormally high interest rates.

When campaigning for the presidency, Reagan promised to improve *Defense* and to cut domestic spending. He assigned top priority to *Defense* and rebuilt the military despite the fact that Congress refused to cooperate by reducing the cost of the welfare state. Why was Congress so intransigent?

By claiming for *Defense* its rightful position in the hierarchy of cost centers, Reagan made it painfully clear to liberals that the entitlement system they had created could not be cut—to reduce cost, it had to be substantially modified. To do this, liberals would have to admit that they had been wrong for years, and they would have to share the unpopular responsibility for cutbacks.

They were not prepared for that. They preferred to underrate the Soviet problem and blame Reagan for overspending.

Under Jimmy Carter, the misery index was 40.6 percent. In 1984, it was down to 23.1 percent—44 percent lower. The combination of prime interest and inflation rates was 33.5 percent in 1980; it was 15.6 percent in 1984—53 percent lower.

The latter comparison had pocketbook importance which, when combined with the tax decrease, made 1981–1984 a good period for all Americans. But the problems of the period, large deficits, were hidden in the form of higher public debt, that handy shelf in the federal closet where the true costs of expanded government are stored.

Unemployment was a continuing problem in the country and an expensive budget item for Reagan. From Eisenhower to Nixon, the rate ran from 5.2 percent to 5.6 percent (except for the war years under Johnson). It accelerated under Ford and Carter to the 7 percent level and carried over into the Reagan era, peaking in 1982 at 9.7 percent. By 1984 it was down to 7.5 percent and still dropping.

It is fashionable among liberals to classify Reagan as a war hawk who spent America into the largest deficits and the hugest debt buildup in history. In fact, since Eisenhower, only Carter and Ford spent less on *Defense* than Reagan did in 1984 when measured as a percent of GDP, or of total spending (see *What Did It?—Defense*). The liberals' charge against Reagan was poppycock, designed to move the critical eye away from the costs of the welfare state.

Table 12.8
Spending Priorities[a]

	1960	1980	1984	1996
Defense	52.2%	22.7%	26.7%	17.0%
Interest	7.5	8.9	13.0	15.5
Total	59.7	31.6	39.7	32.5
Government	11.9	15.4	9.5	6.1
Soc. Sec.	12.6	20.1	20.9	22.4
Medicare	0.0	5.4	6.8	11.2
Veterans	5.9	3.6	3.0	2.4
Welfare	9.9	23.9	20.1	25.4
Total	100.0%	100.0%	100.0%	100.0%

a) See discussion following Table 2.4.

In 1960, Dwight Eisenhower devoted about 52 percent of his total spending to *Defense*. In 1980, under Jimmy Carter, 23 percent went for the same purpose; under Reagan, 27 percent. How a president spends, modified by the control he exercises over Congress, says more about his philosophy of government than all his speeches placed end to end.

Under Dwight Eisenhower, about 93 percent of spending went to the basic (see below) functions of government. Then came the New Frontier/ Great Society programs that created a new American world. Funds poured into society in search of a monetary solution to the ills of mankind. Government moved away from classic and toward more intrusive duties. In 1980 (Carter), the shift in priorities was remarkable. In 1984 the trend was reversed.

Table 12.9
Summary of Federal Spending—Base vs Other
(In Billions of Dollars)

	1960	1980	1984	1996
Defense	$ 48.1	$ 134.0	$ 227.4	$ 265.7
Interest	6.9	52.5	111.1	241.1
Soc. Sec.	11.6	118.5	178.2	349.7
Medicare	0.0	32.1	57.5	174.2
Unemployment	2.9	18.1	18.4	24.9
Veterans	5.4	21.2	25.6	37.0
Government	11.0	91.1	81.2	95.4
Base	$ 85.9	$ 467.5	$ 699.4	$ 1188.0
Other	6.3	123.4	152.4	372.5
Total	$ 92.2	$ 590.9	$ 851.8	$ 1560.5
Base as percentage of total				
	93.2%	79.1%	82.1%	76.1%

Some pundits say America was emancipated in the 1960s. Women were liberated. Civil rights, especially of blacks, were solidified. Objective morality gave way to individual choice. Government became the caring, cuddling force that protected the many "victims" in America's racist society. Lyndon Johnson's Great Society programs led the way to a new America that would be proud and strong—and very nice.

The chart below suggests, however, that the people of 1985 were not happier.

Table 12.10
American Social Statistics

	1965	1980	1985	1994
Murders	8773	21860		22084
Rapes		82990	88670	102100
Prisoners		315974	480568	1016760
Divorces	479000	1189000	1190000	1191000
Abortions		1554000	1589000	1529000[a]
Population (millions)	194.3	227.7	238.4	260.7

a)1992 figure.

When individuals try something new and the project fails to yield promised rewards, they drop the project and rethink their objectives and resources. Corporations, sports organizations, and artists do the same, but not the federal government.

By any objective measurement, the Great Society, its unbelievably expensive programs, and its intrusions into the daily life of people and businesses was a flop. To liberals and entrenched Washingtonocrats, negative results seem to perversely increase their desire to do more of the same, a characteristic that postpones forever a day of reckoning.

In the five years ended in 1985, prison population increased 52.2 percent. Blacks were 40 percent of the prison population in 1985, although they constituted 12 percent of total population.

Transactions

Political warfare was in full swing in 1981–1984. On one side were entrenched strong-minded Democrats and weak-kneed Republicans; on the other, the intrepid Reagan and the staunch fiscal conservatives from both parties who had, finally, a champion who would take their case to the people. The issue was Reagan's determination to rebuild the military and win the cold war versus the refusal of liberals to accept his cause as necessary or possible.

The comparative transactions shown below silently report the result of the collision between these political forces.

Table 12.11
Transactions (In Billions of Dollars)

		1981–1984		1977–1980
Taxes		$2484.2		$1735.6
Less:				
Defense	$ 780.0		$ 452.0	
Interest	354.7		160.5	
Total		1134.7		612.5
Net		$1349.5		$1123.1
Less:				
Government	$ 340.7		305.1	
Hum. Resources	1608.8		1045.2	
Total		1949.5		1350.3
Net		-$ 600.0		-$ 227.2
Debt, beginning		- 709.8		- 477.4
Total		-$1309.8		-$ 704.6
Adjustment[a]				- 14.8
Total				- 719.4
Adjustment[b]		- 9.3		9.6
Debt, end		-$1300.5		-$ 709.8

a) See Table 11.2, note a. b) See Table 12.1, note d.

Taxes

Reagan believed Americans were overtaxed. It was also his view that a tax cut would stimulate the sagging economy. These beliefs led to major changes in tax law (1981, 1982, 1984) which contributed to the following results.

Table 12.12
Real Growth in GDP and Federal Income

President	Year	Real Growth GDP	Real Growth Income
Carter	1979	- 1.2%	4.7%
Carter	1980	- 3.2	- 1.5
Reagan	1981	- .8	5.7
Reagan	1982	- 2.4	- 2.9
Reagan	1983	7.6	- 6.3
Reagan	1984	4.5	6.5
Reagan	1985	3.5	6.4
Reagan	1986	3.1	2.9
Reagan	1987	3.6	7.3
Reagan	1988	3.4	2.1

Note: The extension of the above table beyond Reagan's first term was necessary to demonstrate the long-term impact of his tax policy.

The early results of changes in the tax law gave Reagan's critics a chance to gloat, but problems of long duration are not fixed overnight. By 1984, Reagan's views were justified.

The mix of taxes has changed over the years in a way that, under the rubric of helping low-income Americans, is hurting them most of all.

Table 12.13
Tax Revenues (In Billions of Dollars)

	Total	Income	Corp.	SS[a]	Excise	Other[b]
1941pw	$ 8.7	$ 1.3	$ 2.1	$ 2.0	$ 2.5	$ .8
1944w	43.7	19.7	14.8	3.4	4.8	1.0
1948p	41.6	19.3	9.7	3.8	7.4	1.4
1952w	66.2	27.9	21.2	6.5	8.9	1.7
1956p	74.6	32.2	20.9	9.3	9.9	2.3
1960p	92.5	40.7	21.5	14.7	11.7	3.9
1964w	112.6	48.7	23.5	22.0	13.7	4.7
1968w	153.0	68.7	28.7	33.9	14.1	7.6
1972w	207.3	94.7	32.2	52.6	15.5	12.4
1976p	298.1	131.6	41.4	90.8	17.0	17.3
1980p	517.1	244.1	64.6	157.8	24.3	26.3
1984p	666.5	298.4	56.9	239.4	37.4	34.4

p = mostly peace. w = mostly war.

a) Social Security. b) Estate and gift taxes, custom duties and fees, Federal Reserve earnings, sundry.

　　　Low and medium income people are hurt most by taxes from which there is no exemption. Payroll taxes and corporate taxes fit that description. Because business must always attempt to maintain its profit margins—its lifeline—corporate taxes result in higher prices or lower wages. They hurt most the unemployed, the retired, and the poor.

　　　The share of Social Security taxes in relation to all taxes has changed radically. In 1960, prior to the Great Society, Social Security taxes were 15.9 percent of all federal income. In 1984 they were 35.9 percent. Social Security taxes hurt most the low-income workers of America.

　　　The Social Security program was in trouble when Reagan took office. During Carter's era, outgo regularly exceeded income. The program had reached the point when it would have been wise to draw on funds that were in lusher times left on deposit with Treasury. Unfortunately, it was at the same point that it was discovered that the Social Security program really was a shell game—the "excess" funds were gone. They were merged with other taxes and spent on the operating expenses of government. The "Social Security Trust Fund" is an IOU from Treasury—there is no cash.

　　　Carter and the Democratic Congress didn't touch the Social Security problem. They turned it over to Reagan and in 1983 he organized a group to fix it. The immediate result was higher payroll taxes.

　　　Given the condition of the economy in 1981 (two years of negative growth in GDP), it would have been foolish to raise income taxes, and Reagan didn't. Along with lower inflation and interest rates, citizens got a tax break in 1981–1984, despite the increase in Social Security taxes.

Table 12.14
Revenues and Spending

Year	Federal Dollars		Per Capita Dollars			Per Capita Percentages of Average Earnings	
	Taxes	Spending	Taxes	Spending	Avg. Earnings	Taxes	Spending
1941[a]	$ 9 bil.	$ 14 bil.	$ 65	$ 102	$ 923	7.0%	11.1%
1944[a]	44 bil.	91 bil.	326	682	1148	28.4	59.4
1948	42 bil.	30 bil.	284	203	1388	20.5	14.6
1952[a]	66 bil.	68 bil.	420	430	1653	25.4	26.0
1956	75 bil.	71 bil.	442	418	1949	22.6	21.4
1960	93 bil.	92 bil.	512	510	2219	23.1	23.0
1964[a]	113 bil.	119 bil.	587	618	2662	22.1	23.2
1968	153 bil.	178 bil.	762	887	3445	22.1	25.7
1972[a]	207 bil.	231 bil.	988	1099	4677	21.1	23.5

Table 12.14 *(continued)*
Revenues and Spending

Year	Federal Dollars		Per Capita Dollars			Per Capita Percentages of Average Earnings	
	Taxes	Spending	Taxes	Spending	Avg. Earnings	Taxes	Spending
1976[a]	298 bil.	372 bil.	1367	1705	6548	20.9	26.0
1980[a]	517 bil.	591 bil.	2271	2595	9910	22.9	26.2
1984[a]	667 bil.	852 bil.	2821	3605	13114	21.5	27.5

a) deficit year

The tax break per capita was as welcome to taxpayers as the more subtle benefits they received as the result of lower interest rates and lower prices.

The increase in spending per capita was not good news. It is probable that a portion of the increase related to special circumstances that have been historically financed with debt. But until that angle is examined in the next section, the initial conclusion must be that fiscal problems of the nation were again swept into the federal closet that hides Washington's biggest fiscal secret, the true cost of the welfare state.

What Did It?

DEFENSE

Given Reagan's objectives, those who shared his goals were not surprised that part of the deficit was caused by *Defense*, the other side of that coin being the belief (hope?) that nondefense spending would be cut back until the cold war was resolved.

Those who opposed Reagan could not afford to take his objectives seriously. To do so would have forced them, as patriots, to control domestic spending while the commander in chief went about his business, a road they had refused to take during the Korean and Vietnam wars. Perhaps that was the reason why war was never declared in those conflicts and our participation was always described with weasel words like "police action."

With that as a background, liberals were not about to cut spending during a nonshooting cold war. The MAD doctrine had kept the peace for 40 years, the argument went. There was no reason to change. Reagan's military buildup was arbitrary, unnecessary, and useless. The cold war can't be won, they said. The USSR is too strong. Anyway, America's resources are needed for social projects, not guns.

Given this clash of views, it was inevitable that a deficit would result and that *Defense* would be part of it.

In 1981–1984, *Defense* increased 72.6 percent, revenue increased 43.1 percent, and inflation was 28.4 percent. Revenue financed increased costs attributable to inflation plus some of the costs of the buildup. The unfunded cost of *Defense*, therefore, represents the price of the buildup that was not financed by revenue.

Had the increase in Defense *been limited to the rate of revenue increase (43.1 percent), spending would have been $646.8 billion, or $133.2 billion less than actual. To that extent, this cost center added to the 1981–1984 deficit.*

Was the unfunded spending in *Defense* a legitimate addition to debt or another example of spending unwisely?

Those who believe that victories in the cold war and in the Gulf War were directly tied to the military strength that Reagan created by his will and determination will see the expenditure as a legitimate addition to debt of a necessary cost that had been ignored by five previous administrations, presidents and congressmen, who allowed America's military strength to decline to unacceptable levels. In short, as he had done with Social Security, Reagan picked up a check that others had ignored.

Those who see no relationship between Reagan's military program and subsequent international events will regard the unfunded costs of *Defense* as unwise expenditures that could have been better spent on welfare programs.

Evidence favors the acceptance of the unfunded costs of *Defense* as a reasonable addition to debt—non–recurring costs of recovering what should not have been lost in the first place, America's military backbone.

Reagan was a fearsome force to liberal politicians who saw in him a menace to their social engineering plans. With glee they pounced on the 1981–1984 deficits and blamed them all on his promiscuous military spending and insane tax cuts. In fact, the economy thrived under lower taxes, and the charge that his military project was abnormal was poppycock.

Table 12.15
Defense as a Share of GDP and Spending (In Billions of Dollars)

	Defense	GDP	Spending	Percent of GDP	Spending
1960p	$ 48.1	$ 523.9	$ 92.2	9.2%	52.2%
1964w	54.8	675.1	118.5	8.1	46.2
1968w	81.9	936.8	178.1	8.7	46.0
1972w	79.2	1286.8	230.7	6.2	34.3
1976p	89.6	1880.3	371.8	4.8	24.1
1980p	134.0	2911.8	590.9	4.6	22.7
1984p	227.4	3996.7	851.8	5.7	26.7

p = mostly peace; w = mostly war.

The cost of *Defense* under Reagan was modest by historical standards. Only Carter and Ford spent less, and they should have spent more.

INTEREST

In 1981–1984, public debt increased by 83.2 percent. Had *Interest* increased proportionately, its cost would have been $294.0 billion, or $60.7 billion less than actual. The balance of the increase relates to higher interest rates.

The prime rate of interest in 1980 was 20.4 percent; in 1984 it was 11.1 percent. The unfunded *Interest* relates to the extraordinary inflationary influences that began under President Carter and continued into 1981–1984.

The following table represents the growth of interest rates as they existed at the end of each presidential term.

Table 12.16
Prime Interest Rates[a]

President	Yr.	Rate
HST	1952	3.0%
Ike 1	1956	4.0
Ike 2	1960	5.0
JFK/LBJ	1964	4.5
LBJ	1968	6.6
RMN	1972	5.8
RMN/GRF	1976	6.4
JEC	1980	20.4
RWR 1	1984	11.1

a) Commercial rates.

In 1981–1984, Interest *went up 121.0 percent versus a revenue increase of 43.1 percent. Had the growth in* Interest *been limited to the growth in income (43.1 percent), the cost would have been $229.7 billion, $125.0 billion lower than actual. To that extent, this cost center was responsible for the 1981–1984 deficit.* And since the effective interest rate during the period was by definition inflationary, the unfunded *Interest* was a reasonable addition to public debt.

Starting with the analysis of Nixon/Ford, the position has been taken in this book that *Interest* in post–Johnson administrations is largely the result of inherited debt that sitting presidents had no hand in creating and new deficits over which, because of entitlement programs, they had little control. All the more so with Reagan. In addition to the usual inability to overcome past problems absent full cooperation from a liberal Congress (an unlikely development), he was also faced with a money market that featured prime interest rates almost twice the size of Lyndon Johnson's.

GOVERNMENT

Government grew by 11.7 percent in 1981–1984, well below the rate of revenue growth (43.1 percent). For any aspect of domestic spending to show signs of intelligent, controlled growth (see below), given recent history, is a welcome phenomenon.

Table 12.17
Government Operations, Net (In Billions of Dollars)

	1981–84	1977–80	% Change
Energy	$ 45.2	$ 33.2	36.1%
Nat'l Resources/			
Environment	51.9	47.0	10.4
Commerce	28.1	23.5	19.6
Transportation	89.0	69.7	27.7
Community Development	34.2	40.7	- 16.0
International	53.1	34.1	55.7
Science	29.9	20.6	45.1
Agriculture	63.7	38.2	66.7
Justice	20.3	16.2	25.3
General	45.4	50.1	- 9.4
Total	$460.8	$373.3	23.4
Misc. Income	-120.1	- 68.2	76.1
Net	$340.7	$305.1	11.7%

Increases in International, Science, and Agriculture in 1981–1984 draw the analytical eye.

America was busy in Lebanon, Grenada, the Falklands, and elsewhere in 1981–1984. Such responsibilities are costly and are partly borne by the line item International.

Under Reagan, the cost of space flights and associated research increased. In 1984, for example, the price tag for Science was $8.3 billion, 43.1 percent more than it cost in 1980.

Under Carter, the cost of Agriculture went up by 185.1 percent largely because of the Farm Income Stabilization program. Increases in that line item continued in 1981–1984, albeit at a lower rate.

In normal times, one might be reasonably pleased with the overall control shown in *Government*. But 1981–1984 was not normal. Spending had risen at such a clip that any cost increase was unaffordable. The deficit was systemic.

HUMAN RESOURCES

The cost of *Human Resources* grew by 53.9 percent in 1981–1984, well above the rate of revenue increase (43.1 percent) or the inflation rate for the four-year period (28.4 percent).

Table 12.18
Human Resources (In Billions of Dollars)

	1981–84	1977–80	% Change
Education, Training,			
Services, Employment	$ 115.0	$ 109.8	4.7%
Health	113.3	79.5	42.5
Income security[a]	349.4	219.5	59.2
Subtotal	$ 577.7	$ 408.8	41.3
Social Security[b]	$ 644.5	$ 401.6	60.5
Medicare[b]	195.8	100.7	94.4
Unemployment	93.4	56.0	66.8
Veterans	97.4	78.1	24.7
Subtotal	$1031.1	$ 636.4	62.0
Grand total	$1608.8	$1045.2	53.9%

a) Minus unemployment compensation. b) Funded by employers and employees. Note: Major federal programs since the 1960s—Medicaid, 1961; Food Stamps, 1962; Medicare, 1967; Student Aid, 1966; Coal Miners Benefits, 1970; Commodity Donations, 1973; Supplemental Security Income, 1974; Supplemental Feeding, 1976; Earned Income Tax Credit, 1976; Legal Services, 1976; Energy Assistance, 1977.

Health costs are dominated by Medicaid. In 1981–1984, all health care services cost $113.3 billion, 42.5 percent higher than 1977–1980. Cost increases took off in the 1960s and have not stopped since.

Income Security, like the other line items in *Human Resources*, is inflation sensitive. Any increase of 25 percent to 30 percent, however unwelcome, would have been understandable in 1981–1984. But comparisons of 1984 costs with those of 1980 reveal much larger growth in some of the elements of this line item. For example, Federal Employee Retirement was up 43.2 percent and Housing Assistance was up 101.8 percent. *When the possibility of changes in Social Security are inevitably discussed, why is it that programs such as these are not given the same scrutiny?*

Looked at as separated trust funds supported by payroll taxes, Social Security and Medicare were safe in 1981–1984, especially after the 1983 adjustment of the programs went into effect. Thereafter taxes collected easily exceeded outgo. Looked at cynically, as large elements of a welfare state supported by general revenue—of which payroll taxes are a part—the programs were growing at an unsustainable rate. Looked at either way, Social Security and Medicare needed adjustment. But that was easier said than done. Social Security was the "hot rail" issue of politics, and by 1984 Medicare had achieved similar status. It would take politicians more sturdy than the 1984 variety to take on such a perilous, delicate job.

Unemployment costs to the federal government were a reflection of the sick economy inherited by Reagan. They are thus an identifiable part of the passive deficits of 1981–1982 that would be legitimate additions to debt.

Had cost increased at the revenue rate of increase (43.1 percent) it would have been $80.1 billion, or $13.3 billion less, an amount that is a fair estimate of costs imposed by robust inflation.

Had growth in *Human Resources* been limited to 21.2 percent (see below), this cost center would not have contributed to the deficit for the period. Since the actual growth rate was 53.9 percent (see above), its contribution was substantial, as follows:

Table 12.19
Allocation of Deficit, 1981–1984 (In Billions of Dollars)

			Percent
Revenue:			
1977–1980	$ 1735.6		
1981–1984	2484.2	$ 2484.2	
Increase			43.1%
Defense:			
1977–1980	$ 452.0		
Maximum allowed (+43.1%)	646.8	646.8	
1981–1984	780.0		
Variance	-133.2		
Available for Interest		$ 1837.4	
Interest:			
1977–1980	$ 160.5		
Maximum allowed (+43.1%)	229.7	229.7	
1981–1984	354.7		
Variance	-125.0		
Available for other cost centers		$ 1607.7	
Other cost centers:			
1977–1980	$ 1350.3		
Maximum growth rate			19.1%
Government:			
1977–1980	$ 305.1		
Maximum allowed (+19.1%)	363.3		
1981–1984	340.7	340.7	
Variance[a]	22.6		
Available for Human Resources		$ 1267.0	
Human Resources:			
1977–1980	$ 1045.2		
Maximum allowed (+21.2%)	1267.0	1267.0	
1981–1984	1608.8		
Variance	- 341.8	$ 0.0	

a) The benefits of a positive variance are passed along to the next cost center.

In 1981–1984, Reagan did not unwind the welfare state, but he did one great thing about *Human Resources*. He complained, he talked about it. He shone the light of day on spending problems he alone could not fix, and during the course of his dialogue with voters, he changed the political agenda.

For the first time since the days of Dwight Eisenhower, balanced budgets, spending controls, and similar subjects were discussed by power brokers. A preference for deficit spending, once the mark of an economic sophisticate, was now admitted only in the dark corners of the most liberal cocktail parties.

Conclusion

By the end of 1984, Reagan had a strong military force. That was costly. And spending on *Human Resources* had bulled ahead with its characteristic vigor. The result was a four-year deficit of $600.0 billion, as follows:

Table 12.20
Unrecovered Cost (In Billions of Dollars)

Defense	$ 133.2
Interest	125.0
Government	0.0
Human Resources	341.8
Total	$ 600.0

To what extent was unwise spending responsible for the deficits? The following schedule summarizes conclusions reached in the analysis:

Table 12.21
Analysis of Deficit, 1981–1984 (In Billions of Dollars)

Total deficit		$ 600.0
Less adjustments for:		
Defense[a]	$ 133.2	
Interest[b]	125.0	
Unemployment[c]	13.3	271.5
Net		$ 328.5

a) See *Defense* section, pp. 179–180. b) See *Interest* section, p. 181. c) See *Human Resources* section, pp. 182–185.

About 45 percent of the Reagan deficit was a legitimate addition to public debt because of the extraordinary state of the economy in which he functioned and because it fell to him to absorb the neglected costs of *Defense* as the necessary price of winning the cold war, of making the world a more peaceful place in which to live.

No amount of feasible tax increase or cost reduction is alone, or in combination, powerful enough to offset the built-in cost momentum of existing federal programs over an extended period or capable of throwing the federal budget into a surplus position so that debt and tax reduction options are developed. Only a combination of cost control and robust economic growth is up to the task. In 1981–1984, Reagan got the economy working again.

Table 12.22
Gross Domestic Product/Net Growth

	GDP (In Billions of Dollars)		Adjusted GDP (In Billions of Dollars)[a]		Percent Real Growth
	Beginning	End	Beginning	End	4 Yrs
Ike	$ 371	$449	$1402	$1649	17.7%
Ike 2	449	524	1649	1770	7.3
JFK/LBJ	524	675	1770	2178	23.0
LBJ	675	937	2178	2692	23.6
RMN	937	1287	2692	3079	14.4
RMN/GRF	1287	1880	3079	3305	7.3
JEC	1880	2912	3305	3534	6.9
RWR	2912	3997	3534	3847	8.9

a) Expressed in 1983 dollars.

Reagan's first term saw these improvements: *Defense* stronger, interest and inflation rates lower, the recession ended, taxes per capita down as a percent of earnings, federal revenue up sharply, a major simplification of the tax code, spending in *Government* modest, spending in *Human Resources* less extravagant than before.

Such things highlight the accomplishments of Reagan's first term. But there was more to be done. The deeply entrenched problem of spending growth was unsolved, and the investment in *Defense* had yet to pay off.

In a larger context, Reagan's major contribution to the public debt problem was his insistent voice, heard over and over again, deploring spending habits of the government and the tax burdens levied on ordinary citizens. His effective, strong, and conservative voice educated the people. They listened. In 1984 Reagan, 73 years old, ran for a second term and won a landslide victory over Walter Mondale.

Chapter 13

Ronald W. Reagan, 1985–1988

America was heading for a crisis. The results of the 1981–1984 clash between liberals and conservatives had ended in a stalemate and a $600.0 billion deficit. Not even America could afford too many rounds of such a match.

Somewhere, somehow, the race to bone-crushing debt had to stop; recognition that America cannot afford everything had to begin. The ability to fund primary costs had to be preserved; agreement on how to manage debt had to be reached on a firm, bipartisan basis.

Reagan rebuilt the armed forces. Measured historically, the cost was modest and necessary. The logic of the project was pure. America must have the ability to expand its forces through taxes and debt when circumstances dictate. America could not accept as inevitable a life forever threatened by the Soviet Union, an international bully.

The problem? Post-Eisenhower spending on the welfare state had lifted tax rates to their practical maximum level, the budget in peacetime was chronically out of balance, and the nation's credit line was used to finance yesterday's social spending. *America had spent itself into a position where it could not create and keep a military force that was appropriate for its responsibilities as a world power.*

To rebuild the military under such circumstances was to guarantee continuing deficits. But it also put tremendous pressure on those who created and maintained the welfare state. Reagan's insistence on funding an adequate *Defense* forced into the open, for everybody to see, the inability of the government to do so without at the same time incurring huge deficits. And the easy escape routes were closed down. There was no shooting war to justify tax gorging. And debt could not climb much faster because of ongoing deficits without causing alarm.

There is no doubt about it. Reagan caused liberals to lose sleep. "Guns and butter too" did not work for Lyndon Johnson or for them. Trying to make it work had become an issue of national security.

At the beginning of Reagan's second term, public debt was $1300.5 billion, as follows:

Table 13.1
Summary of Deficits/Debt, 1941–1984 (In Billions of Dollars)

Years		Total	Defense	Interest	Govt.	Human Resources
Before 1941		$ 42.8	$ 42.8[a]	$ 0.0	$ 0.0	$ 0.0
1941–44 (FDR)		127.8	127.8	0.0	0.0	0.0
1945–48 (FDR/HST)		47.6	37.4	5.4	0.0	4.8
1949–52 (HST)[b]		- 2.0	- 2.0	0.0	0.0	0.0
1953–56 (Ike)		6.6	6.6	0.0	0.0	0.0
1957–60 (Ike 2)		12.1	0.0	0.0	4.4	7.7
1961–64 (JFK/LBJ)		21.0	0.0	0.0	12.8	8.2
1965–68 (LBJ)		38.9	0.0	.2	14.1	24.6
1969–72 (RMN)		46.1	0.0	1.9	0.0	44.2
1973–76 (RMN/GRF)		148.0	0.0	9.2	17.0	121.8
1977–80 (JEC)		227.2	0.0	17.0	67.7	142.5
1981–84 (RWR)		600.0	133.2	125.0	0.0	341.8
	Deficits	$1316.1	$345.8	158.7	$116.0	695.6
	Adjust[c]	14.8				
	Total	$1330.9				
	Adjust[d]	- 30.4				
	Debt	$1300.5				
	Convert[e]	$1963.9				
	Debt 1996	3732.9				
	Debt 1984					
	% of 1996	52.6%				

a) Includes cost of Great Depression (see p. 19). b) Surplus. c) See Table 11.2, note a. d) Government figures come from a variety of sources and differ somewhat. This adjustment "forces" the above total to agree with the public debt amount reported by the Office of Management and Budget, Historical Tables, 7.1. e) Convert subject debt to 1996 dollars.

Less than 25 percent of the 1981–1984 deficit (above) was related to *Defense.*

Ongoing federal programs piled on top of normal government activities were now so demanding that to spend for anything else, no matter how worthy, was an invitation to increased debt. And as debt grew, so did its offspring, *Interest.* Yet, no matter how high *Interest* went, it was hardly mentioned by Washington's peerless budgeteers.

In four lifetimes, a man with the philosophical bent of Reagan would never have a spending variance in *Human Resources* of $341.8 billion, which makes the point that, for the most part, the deficit amounts assigned to each president in the post-Eisenhower era have little meaning. To identify the culprit, variations in each cost center must be traced back to those who established and nourished the line items therein. With one exception—*Interest*. Nobody invented programs for it; it just happens, like snow happens when temperature and moisture conditions collude. Some of it is normal. Excessive amounts represent flawed fiscal policy.

The unrecovered costs of *Human Resources*, the costs of the welfare state, were the largest component of public debt in 1984. Nothing else came close—Big Brother buying votes with a credit card, a heinous practice fully exposed for the first time in 1981–1984. Would liberals back off in 1985–1988?

Change in Public Debt

In 1985–1988, public debt increased to $2050.8 billion, as follows:

Table 13.2
Change in Public Debt, 1984–1988 (In Billions of Dollars)

Public debt, 1984	$1300.5
Deficit, 1985–1988	738.4
Total	$2038.9
Adjustment[a]	11.9
Public debt, 1988	$2050.8

a) See Table 13.1, note d.

Much of what a president can accomplish depends on the degree of control he has over Congress. Republicans controlled the Senate in 1981–1984 and in 1985–1986. Democrats had the House throughout Reagan's eight years and the Senate during his final two. His power to legislate was marginal.

Table 13.3
Profile of Power, 1949–1988

Cong.	House	Senate	President
81	Rayburn (D)	Lucas (D)	Truman (D)
82	Rayburn (D)	McFarland (D)	Truman (D)
83	Martin (R)	Taft[a] (R)	Eisenhower (R)
83		Knowland (R)	
84	Rayburn (D)	Johnson (D)	Eisenhower (R)
85	Rayburn (D)	Johnson (D)	Eisenhower (R)
86	Rayburn (D)	Johnson[a] (D)	Eisenhower (R)
87	Rayburn (D)	Mansfield (D)	Kennedy (D)
87	Rayburn[b] (D)	Mansfield (D)	Kennedy (D)
87	McCormack (D)		
88	McCormack (D)	Mansfield (D)	Kennedy[c] (D)
88			Johnson[d] (D)

Table 13.3 *(continued)*
Profile of Power, 1949–1988

Cong.	House	Senate	President
89	McCormack (D)	Mansfield (D)	Johnson (D)
90	McCormack (D)	Mansfield (D)	Johnson (D)
91	McCormack[a] (D)	Mansfield (D)	Nixon (R)
92	Albert (D)	Mansfield (D)	Nixon (R)
93	Albert (D)	Mansfield (D)	Nixon[a] (R)
94	Albert[a] (D)	Mansfield (D)	Ford[d] (R)
95	O'Neil (D)	Mansfield[a](D)	Carter (D)
95		Byrd (D)	
96	O'Neil (D)	Byrd (D)	Carter (D)
97	O'Neil (D)	Baker (R)	Reagan (R)
98	O'Neil (D)	Baker (R)	Reagan (R)
99	O'Neil[a] (D)	Dole (R)	Reagan (R)
100	Wright (D)	Byrd (D)	Reagan (R)

a) Resigned. b) Died in office. c) Assassinated. d) VP succession.

Increases in public debt stimulate negative vibrations, as well they should. And increasingly they were entering the conversations and news reports of 1985–1988 as topics of interest. Concern would have been justifiable much sooner. Double-digit growth in debt had begun under Lyndon Johnson, and by the 1970s and 1980s, it had reached scary proportions. The unbroken line of ever-higher debt was an accurate indicator that a dangerous virus was loose in the budget process. And the simplistic assignment of the deficit problem to the sitting president was obviously outdated.

Table 13.4
Public Debt (In Billions of Dollars)

	Beginning	End	Percent
FDR	$ 42.8	$ 184.8	331.8%
FDR/HST	184.8	216.3	17.0
HST	216.3	214.8	- .7
Ike	214.8	222.2	3.4
Ike 2	222.2	236.8	6.7
JFK/LBJ	236.8	256.8	8.4
LBJ	256.8	289.5	12.7
RMN	289.5	322.4	11.4
RMN/GRF	322.4	477.4	48.1
JEC	477.4	709.8	48.7
RWR	709.8	1300.5	83.2
RWR 2	1300.5	2050.8	57.7

Only Franklin Roosevelt/Harry Truman during World War Two had a larger percent increase in public debt than Reagan during his two terms. Here, Reagan's record is attacked. His tax cuts did it. His *Defense* program did it. This is fallacious reasoning. The increase in revenue in 1985–1988 was above average. And as analysis continues it will become plain that the size of government was the issue, not the size of the military.

Perspectives

Reagan put the armed forces back on their feet in 1981–1984. It was his primary objective to finish the project because, as he looked at things, it was the only way to end the cold war, the only way to win it. No doubt at times Richard Nixon, Gerald Ford, and Jimmy Carter believed the same, but they were confronted by three roadblocks: 1) domestic costs were rising much faster than revenue, 2) it was political suicide to downsize the welfare state absent support from liberals, and 3) Americans were taxed to the hilt, and apart from the unpopularity of tax increases, these increases could hurt economic growth. Nixon, Ford, and Carter were caught between a rock and a hard place. And to add to the problem by rebuilding *Defense* was something they didn't have the stomach for.

But Reagan did. It was right to restore America's military might, he reasoned, wrong to overspend on things that people or states could do for themselves. And so he forged ahead, no doubt hoping that along the way enough liberals would open doors that could lead to an affordable realignment of welfare programs.

Reagan pursued an institutional approach in his search for fiscal sanity, approving in 1985 the Gramm, Rudman, Hollings Act that was supposed to lead to a balanced budget in 1990. It missed by $221 billion, but that was an improvement and, more importantly, it was an indication that conservatives were asserting themselves.

Foreign affairs occupied much of Reagan's time in his second term, as he sought to cash in on America's rebuilt military muscle. With typical optimism, he set out to tame the Russian bear, to deal with the terrorists who committed senseless crimes all over the world, and to keep Central America free from Soviet influence.

In March 1985, Mikhail Gorbachev took control of the Soviet Union. The state of relations between America and the Soviet Union since President Carter's days was symbolized by the refusal of the Soviets to participate in the 1984 Olympic Games held in Los Angeles.

Reagan and Gorbachev first met in late 1985. At that time Reagan mentioned, as an alternative to the MAD doctrine, a program that would, in effect, put a roof over both countries, one that could defend against nuclear weapons. And he proposed disarmament schemes that had at their core his "trust but verify" point of view.

Reagan's ideas were not well accepted by either Gorbachev or American politicians and journalists, but he persisted and kept the heat on.

The leaders met again in October 1986, but the meeting broke up when Reagan stuck to his bargaining positions, an attitude that angered Gorbachev. The American press and Reagan's political opponents faulted the president for not being more conciliatory.

By the end of 1987, however, Gorbachev was ready to deal. Arms reduction agreements were signed. The destruction of many weapons with provisions for mutual investigation of military sites was agreed to.

The cold war was over.

A new tone was set. The Soviet empire crumbled. Two years later the Berlin wall, the most significant physical symbol of the cold war, became a bad memory.

Never-ending strife between Israel and the Arab world gave birth to a campaign of widespread terrorism. Rogue nations were supporters of these international gangsters, chief among them being Iran, Syria, and Libya. Reagan focused on Libya.

Early in 1986, Reagan froze Libyan assets in the United States. American ships patrolled the Mediterranean Sea off the Libyan coast. There were clashes between American and Libyan forces. In April a GI hangout in Berlin was bombed. German authorities suspected Libyans. Soon after, a bomb exploded aboard a plane during a flight from Athens to Rome. An Arab group took responsibility and cited the harassment of Libya as the cause.

Eighteen American bombers left England, joined planes from the American carriers that patrolled the Mediterranean Sea, and flattened the port of Tripoli, a nearby airport, and a military installation.

Occasional incidents of terrorism continue to haunt the world, but compared to the plague of the post–World War Two years, after April 1986 the number of Arab-related incidents in the West dropped to a trickle.

Strife with Arab nations over terrorism brought to the Reagan presidency its most serious problem—the Iran-Contra affair.

Before the USSR's demise, it fomented revolution in the Americas, including Nicaragua. From the beginning, Reagan had resisted a Soviet presence in the Americas. He suspended aid to Nicaragua, accusing it of supplying arms to the rebels in El Salvador. In the same year, a revolutionary group called the Contras began a campaign to overthrow the ruling party in Nicaragua. Reagan assisted the dissidents.

Reagan skirmished with the liberal Congress over aid to the Contras in Nicaragua, and during the course of this skirmish, some of his aides stepped over the boundaries of propriety. They linked certain transactions with Iran to the problem of funding the Contras in a way that violated law and evaded the will of Congress. Congress, hostile to the Nicaraguan project to begin with, saw an opportunity to embarrass the man who so eloquently opposed the welfare state. Hearings were held and charges brought. Heads rolled. Reagan was found innocent of illegality, but his image was scarred. Those were his darkest days.

The 1985–1988 years were momentous, and the battle for America's future between the conservative president and his liberal opponents changed again its financial profile.

Table 13.5
Financial Profile

	1960	1984	1988	1996
	(pop: 180.7 mil)[a]	(pop: 236.3 mil)	(pop: 245.0 mil)	(pop: 265.5 mil)

Federal Income and Outlay, in Billions of Dollars

	1960	1984	1988	1996
GDP[b]	$ 523.9	$3996.7	$5205.3	$7636.0
Taxes	92.5	666.5	909.0	1453.1
Spending	92.2	851.8	1064.1	1560.5
Debt	236.8	1300.5	2050.8	3732.9
Interest	6.9	111.1	151.8	241.1

Federal Income and Outlay—Proportional Comparisons, in Percentages

	1960	1984	1988	1996
Taxes/GDP	18%	17%	17%	19%
Spending/GDP	18	21	20	20
Debt/GDP	45	33	39	49
Taxes/Debt	39	51	44	39
Interest/Taxes	7	17	17	17

Federal Income and Outlay Per Capita, in Dollars

	1960	1984	1988	1996
Taxes	$ 512	$ 2821	$ 3710	$ 5473
Spending	510	3605	4343	5878
Debt	1310	5504	8371	14060
Interest	38	470	620	908

Average Per Capita Income, in Dollars[c]

	1960	1984	1988	1996
	$ 2219	$ 13114	$ 16615	$ 24231

Federal Income and Outlay as Percentage of Avg. Per Capita Income

	1960	1984	1988	1996
Taxes	23.0%	22.0%	22.0%	23.0%
Spending	23.0	27.0	26.0	24.0
Debt	59.0	41.0	50.0	58.0
Interest	1.7	3.6	3.7	3.7

Misery index, in percentages[d]

	1960	1984	1988	1996
Prime interest	5.0%	11.1%	10.5%	8.3%
Unemployment	5.5	7.5	5.4	5.3
Inflation	1.7	4.5	4.3	3.0

a) Population: U.S. Bureau of Census. b) GDP: 1940, 1942, 1944—Salem State College; other years—Federal Reserve Board, Chicago. c) Average income was not available for all years. Figures for missing years were estimated on a linear basis. d) Rates taken from several U.S. government sources.

After four straight fiscal years of negative growth in GDP (1979–1982), the American economy got rolling again in December 1982 and was in its 25th month of growth when Reagan returned to office (1985). Good times continued to the end of his second term and beyond.

The tax cuts of 1982 were followed in 1986 by another major reform of the tax code. The end product featured lower rates, fewer rates, and the elimination of bracket creep (the automatic tax increase levied by the old system that became odious under Carter when inflation moved wages into higher tax brackets).

The turnaround in the economy under Reagan was nothing short of astounding. Why then the huge deficit? A loss in revenue? No. In 1985–1988, net growth in federal revenue was an above-average 15.6 percent. The deficit was cost, not income, driven.

Table 13.6
Economic Indicators, 1953–1996

President	Year[a]	Cycle[b]	GDP[c]	CPI[d]	Rev.[e]
Eisenhower	1956	79%	18%	3%	39%
Eisenhower	1960	65	7	10	9
Kennedy/Johnson	1964	96	23	6	19
Johnson	1968	100	24	15	18
Nixon	1972	77	14	23	18
Nixon/Ford	1976	67	7	39	0
Carter	1980	88	7	48	14
Reagan	1984	67	9	28	15
Reagan	**1988**	**100**	**14**	**16**	**16**
Bush	1992	83	3	19	8
Clinton	1996	100	7	13	13
Range:					
High		97	19	33	24
Low		70	6	7	6
Average[f]		82	10	18	14

a) The final year of the term. b) Ratio of months of growth in GDP to 48 months. c) Real growth, four years. d) Inflation, four years. e) Real growth in federal revenue, four years. f) The working average of those within the range.

The Reagan program came together in 1985–1988. There was growth in GDP throughout his second term, and the rate of growth seemed to solidify, a large first step toward solving the debt problem—a healthy GDP.

The increase in revenue was strong. But the second element in the problem-solution path was missing—cost control. For deficits and debt to diminish, the fruits of a healthy economy must flow in positive directions, like deficit/debt/tax reduction. That did not occur in 1985–1988, and it will not occur with persistence in the future until the momentum of social spending is reversed.

Policy from Washington is not the sole cause of fluctuations in the economy, but the "two plus two equals four" school of economics says that more money in the private sector means more growth in GDP, and a healthy GDP is the essential long-term treatment for the fiscal disease of the nation. In 1985–1988, growth reached levels hardly dreamed of a decade earlier.

Table 13.7
Inflation; Debt/GDP; Real Growth

President	Inflation			Debt/ GDP[a]	Real Growth[b]
	Peak Year	Peak Rate	4 Yr. Rate		
Ike	1956	1.5%	3.1%	50%	17.7%
Ike 2	1957	3.3	9.5	45	7.3
JFK/LBJ	1963	1.4	5.8	38	23.0
LBJ	1968	4.4	15.2	31	23.6
RMN	1970	5.7	23.0	25	14.4
RMN/GRF	1974	10.7	38.8	25	7.3
JEC	1980	13.1	47.9	24	6.9
RWR	1981	10.2	28.4	33	8.9
RWR 2	1988	4.3	15.9	39	14.4

a) Debt to GDP relationship at the end of the term. b) GDP growth adjusted for inflation.

Inflation was retreating, GDP and collections were up. Yet deficits continued. Why? Because the deficit was now systemic. The cost base was too high. Until it was cut, deficits would continue.

Only one good thing can be said about a debt that grows and grows. Eventually borrowing capacity is reached, and the profligate spender must pause and learn new habits which in the future might cause less damage.

If the public debt is ever reduced over an extended period of time, it will not be as a result of tax increases. And given the political climate of the times, the reduction will not be the result of a wholesale destruction of welfare programs. Revenues from a healthy, growing economy will be the primary prescription, combined with the imposition of spending disciplines and a rethinking of federal programs—all of them—eliminating, combining, and sending most back to the states, where local concerns can be better addressed by local problem solvers using local tax receipts.

Spending in 1988 was 24.9 percent more than in 1984; its rate of increase slowed under Reagan. And the cold war was over. The stage was set for future presidents to take advantage of these trends and use fiscal benefits in view to whittle away at the deficit, and then debt, and then taxes.

In 1980 the misery index was 40.6 percent. In 1981–1984, interest and inflation rates dropped substantially and the index fell to 23.1 percent. In 1985–1988 the final member of the miserable three, the unemployment rate, dropped from 7.5 percent in 1984 to 5.4 percent, bringing the index to 20.2 percent. The period 1981–1988 was a productive era at a time when America badly needed one.

Day-to-day political wars between Reagan and liberals had to do with spending priorities. But behind these mundane issues, a more fundamental difference lurked.

Liberals, driven by a welfare mentality and an appetite for control, need a large, centralized government to achieve their ends. For every social ill, they have a program and a money belt. In effect, liberals favor a covert invasion of states' rights.

Reagan was driven by admiration for the human spirit and a respect for human initiative and individual responsibility. His ends were best served with a small federal bureaucracy. To deal with social problems relative to age, poverty, or need, he would approve historic federal responsibilities and refer others to the states. He was a strong supporter of states' rights.

Both sides in this battle had a hand in setting the priorities of 1985–1988.

Table 13.8
Spending Priorities[a]

	1960	1984	1988	1996
Defense	52.2%	26.7%	27.3%	17.0%
Interest	7.5	13.0	14.3	15.5
Total	59.7	39.7	41.6	32.5
Government	11.9	9.5	8.3	6.1
Soc. Sec.	12.6	20.9	20.6	22.4
Medicare	0.0	6.8	7.4	11.2
Veterans	5.9	3.0	2.8	2.4
Welfare	9.9	20.1	19.3	25.4
Total	100.0%	100.0%	100.0%	100.0%

a) See discussion following Table 2.4.

Under Dwight Eisenhower, *Defense* took 52.2 percent of all dollars spent; in 1980 under a liberal president, 22.7 percent; in 1984 and 1988, under a conservative president, 26.7 percent and 27.3 percent; under a liberal president in 1996, 17.0 percent. Behind most myths there is some truth. According to the numbers, conservatives take their duties as commander in chief more seriously than liberals.

Names and faces have changed, but the dominant trend in Washington since Lyndon Johnson became Senate majority leader, and especially since his presidency, has been the expansion of federal power at the expense of states' rights and individual liberty. Reagan inherited the new priorities and with them the leaders who had spent a lifetime turning Washington into the largest welfare agency in the world. Although he threw the light of publicity on the welfare program and unwaveringly wailed about the cost of it, he had only limited success in changing it.

Table 13.9
Summary of Federal Spending—Base vs. Other
(In Billions of Dollars)

	1960	1984	1988	1996
Defense	$ 48.1	$ 227.4	$ 290.4	$ 265.7
Interest	6.9	111.1	151.8	241.1
Soc. Sec.	11.6	178.2	219.3	349.7
Medicare	0.0	57.5	78.9	174.2
Unemployment	2.9	18.4	15.3	24.9
Veterans	5.4	25.6	29.4	37.0
Government	11.0	81.2	88.5	95.4
Base	$ 85.9	$ 699.4	$ 873.6	$ 1188.0
Other	6.3	152.4	190.5	372.5
Total	$ 92.2	$ 851.8	$1064.1	$ 1560.5
Base as percentage of total				
	93.2%	82.1%	82.1%	76.1%

Under Dwight Eisenhower, federal priorities were clear and limited, following the dictum of the Constitution to do only what states and individuals can't do, national defense being the best example. Only 6.8 percent of total spending in 1960 was devoted to the federal programs that later threatened to consume the federal government's resources.

Value and capacity are the tests of expenditures. Is it worth it? Can I afford it? These are the questions that everyone asks when considering a major purchase. The case has been made that the Great Society is too expensive for America. However worthy the goals, price exceeds capacity to pay. But apart from capacity, is the materialistic approach to social problems effective? Wise or unwise, do massive amounts of federal spending make Americans happier?

Table 13.10
American Social Statistics

	1965	1985	1990	1994
Murders	8773		20273	22084
Rapes		88670	102560	102100
Prisoners		480568	739980	1016760
Divorces	479000	1190000	1182000	1191000
Abortions		1589000	1609000	1529000[a]
Population (millions)	194.3	238.4	249.9	260.7

a)1992 figure.

Had government restricted its role, reserving its fiscal capacities for those things that local governments and organizations could not reasonably do, would the numbers in the above table be worse? With lower taxes, higher savings, less regulation and more freedom, would an America unblessed by the gifts of the Great Society be worse off? Would debt be as high? Absent its centralized power, would Washington be the snake pit for special interest groups that it is today? Would the political system be as corrupt?

Transactions

In an earlier section of this chapter, the amount added to the public debt was summarized. It wasn't good news. The spending habits of three decades were alive and well.

Good intentions, ignorance, or exuberance were no longer acceptable excuses for the spending orgy that battered the sides of America's fiscal ship of state with a broadside of blows which, unchecked, were sure to penetrate its sturdy hull.

The usual table of *Transactions* provides the basic data from which one can extract the meaning of this latest budget travesty.

Table 13.11
Transactions (In Billions of Dollars)

		1985–1988		1981–1984
Taxes		$3266.3		$2484.2
Less:				
Defense	$1098.5		$ 780.0	
Interest	556.0		354.7	
Total		1654.5		1134.7
Net		$1611.8		$1349.5
Less:				
Government	$ 361.1		$ 340.7	
Hum. Resources	1989.1		1608.8	
Total		2350.2		1949.5
Net		-$ 738.4		-$ 600.0
Debt, beginning		- 1300.5		- 709.8
Total		-$2038.9		-$1309.8
Adjustment[a]		11.9		- 9.3
Debt, end		-$2050.8		-$1300.5

a) See Table 13.1, note d.

Taxes

Tax revenue in 1988, despite lower rates, was 36.4 percent higher than Reagan's startup base (1984). Increases were persistent from year to year: 1985, 10.1 percent; 1986, 4.8 percent; 1987, 11.1 percent; 1988, 6.4 percent.

Table 13.12
Tax Revenues (In Billions of Dollars)

	Total	Income	Corp.	SS[a]	Excise	Other[b]
1941pw	$ 8.7	$ 1.3	$ 2.1	$ 2.0	$ 2.5	$ .8
1944w	43.7	19.7	14.8	3.4	4.8	1.0
1948p	41.6	19.3	9.7	3.8	7.4	1.4
1952w	66.2	27.9	21.2	6.5	8.9	1.7
1956p	74.6	32.2	20.9	9.3	9.9	2.3
1960p	92.5	40.7	21.5	14.7	11.7	3.9
1964w	112.6	48.7	23.5	22.0	13.7	4.7
1968w	153.0	68.7	28.7	33.9	14.1	7.6
1972w	207.3	94.7	32.2	52.6	15.5	12.4
1976p	298.1	131.6	41.4	90.8	17.0	17.3
1980p	517.1	244.1	64.6	157.8	24.3	26.3
1984p	666.5	298.4	56.9	239.4	37.4	34.4
1988p	909.0	401.2	94.5	334.4	35.2	43.7

p = mostly peace. w = mostly war.

a) Social Security. b) Estate and gift taxes, custom duties and fees, Federal Reserve earnings, sundry.

Just as Americans are fundamentally unaware of the cost of building the welfare state (financed by public debt that nobody talks about), so also are they fundamentally unaware of the change in the tax system.

The business world cannot exist without profit. With profit, attractive dividends can be paid that attract new investors. With profit and new investment, industry spends more on research, buys more equipment, modernizes and builds plants, and otherwise acts in ways that create jobs.

Taxes are a cost of doing business and, like other costs, are passed along to consumers as part of the selling price or act as depressants against wage demands. In effect, business taxes are hidden sales taxes.

Nevertheless, because of the antibusiness environment that liberals have created in America, corporate taxes are the most popular ones for a politician to support. When they go up, people think they are getting a free lunch. They are not. They are paying a higher "sales" tax with every purchase they make.

So the least troublesome tax increase for politicians to support (a corporate tax) is in reality a hidden "sales" tax that is the cruelest one of all because it attaches to all products, even those usually exempt from sales taxes. And it is paid by all people, from welfare recipients to millionaires. Low income people are hurt the most because they spend all of their income; wealthier ones do not.

Social Security taxes are supposed to fund Social Security and the basic Medicare programs. Employees never touch the part of their wages that is sent to Washington for those purposes. But when the money gets there, it is not set aside in a separate fund to remain untouched except for benefit payments.

Rather, it is merged with other federal income and used for general purposes. Social Security taxes, in effect, are simply another form of general taxation that politicians merchandise under a more attractive name.

They are also cruel taxes that apply to all workers, even those who earn minimum wages. There are no exemptions. And unlike normal sales taxes that are activated when a purchase is made, for most Americans they are applied to every dollar earned (up to $68,400 in 1998).

In 1960, 39 percent of taxes collected came from corporate and payroll taxes; the amount was 47 percent in 1988. The unfairest, sneakiest, most punishing taxes of all accounted for more revenue in 1988 than the individual income tax. This has been the case since the mid-1970s. Someday Americans will comprehend this, and they will demand that the entire tax system be jettisoned and a fair one substituted which, among other things, will destroy the ability of politicians to manipulate people and businesses by creating benefits and loopholes that attract lobbyists like sugar attracts flies.

Taxes per capita were slightly higher in 1988 than in 1984 but were roughly in the same range that had existed for three decades. Spending per capita improved but was still too high.

Table 13.13
Revenues and Spending

Year	Federal Dollars		Per Capita Dollars			Per Capita Percentages of Average Earnings	
	Taxes	Spending	Taxes	Spending	Avg. Earnings	Taxes	Spending
1941[a]	$ 9 bil.	$ 14 bil.	$ 65	$ 102	$ 923	7.0%	11.1%
1944[a]	44 bil.	91 bil.	326	682	1148	28.4	59.4
1948	42 bil.	30 bil.	284	203	1388	20.5	14.6
1952[a]	66 bil.	68 bil.	420	430	1653	25.4	26.0
1956	75 bil.	71 bil.	442	418	1949	22.6	21.4
1960	93 bil.	92 bil.	512	510	2219	23.1	23.0
1964[a]	113 bil.	119 bil.	587	618	2662	22.1	23.2
1968[a]	153 bil.	178 bil.	762	887	3445	22.1	25.7
1972[a]	207 bil.	231 bil.	988	1099	4677	21.1	23.5
1976[a]	298 bil.	372 bil.	1367	1705	6548	20.9	26.0
1980[a]	517 bil.	591 bil.	2271	2595	9910	22.9	26.2
1984[a]	667 bil.	852 bil.	2821	3605	13114	21.5	27.5
1988[a]	909 bil.	1064 bil.	3710	4343	16615	22.3	26.1

a) deficit year

With the close of Reagan's second term, seven straight presidents had outspent their income, producing 28 profligate years of climbing debt. Was this because of wars, recession and inflation as Treasury says? Hardly. Washington has a serious problem that no amount of "spin" will take away.

What Did It?

The method of allocating the elements of the deficits was changed in the previous analysis because deficits had become systemic and unavoidable, except, perhaps, for short periods when the gods of revenue and cost become hyperactive.

Cost control was no longer enough; downsizing was needed. Lawmakers will voluntarily organize it, or fate will eventually shove it down their throats.

Because of the above factors, a changed analytical presentation for the allocation of deficit responsibility was used in 1981–1984 and is repeated below (p. 204).

DEFENSE

Before getting into the details of the buildup in *Defense*, more data are needed to make the numbers meaningful.

Table 13.14
Analysis of Defense (In Billions of Dollars)

Items	1962 (JFK)	1976 (JEC)	1980 (JEC)	1984 (RWR)	1988 (RWR)
Personnel	$ 16.3	$ 32.6	$ 40.9	$ 64.2	$ 76.3
Operations	11.6	27.8	44.8	67.4	84.5
Material	14.5	16.0	29.0	61.9	77.2
R&D	6.3	8.9	13.1	23.1	34.8
Atomic	2.1	1.6	2.9	6.1	7.9
Other	1.5	2.7	3.3	4.7	9.7
Total	$ 52.3	$ 89.6	$ 134.0	$ 227.4	$ 290.4
1983[a]	$ 173.2	$ 157.5	$ 162.6	$ 218.9	$ 245.5
Men (millions)	2806	2082	2051	2138	2138
Per man:[b]					
Personnel	$ 19237	$ 27524	$ 24198	$ 28906	$ 30170
Other	42488	48124	55080	73479	84657
Total	$ 61725	$ 75648	$ 79278	$ 102385	$ 114827

a) Totals in 1983 dollars (billions). b) In 1983 dollars.

Reagan had a smaller active force than John Kennedy had in 1962 (pre–Vietnam). He had about 4 percent more men in uniform than Jimmy Carter. Those who tried to paint Reagan as another Attila the Hun with hordes of new soldiers at his back were guilty of demagoguery.

The increase in Research and Development on Reagan's watch made credible to Gorbachev his plans for a Strategic Defense System (a shield against nuclear attack) as a substitute for the MAD doctrine—that insane standoff that had kept the world on the edge of its seat for decades. The increase in *Defense* was long overdue, extraordinarily useful, and by any reasonable historic measurement, modest, as follows:

Table 13.15
Defense as a Share of GDP and Spending
(In Billions of Dollars)

	Defense	GDP	Spending	Percent of GDP	Spending
1960p	$ 48.1	$ 523.9	$ 92.2	9.2%	52.2%
1964w	54.8	675.1	118.5	8.1	46.2
1968w	81.9	936.8	178.1	8.7	46.0
1972w	79.2	1286.8	230.7	6.2	34.3
1976p	89.6	1880.3	371.8	4.8	24.1
1980p	134.0	2911.8	590.9	4.6	22.7
1984p	227.4	3996.7	851.8	5.7	26.7
1988p	290.4	5205.3	1064.1	5.6	27.3

p = mostly peace; w = mostly war

Defense increased by 40.8 percent in 1985–1988; inflation, 15.9 percent; revenue, 31.5 percent. Revenues easily financed cost increases related to inflation, and a good portion of expansion cost as well. Unfunded *Defense* was a legitimate addition to public debt on the same grounds advanced in the analysis of 1981–1984—it represented the necessary costs of public security that had been evaded by previous presidents and congresses.

Had the growth in Defense *been limited to the rate of revenue increase (31.5 percent), the cost would have been $1025.7 billion, or $72.8 billion less than actual. To that extent, this cost center added to the 1985–1988 deficit.*

INTEREST

The effective rates of interest in 1985–1988 went down, but were still well above the average (extremes eliminated) for all presidents (6.5 percent).

Table 13.16
Prime Interest Rates[a]

President	Yr.	Rate
HST	1952	3.0%
Ike 1	1956	4.0
Ike 2	1960	5.0
JFK/LBJ	1964	4.5
LBJ	1968	6.6
RMN	1972	5.8
RMN/GRF	1976	6.4
JEC	1980	20.4
RWR 1	1984	11.1
RWR 2	1988	10.5

a) Commercial rates.

Interest was now a major budget item in its own right and in 1988 was more expensive than the entire cost of *Government* or all Income Security programs. It cost twice as much as all Education and Health programs, and was twice as costly as Medicare. Yet when budget experts drone on about deficits, the same two chestnuts are trotted out for examination, *Defense* and Social Security.

"Let's cut the COL index, or cancel a submarine" is the typical budget war cry. The flimflam game. Now you see it, now you don't. These diversionary tactics are designed to move the eye away from entitlement programs (including retirement plans for politicians). Why? Because to reduce *Interest*, debt must drop. And to reduce debt, spending must decrease.

Had the growth in Interest *been limited to the rate of revenue increase (31.5 percent), the cost would have been $466.4 billion, $89.6 billion less than actual. To that extent,* Interest *added to the 1985–1988 deficit.*

Interest rates were on a downward slope in 1985–1988 but were, nonetheless, well above average throughout the period. Extraordinary costs are legitimate additions to the public debt.

GOVERNMENT AND HUMAN RESOURCES

The 1985–1988 period presented a unique problem. Funds available for *Government/Human Resources* after deducting from revenue the primary costs *(Defense/Interest)* were less than the total amount paid out by those cost centers in 1981–1984 (see p. 198). Worse still, when the primary cost deduction was reduced to the level of revenue growth (31.5 percent), the same situation pertained, albeit to a lesser degree (see p. 204).

The following table shows the central problem that has haunted Washington since Lyndon Johnson became a figure of power in 1955. It compares the rate of revenue increase with the rate of increase in *Government, Human Resources*, and Public Debt.

Table 13.17
Percent Increase
Revenue, Government, Human Resources, & Debt

	Taxes	Govt.	HR	Govt. & HR	Debt
LBJ	32.9%	49.3%	46.4%	47.4%	12.7%
RMN	40.9	3.5	78.8	53.5	11.4
RMN/GRF	38.4	66.8	85.5	81.3	48.1
JEC	62.0	83.5	65.3	69.1	48.7
RWR	43.1	11.7	53.9	44.3	83.2
RWR2	31.5	6.0	23.6	20.5	57.7

Note that the healthiest relationship between taxes and *Government/*

Human Resources existed at a time when debt went up the most. Contradictory? Apparently, yes. Actually, no. By the time the improvement arrived, the cost base was so high that control of it was yesterday's solution. The only way out thereafter would be cost reduction. The infection of the 1960s had metastasized to such an extent that by the 1980s major surgery was required to cure it.

No financial system can absorb the kind of revenue-to-cost relationships that have battered the federal fiscal system since the 1960s. And how they ravaged yet another presidency is outlined below.

Table 13.18
Allocation of Deficit, 1985–1988
(In Billions of Dollars)

			Percent
Revenue:			
1981–1984	$ 2484.2		
1985–1988	3266.3	$ 3266.3	
Increase			31.5%
Defense:			
1981–1984	$ 780.0		
Maximum allowed (+31.5%)	1025.7	1025.7	
1985–1988	1098.5		
Variance	- 72.8		
Available for Interest		$ 2240.6	
Interest:			
1981–1984	$ 354.7		
Maximum allowed (31.5%)	466.4	466.4	
1985–1988	556.0		
Variance	- 89.6		
Available for other cost centers		$ 1774.2	
Other cost centers:			
1981–1984	$ 1949.5		
Maximum growth rate			-9.0%
Government:			
1981–1984	$ 340.7		
Maximum allowed (-9.0%)	310.0	310.0	
1985–1988	361.1		
Variance	-51.1		
Available for Human Resources		$ 1464.2	
Human Resources:			
1981–1984	$ 1608.8		
Maximum allowed (-9.0%)	1464.2	1464.2	
1985–1988	1989.1		
Variance	- 524.9	$ 0.0	

The above table demonstrates that America could not afford what it was trying to do. The demand for funds for *Government/Human Resources* was, in the context of a balanced budget, excessive.

GOVERNMENT

Government, according to the previous analysis, added $51.1 billion to the deficit in 1985–1988. The problem was not the rate of growth (6.0 percent). It was the accumulated size of the cost center. Reorganization of *Government* had to be the future objective.

Table 13.19
Government Operations, Net (In Billions of Dollars)

	1985–88	1981–84	% Change
Energy	$ 16.8	$ 45.2	- 62.8%
Nat'l Resources/ Environment	55.0	51.9	6.0
Commerce	34.1	28.1	21.4
Transportation	107.3	89.0	20.6
Community Development	25.3	34.2	- 26.0
International	52.5	53.1	- 1.1
Science	37.6	29.9	25.8
Agriculture	100.7	63.7	58.1
Justice	29.7	20.3	46.3
General	41.3	45.4	- 9.0
Total	$500.3	$460.8	8.6
Misc. Income	-139.2	-120.1	15.9
Net	$361.1	$340.7	6.0%

Inflation was 15.9 percent in 1985–1988. In real terms the cost of *Government* shrunk, a step in the right direction.

Agriculture and General were the only two items badly out of line, a condition that in normal times might be acceptable. But these were not normal times. Any increase was threatening. It is the duty of subordinate cost centers in such an era to give way, to make room, to cut back. So, the record in 1985–1988 was good but not good enough.

HUMAN RESOURCES

The deficit of 1985–1988 was primarily caused by the now familiar cash-eating federal monster, *Human Resources.*

Table 13.20
Human Resources (In Billions of Dollars)

	1985–88	1981–84	% Change
Education, Training, Services, Employment	$ 121.5	$ 115.0	5.7%
Health	153.9	113.3	35.8
Income Security[a]	433.0	349.4	23.9
Subtotal	$ 708.4	$ 577.7	22.6%

Table 13.20 *(continued)*
Human Resources (In Billions of Dollars)

	1985–88	1981–84	% Change
Social Security[b]	$ 814.1	$ 644.5	26.3
Medicare[b]	290.0	195.8	48.2
Unemployment	67.7	93.4	-27.5
Veterans	108.9	97.4	11.8
Subtotal	$ 1280.7	$ 1031.1	24.2
Grand total	$ 1989.1	$ 1608.8	23.6%

a) Minus unemployment compensation. b) Funded by employers and employees. Note: Major federal programs since the 1960s—Medicaid, 1961; Food Stamps, 1962; Medicare, 1967; Student Aid, 1966; Coal Miners Benefits, 1970; Commodity Donations, 1973; Supplemental Security Income, 1974; Supplemental Feeding, 1976; Earned Income Tax Credit, 1976; Legal Services, 1976; Energy Assistance, 1977.

The overall increase was less than the rate of revenue increase (31.5 percent). A good sign of progress, but not good enough. The cost base, long established and constantly growing, was not affordable.

Essential tasks of government were being crowded out by optional ones. Discretionary costs must be lowered by those who created them. If they don't, money markets will do it for them.

Conclusion

It isn't the purpose here to evaluate the performance of presidents in the international arena. In the case of Reagan, however, some aspects of his foreign affairs activities must be touched upon because of their close relationship to the budgetary decisions he made at home.

The rebuilding of America's military presence and the demonstrated will to use it when circumstances dictated was the cornerstone of Reagan's foreign policy. Let others make a hero out of Gorbachev for ending the cold war. Here the position is taken that Reagan restored America's strength and the USSR went bankrupt trying to keep up. Determination, steadiness, and carrying Teddy Roosevelt's "big stick," Reagan convinced Gorbachev that he meant business and, like the good salesman he is, Gorbachev put the best face on it that he could as the Soviet empire collapsed beneath him.

Mikhail Gorbachev, a loyal Communist who was promoted through the ranks, did not assume office to turn the USSR into a democracy. He loosened central controls because he had to, because Reagan's policies made it impossible to continue the old ways.

The American media, perfectly willing to lionize Gorbachev, has been strangely unwilling to decorate the chest of the old cold war warrior who more than anyone else brought the Russian bear to heel. Nor is it often mentioned that Arab-sponsored terrorism declined sharply after Reagan approved an air attack on Libya or that Central America was saved from Communist infiltration because of his policies relative to El Salvador, Panama, Grenada and Nicaragua, policies that were constantly opposed.

These accomplishments were directly related to Reagan's attitude toward spending for the military. Absent his determination on the budget front, there would not have been the same progress on the international front. Americans' ability to sleep without fear of nuclear attack is the result in no small measure of Reagan's spending priorities of 1981–1988.

During Reagan's second term, public debt went up $738.4 billion, as follows:

Table 13.21
Unrecovered Cost (In Billions of Dollars)

Defense	$ 72.8
Interest	89.6
Government	51.1
Human Resources	524.9
Total	$ 738.4

It has long been accepted that extraordinary expenses may be legitimately funded with debt, with the caveat that debt is reduced when normalcy returns. Reagan was faced with unusual circumstances in his first term and, to a lesser degree, encountered them again in his second.

Table 13.22
Analysis of Deficit, 1985–1988 (In Billions of Dollars)

Total Deficit		$ 738.4
Adjusted:		
Defense[a]	$ 72.8	
Interest[b]	89.6	162.4
Net		$ 576.0

a) See *Defense* section, pp. 201–202. b) See *Interest* section, pp. 202–203.

The economy surged in 1985–1988. Tax receipts were above average, and inflation tapered off, producing good times.

And America had an adjusted deficit of more than a half-trillion dollars. What will happen when bad times return?

For so long as the welfare state was financed with debt or by the avoidance of military costs, no clamor was raised. But when *Defense* took its necessary share and deficits exploded, the costs of social engineering were exposed. Spin doctors might work overtime to point the finger the other way, to change suspect "spending" into noble "investments," but excuses are wearing thin.

The truth will surface. If enough people care about preserving America and its institutions, maybe they will do something about it.

Ronald Reagan did not reduce the size of government as he had hoped. But he did repair the most powerful economic tool in America, the only one mighty enough to balance the budget and reduce debt and taxes on a sustained basis—the American economy.

Table 13.23
Gross Domestic Product/Net Growth

	GDP (In Billions of Dollars)		Adjusted GDP (In Billions of Dollars)[a]		Percent Real Growth
	Beginning	End	Beginning	End	4 Yrs
Ike	$ 371	$ 449	$ 1402	$ 1649	17.7%
Ike 2	449	524	1649	1770	7.3
JFK/LBJ	524	675	1770	2178	23.0
LBJ	675	937	2178	2692	23.6
RMN	937	1287	2692	3079	14.4
RMN/GRF	1287	1880	3079	3305	7.3
JEC	1880	2912	3305	3534	6.9
RWR	2912	3997	3534	3847	8.9
RWR 2	3997	5205	3847	4400	14.4

a) Expressed in 1983 dollars.

The economy was in a shambles in 1980. Eight years later it was purring like a Mercedes Benz. The cold war was at its peak in 1980. It was over in 1988. Terrorism frightened the world in 1980. It was greatly muted in 1988. As the result of the agitations of Cuba and the USSR, Central America was in turmoil in 1980. In 1988, Cuba was a client without a sponsor; democracy was beginning to thrive in Central America.

It will someday be more generally recognized that Ronald Reagan had a hand in these developments.

Chapter 14

George H. W. Bush, 1989–1992

George Herbert Walker Bush, by entering the world in 1924 in the Milton, Massachusetts, home of his parents, Prescott and Dorothy, preserved Jimmy Carter's status as the only president of the first 41 to be born in a hospital. Calvin Coolidge was president when baby George uttered his first sound. Public debt was $21.3 billion.

Many presidents have had royal political blood in their veins, albeit remotely. Bush was no exception. The New England National Historic Genealogical Society has verified that names like Winston Churchill, Abraham Lincoln, Theodore Roosevelt, and Gerald Ford are found in distant branches of the Bush family tree.

The Bushes settled in Massachusetts in the 1600s. Great-great-grandfather James, who chased gold with the forty niners, bequeathed to Bush his taste for travel. Great-grandfather James, a minister, was a fitting ancestor for Bush, who is a devout Christian.

A successful businessman/civil servant, grandfather Samuel left behind enough money for the Bush progeny to enjoy a rich life style, and the family fortune was increased even more by Bush's maternal grandfather, George Herbert Walker, founder of a prosperous investment banking firm. Athletic skills that Bush demonstrated in later years may have had their origin in this talented man, who was an accomplished boxer and golfer.

Until one reaches the parental level, the background of the Bushes reads much like that of the Roosevelts. In both cases, the family fortune was established before the parents of the presidents-to-be were born. But thereafter, there is no similarity. Where the Roosevelts leaned back and enjoyed the fruits of wealth, George Bush's parents were actively involved in the day-by-day affairs of the world.

Father Prescott Bush (1895–1972), born in Ohio, went to Yale and served with distinction as a soldier in the expedition against Pancho Villa and in

World War One. Duty to country behind him, Prescott built a prosperous business career that peaked when he became a partner in a prestigious investment banking firm in New York. In the 1950s, politics attracted his interest, and in 1952 he became a member of the United States Senate. In his private time, Prescott was a golfer of almost professional skill. He died of cancer in 1972 when his son George was ambassador to the United Nations.

Mother Dorothy is the Maine influence in Bush's life that draws him back to the rocky New England coast every year. Born in Kennebunkport, she was a very active woman, a remarkable athlete in her own right and the author of a newspaper column during her husband's days in the Senate. She married Prescott in 1921. The couple had five children of whom George was the second.

During most of his lifetime, Bush moved from place to place. As a child, his residence changed from Massachusetts to Connecticut. His was a privileged upbringing. His parents were supportive and loving, and servants eased the way. But his activities were typical—sports, games, and quiet time. He attended private day school until he was 13, after which he studied at Phillips Academy in Massachusetts. He was an ordinary student, a great athlete, and a popular and active campus figure.

Bush was ready for Yale in 1942, but his genes got in the way. His father's son to the core, he joined the navy and developed a record of heroics and bravery that compares favorably with that of any veteran. The youngest pilot in the navy when he won his wings in 1943, Bush flew 58 combat missions from the deck of the carrier *San Jacinto* over hot spots like Wake Island, Guam, and Saipan. Once he was forced to land in the sea; a second time he had to bail out of his bullet-riddled plane. In the first case, he was saved by the *USS Bronson*; the second, by the *Finback*, a submarine that halted its own tour to pull him in. Bush stayed with the *Finback* on its combat missions before it returned to port.

By December 1944, Bush was ready to go again as a member of a bomber squadron assigned to assault Japan. Harry Truman's decision to drop the big bomb may have saved his life and that of tens of thousands of other Americans who would have been part of that bloody battle.

Bush was one of four pilots of his original squadron to survive. The Distinguished Flying Cross was on his chest when he was discharged in 1945. Even so, members of the Washington press had the effrontery to call this man a "wimp."

Bush and Barbara Pierce were married in January 1945 while he was still in the navy, a union of both love and wealth; her father was publisher of two popular magazines, *Redbook* and *McCall's*. The marriage was blessed with six children—four boys and two girls. One girl, Robin, died of leukemia when she was four years old, a family tragedy that left enduring marks on both parents.

Bush was a mature 21 when he returned to Yale, and it showed in his marks—he graduated with honors in 1948. In his senior year, Bush realized a boyhood dream when as captain of the baseball team, he rubbed elbows with Babe Ruth, the unforgettable Sultan of Swat, a visiting dignitary at the Yale/Princeton game. Harry Truman was still president. Public debt was $216.3 billion.

Can a young man from a wealthy family with country-wide connections "strike out on his own?" Probably not. Like it or not, the family name and reputation precede him. But Bush came close. He passed up the chance to go into investment banking with his father, but he did take advantage of family influence to get himself into the oil business in Texas. He sold oil drilling equipment from Texas to California until in 1950 he started the Bush-Overby Oil Development Company with money raised by his uncle. This operation evolved into the Zapata Petroleum Corporation, which in 1953 struck it rich. Other ventures followed into the 1960s; then Bush, like his father, sold his holdings (1966) and turned his interests toward politics. Bush was a self-made millionaire. Lyndon Johnson was president, and public debt was $263.7 billion.

Bush's public career began in Texas a few years before he sold his businesses. He ran for the United States Senate in 1964 against the incumbent senator from Texas, Ralph Yarborough. Bush lost but did much better in his state than the presidential candidate, Barry Goldwater. In 1966 he tried again, this time for a seat in the House of Representatives. He won and repeated his victory in 1968.

After the 1968 election, in an unexpected but typically courtly show of loyalty, Bush passed up Nixon's inaugural parade so he could say good-bye, at Andrews Air Force Base, to the departing president, Lyndon Johnson, who had been helpful to Bush's father in the Senate.

In 1970, responding to party pressures, Bush ran again for the United States Senate against Ralph Yarborough. His chances were rated high because of the liberal views of his opponent. But the strategy hit the rocks when Yarborough lost the primary to Lloyd Bentsen, a former congressman with a conservative reputation as good as Bush's. Bentsen won and Bush's career in elected politics was temporarily over.

"Politicians take care of their own," is an observation that is hardly original. The Republican party and Richard Nixon appreciated the fact that Bush had given up a safe seat in the House in order to run for the Senate in 1970. The debt to Bush was repaid in the form of an appointive career that would take him to the far corners of the earth.

From 1971–1977, Bush served in a variety of positions: ambassador to the United Nations (1971–1973); chairman of the Republican National Committee (1973–1974); ambassador (unofficial) to China (1974–1975); director of the Central Intelligence Agency (1976–1977). When Jimmy Carter defeated Gerald Ford, Bush stepped down from the CIA post and started to organize his most ambitious political effort—a run for the presidency.

Ronald Reagan was Bush's primary opponent for the 1980 Republican nomination. Reagan won the race, but he picked Bush as his running mate. The two went on to serve for eight years at the top of the Golden City.

It was Bush's turn in 1988, with the full support of Ronald Reagan. His opponent was Michael Dukakis, a liberal from Massachusetts. Bush won handily.

Ronald Reagan slowed growth in domestic spending but did not solve the underlying problems that made continuing deficits inevitable. Bush inherited them (as had the four previous presidents) and an *Interest* cost which, by itself, was a major budget problem. On the plus side, the cold war was over and with it the surge of military spending. Bush controlled the most powerful military machine in the world, and there was no rival in view.

Public debt in 1988 was $2050.8 billion and growing, as follows:

Table 14.1
Summary of Deficits/Debt, 1941–1988 (In Billions of Dollars)

Years		Total	Defense	Interest	Govt.	Human Resources
Before 1941		$ 42.8	$ 42.8[a]	$ 0.0	$ 0.0	$ 0.0
1941–44 (FDR)		127.8	127.8	0.0	0.0	0.0
1945–48 (FDR/HST)		47.6	37.4	5.4	0.0	4.8
1949–52 (HST)[b]		- 2.0	- 2.0	0.0	0.0	0.0
1953–56 (Ike)		6.6	6.6	0.0	0.0	0.0
1957–60 (Ike 2)		12.1	0.0	0.0	4.4	7.7
1961–64 (JFK/LBJ)		21.0	0.0	0.0	12.8	8.2
1965–68 (LBJ)		38.9	0.0	.2	14.1	24.6
1969–72 (RMN)		46.1	0.0	1.9	0.0	44.2
1973–76 (RMN/GRF)		148.0	0.0	9.2	17.0	121.8
1977–80 (JEC)		227.2	0.0	17.0	67.7	142.5
1981–84 (RWR)		600.0	133.2	125.0	0.0	341.8
1985–88 (RWR 2)		738.4	72.8	89.6	51.1	524.9
	Deficits	$ 2054.5	$ 418.6	248.3	$ 167.1	1220.5
	Adjust[c]	14.8				
	Total	$ 2069.3				
	Adjust[d]	- 18.5				
	Debt	$ 2050.8				
	Convert[e]	$ 2720.0				
	Debt 1996	$ 3732.9				
	Debt 1988					
	% of 1996	72.9%				

a) Includes cost of Great Depression (see p. 19). b) Surplus. c) See Table 11.2, note a. d) Government figures come from a variety of sources and differ somewhat. This adjustment "forces" the above total to agree with the public debt amount reported by the Office of Management and Budget, Historical Tables, 7.1. e) Convert subject debt to 1996 dollars.

As a causative force behind climbing public debt, *Defense* was not a major concern. What had to be fixed militarily, Ronald Reagan had fixed. At worst, military spending would stay even and it could soon decrease. *Interest, Government*, and *Human Resources* were the cost centers of immediate concern.

Interest would not drop substantially until total debt dropped; it was a consequence, not a cause. *Government* and *Human Resources* were targets for action. Fix them, fix the problem; ignore them, face fiscal ruin.

Under Ronald Reagan, the costs of the welfare state that were buried in *Government/Human Resources* were fully revealed for the first time. The piper had arrived for his payment. Somebody would be stuck with the bill. The policy of "charge it," finally out in the open, was exposed as an act of fraud against the American people and their children. The inability of presidents to stop the systemic deficits was increasingly understood.

Realizing he was a victim of circumstances before he walked into the White House didn't give Bush much comfort. He must have known that the media's time-worn practice of hanging each president with the numbers of his time would leave him looking like a fiscal failure unless he could build a coalition of reformers who would broadcast that a change, painful for some, was in the making.

Change in Public Debt

A president with control over both houses of Congress can effect great change. Harry Truman, John Kennedy, Lyndon Johnson, and Jimmy Carter were in such a position. Dwight Eisenhower had control of both houses in one Congress (83d) and no control over three (84th–86th). Richard Nixon never controlled either house. Ronald Reagan had the Senate for six years, lost it for his last two, and never had the House. Bush, like Nixon/Ford, had no control over Congress, not good news at a time when great reforms were needed.

Table 14.2
Profile of Power, 1949–1992

Cong.	House	Senate	President
81	Rayburn (D)	Lucas (D)	Truman (D)
82	Rayburn (D)	McFarland (D)	Truman (D)
83	Martin (R)	Taft[a] (R)	Eisenhower (R)
83		Knowland (R)	
84	Rayburn (D)	Johnson (D)	Eisenhower (R)
85	Rayburn (D)	Johnson (D)	Eisenhower (R)
86	Rayburn (D)	Johnson[a] (D)	Eisenhower (R)
87	Rayburn (D)	Mansfield (D)	Kennedy (D)

Table 14.2 *(continued)*
Profile of Power, 1949–1992

Cong.	House	Senate	President
87	Rayburn[b] (D)	Mansfield (D)	Kennedy (D)
87	McCormack (D)		
88	McCormack (D)	Mansfield (D)	Kennedy[c] (D)
88			Johnson[d] (D)
89	McCormack (D)	Mansfield (D)	Johnson (D)
90	McCormack (D)	Mansfield (D)	Johnson (D)
91	McCormack[a] (D)	Mansfield (D)	Nixon (R)
92	Albert (D)	Mansfield (D)	Nixon (R)
93	Albert (D)	Mansfield (D)	Nixon[a] (R)
94	Albert[a] (D)	Mansfield (D)	Ford[d] (R)
95	O'Neil (D)	Mansfield[a] (D)	Carter (D)
95		Byrd (D)	
96	O'Neil (D)	Byrd (D)	Carter (D)
97	O'Neil (D)	Baker (R)	Reagan (R)
98	O'Neil (D)	Baker (R)	Reagan (R)
99	O'Neil[a] (D)	Dole (R)	Reagan (R)
100	Wright (D)	Byrd[a] (D)	Reagan (R)
101	Wright[a] (D)	Mitchell (D)	Bush (R)
101	Foley (D)		
102	Foley (D)	Mitchell (D)	Bush (R)

a) Resigned. b) Died in office. c) Assassinated. d) VP succession.

Given the above disposition of power, only a magician could have developed the consensus necessary to continue Ronald Reagan's attempts to affect fundamental change. And Bush was no magician. The deficit, of course, continued, and debt increased by $933.4 billion to $2998.8 billion.

Table 14.3
Change in Public Debt, 1988–1992 (In Billions of Dollars)

Public debt, 1988	$2050.8
Deficit, 1989–1992	933.4
Total	$2984.2
Adjustment[a]	14.6
Public debt, 1992	$2998.8

a) See Table 14.1, note d.

It was a startling fact that the country was facing a deficit of almost $1 trillion. One can only wonder why politicians of that era could not put party ambitions aside long enough to acknowledge in a unified voice that the federal fiscal system was badly in need of overhaul.

Not a chance. "He did it" was the most popular game in town. Doublespeak became an art form. Nobody "spent"; they "invested." On what? Children, of course, or health. No matter how disassociated, new programs were sold as benefits for children, or health. To oppose the idea was to hate kids or sponsor illness.

There is little comfort in the fact that debt grew at a lower rate under Bush. Small things can grow at rapid rates; large things grow more slowly.

Table 14.4
Public Debt (In Billions of Dollars)

	Beginning	End	Percent
FDR	$ 42.8	$ 184.8	331.8%
FDR/HST	184.8	216.3	17.0
HST	216.3	214.8	- .7
Ike	214.8	222.2	3.4
Ike 2	222.2	236.8	6.7
JFK/LBJ	236.8	256.8	8.4
LBJ	256.8	289.5	12.7
RMN	289.5	322.4	11.4
RMN/GRF	322.4	477.4	48.1
JEC	477.4	709.8	48.7
RWR	709.8	1300.5	83.2
RWR 2	1300.5	2050.8	57.7
GHWB	2050.8	2998.8	46.2

Perspectives

Bush was one of the best-trained men ever to assume the presidency. What there was to know about Washington, he knew. Whom one should know in Washington, he knew. Many things may have troubled Bush during his presidency, but not much surprised him.

It is understandable that Bush wanted to split from the shadow of one of the most popular presidents in history and make his own mark. But except for breaking his "no new taxes" pledge in 1990, he made his most strategic blunder when he separated himself from his popular predecessor.

Bush hardly mentioned Ronald Reagan, gave him little credit for the more peaceful world he (Bush) inherited, and when he added the devastating mistake of breaking his tax promise, his separation from the ex-president was complete, and his destruction as a continuing political presence was assured.

In June 1990, Bush indeed became his own man when he raised taxes. But the price was ruinous. By that act, Bush doubled the chances that a Democrat would be the next president, any Democrat.

Bush did not present the stern resistance to federal spending that had characterized Ronald Reagan's stance. He bargained with Democratic leaders, trying to persuade them to more conservative positions. They ignored him because they didn't fear new public debt as much as they desired to protect the welfare state which they reasoned had given them the popular support needed to rule Congress for most of a half century. With his veto power, Bush slowed down the spending orgy (he cast 35 vetoes that held), but the balance of power favored the liberals and they used it effectively, their greatest success being his collapse on the tax issue (despite "read my lips.").

Thanks to Ronald Reagan, the world Bush inherited was a less stressful place, but hardly peaceful. Just prior to his inauguration, for example, American planes shot down two Libyan fighters in the Mediterranean skies, a final reminder to terrorists from Dutch Reagan to behave.

The Berlin Wall became a memory in 1989. The media made much of meetings between Bush and Gorbachev, but they were all an aftermath to a cold war that ended in 1988. Neither man had much influence over the inevitable collapse of the Soviet empire that followed its unsuccessful attempts to compete for world leadership with Reagan's America.

In 1991, Gorbachev was a memory and Boris Yeltsin was the first freely elected president of the Russian Republic. To the United States, the Russian problem had boiled down to one more significant issue: What would they do with their weapons? a subject sure to keep Bush and future presidents busy and the world on edge.

The arrest (1990) and conviction (1992) of General Manuel Noriega, the strong man in Panama, as a key player in the trafficking of drugs, symbolized America's deep state of addiction to dream worlds, a curse that would keep high the budgets of Justice for years to come.

Margaret Thatcher played a part in the formation of Bush's budgets in the sense that before her resignation in 1990 she pledged her support to Bush when he warned Iraq of dire consequences if it did not retreat from Kuwait. Her support was especially valuable when Bush was organizing an international military force to deal with Iraq. Out of the confrontation with Iraq came Bush's finest hour as president. It was almost sufficient to overcome his domestic mistakes, almost but not quite.

The Gulf War against Iraq began and ended in January 1991. The demonstrated power of the United States was of a mind-boggling variety. Saddam Hussein survived because America's license to pursue the war with Allied support expired when Iraq surrendered and left Kuwait. It is one of the miracles of international politics that he has survived.

The Gulf War drew headlines while the increase in debt of 46.2 percent in 1989–1992 went, relatively speaking, unnoticed.

Table 14.5
Financial Profile

	1960	1988	1992	1996
	(pop: 180.7 mil)[a]	(pop: 245.0 mil)	(pop: 255.4 mil)	(pop: 265.5 mil)

Federal Income and Outlay, in Billions of Dollars

GDP[b]	$ 523.9	$ 5205.3	$ 6383.1	$ 7636.0
Taxes	92.5	909.0	1090.5	1453.1
Spending	92.2	1064.1	1380.9	1560.5
Debt	236.8	2050.8	2998.8	3732.9
Interest	6.9	151.8	199.4	241.1

Federal Income and Outlay—Proportional Comparisons, in Percentages

Taxes/GDP	18%	17%	17%	19%
Spending/GDP	18	20	22	20
Debt/GDP	45	39	47	49
Taxes/Debt	39	44	36	39
Interest/Taxes	7	17	18	17

Federal Income and Outlay Per Capita, in Dollars

Taxes	$ 512	$ 3710	$ 4270	$ 5473
Spending	510	4343	5407	5878
Debt	1310	8371	11742	14060
Interest	38	620	781	908

Average Per Capita Income, in Dollars[c]

	$ 2219	$ 16615	$ 20105	$ 24331

Federal Income and Outlay as Percentage of Avg. Per Capita Income

Taxes	23.0%	22.0%	21.0%	23.0%
Spending	23.0	26.0	27.0	24.0
Debt	59.0	50.0	58.0	58.0
Interest	1.7	3.7	3.9	3.7

Misery index, in percentages[d]

Prime interest	5.0%	10.5%	6.0%	8.3%
Unemployment	5.5	5.4	7.4	5.3
Inflation	1.7	4.3	3.1	3.0

a) Population: U.S. Bureau of Census. b) GDP: 1940, 1942, 1944—Salem State College; other years—Federal Reserve Board, Chicago. c) Average income was not available for all years. Figures for missing years were estimated on a linear basis. d) Rates taken from several U.S. government sources.

The economy had turned around under Ronald Reagan. When Bush took power, the recovery was 73 months old. He enjoyed 19 more months of growth in GDP before the downturn in 1990 that lasted for eight months and led to nine more months of growth, on the surface, an attractive business cycle. Why then, the huge deficit?

Table 14.6
Economic Indicators, 1953–1992

President	Year[a]	Cycle[b]	GDP[c]	CPI[d]	Rev.[e]
Eisenhower	1956	79%	18%	3%	39%
Eisenhower	1960	65	7	10	9
Kennedy/Johnson	1964	96	23	6	19
Johnson	1968	100	24	15	18
Nixon	1972	77	14	23	18
Nixon/Ford	1976	67	7	39	0
Carter	1980	88	7	48	14
Reagan	1984	67	9	28	15
Reagan	1988	100	14	16	16
Bush	**1992**	**83**	**3**	**19**	**8**
Clinton	1996	100	7	13	13
Range:					
High		97	19	33	24
Low		70	6	7	6
Average[f]		82	10	18	14

a) The final year of the term. b) Ratio of months of growth in GDP to 48 months. c) Real growth, four years. d) Inflation, four years. e) Real growth in federal revenue, four years. f) The working average of those within the range.

The old question: How high is up? is relevant here. Bush had above average luck with the business cycle in terms of frequency; below average, in terms of intensity. Times were good, but not very good, and the real increase in federal revenue for the period (8.4 percent) was well below average (14 percent).

To a significant extent, the deficit for 1989–1992 was revenue driven. Had tax collections been normal, they would have been $4350.7, or $183.9 billion higher. This amount may realistically be considered as the cost of the weak recovery during the period.

Concerning the slump in revenue, some point an accusing finger at the elimination of bracket creep and the reduction in the number of tax brackets, both legacies of the Reagan years that made the tax system, they say, less rewarding than before. There is no denying the logic of that position if one accepts the mechanistic model of an economy that supports it. But people tend to foul up the "inevitable" reactions that flow from the Keynesian model. Only time will tell if lost revenue from "undeclared tax hikes" is more powerful than improved receipts from a high-employment economy operating under a simpler system with lower rates.

In 1989–1992 in particular, the "bracket" argument is weak. Low growth and high unemployment were clearly the dominant reasons for the low rate of increase in federal revenues.

Revenue and spending profiles indicate that deficits will continue as usual: taxes in 1992 were 20.0 percent higher than in 1988, spending was 29.8

percent higher. Liberals conclude that more revenue is needed; conservatives think that spending is too high. *This book says, manage your revenue, whatever it is, well. And it isn't good management to consistently outspend the revenue base.*

Public debt from 1988 to 1992 rose by 46.2 percent. Granted that Bush was not the stonewall of resistance to the spending ways of Congress that one might have preferred, it would be the height of unfairness to lay blame for the ballooning debt solely on his shoulders. President Lyndon Johnson and congressional leaders Sam Rayburn and Mike Mansfield had more to do with the 1989–1992 deficit, and therefore the climbing debt, than Bush did.

The misery index was down again, from 20.2 percent to 16.5 percent, but the member of the troika that had the worst impact on voters, unemployment, increased from 5.4 percent to 7.4 percent. Most of the public unthinkingly absorbed the quiet benefits of lower interest and inflation rates, but the unemployed were loud and brought with them the double whammy of lower revenue and higher cost.

At the end of Ronald Reagan's term, the economy was filling its ordained role in the problem-solving formula. After four years of negative growth in GDP (unprecedented since the 1930s), the American economy was on the move again. But it faltered thereafter.

Table 14.7
Adjusted Four-Year Growth (In Billions of Dollars)

	GDP		Four-Year Growth	
	Beginning	End	Actual	Real[a]
Johnson	$ 675.1	$ 936.8	38.8%	23.6%
Nixon	936.8	1286.8	37.4	14.4
Nixon/Ford	1286.8	1880.3	46.1	7.3
Carter	1880.3	2911.8	54.9	6.9
Reagan	2911.8	3996.7	37.3	8.9
Reagan 2	3996.7	5205.3	30.2	14.4
Bush	5205.3	6383.1	22.6	3.4

a) Measured in 1983 dollars.

If economic growth plus cost containment means lower debt, then a weak economy plus spending-as-usual invites trouble. And in economic terms, that's what happened under Bush: low growth, less than normal tax revenue, and a big deficit.

Washington policy is followed by the private sector. It reacts to intangible and tangible data. Few businessmen applaud the exit of a conservative like Ronald Reagan. The mere fact of such a change invites caution. The new leader and his circumstances are appraised. Bush's zero control of Congress, for example, would be noted. And the budget deal he swung with liberals in 1990 was a clear indication to businessmen that taxes would rise, cost containment would be doubtful, deficits would probably rise, and Washington would again be an aggressive competitor for investment dollars. Information of that type does not add to confidence in the marketplace. It affects GDP.

Cost containment is almost as important an element in the debt reduction project as a growing GDP. Why? Because history says that when debt-reduction capital appears from higher revenue or reduced *Defense*, debt will not decrease because politicians will spend it on current projects. In this regard, the relationship between *Defense* and Welfare in the following table is informative.

Table 14.8
Spending Priorities[a]

	1960	1988	1992	1996
Defense	52.2%	27.3%	21.6%	17.0%
Interest	7.5	14.3	14.4	15.5
Total	59.7	41.6	36.0	32.5
Government	11.9	8.3	8.0	6.1
Soc. Sec.	12.6	20.6	20.8	22.4
Medicare	0.0	7.4	8.6	11.2
Veterans	5.9	2.8	2.5	2.4
Welfare	9.9	19.3	24.1	25.4
Total	100.0%	100.0%	100.0%	100.0%

a) See discussion following Table 2.4.

The formula at work during the Bush administration was lower *Defense* equals higher welfare. *That is a recipe for ruin, one which, in one form or another, has destroyed the budget since the 1960s.*

Priorities under Ronald Reagan had begun to return to the classic form represented during the administration of Dwight Eisenhower. Under Bush, they reversed and headed the other way again.

Table 14.9
Summary of Federal Spending—Base vs. Other
(In Billions of Dollars)

	1960	1988	1992	1996
Defense	$ 48.1	$ 290.4	$ 298.4	$ 265.7
Interest	6.9	151.8	199.4	241.1
Soc. Sec.	11.6	219.3	287.6	349.7
Medicare	0.0	78.9	119.0	174.2
Unemployment	2.9	15.3	39.5	24.9
Veterans	5.4	29.4	34.1	37.0
Government	11.0	88.5	110.6	95.4
Base	$ 85.9	$ 873.6	$ 1088.6	$ 1188.0

Table 14.9 *(continued)*
Summary of Federal Spending—Base vs. Other
(In Billions of Dollars)

	1960	1988	1992	1996
Other	6.3	190.5	292.3	372.5
Total	$ 92.2	$ 1064.1	$ 1380.9	$ 1560.5
Base as percentage of total	93.2%	82.1%	78.8%	76.1%

When government subtracts from states' powers, involves itself in the personal affairs of citizens in matters like child care, abortion, baby-sitting, and the right to pray in school, it must produce something of commensurate value. When government intrudes into these affairs on the grounds that it is building a Great Society, it had better build it, but the following table suggests this is not the case.

Table 14.10
American Social Statistics

	1965	1985	1990	1994
Divorces	479000	1190000	1182000	1191000
Abortions		1589000	1609000	1529000[a]
Population (millions)	194.3	238.4	249.9	260.7

a) 1992 figure.

It is not original to observe that the family is the basic social unit, that as the family goes, so goes the society at large. From the above, one might dare to infer that the Great Society has not been good for the American family.

Transactions

The cold war ended with Ronald Reagan. The years of abrupt increases in military spending were over. Yet the growth in public debt exploded again in 1989–1992. It was no longer possible for liberals to blame *Defense* for huge deficits. With no war to hide behind, even they were forced to look at other cost centers with a critical eye.

Setting forth the transactions during recent four-year periods is the first step toward problem identification in 1989–1992.

Table 14.11
Transactions (In Billions of Dollars)

		1989–1992		1985–1988
Taxes		$4166.8		$3266.3
Less:				
Defense	$ 1174.6		$ 1098.5	
Interest	747.4		556.0	
Total		1922.0		1654.5
Net		$ 2244.8		$ 1611.8
Less:				
Government	$ 528.1		$ 361.1	
Hum. Resources	2650.1		1989.1	
Total		3178.2		2350.2
Net		-$ 933.4		-$ 738.4
Debt, beginning		- 2050.8		- 1300.5
Total		-$ 2984.2		-$ 2038.9
Adjustment[a]		- 14.6		- 11.9
Debt, end		-$ 2998.8		-$ 2050.8

a) See Table 14.1, note d.

Taxes

The major news in the distribution of tax revenue has been the increasing prominence of Social Security taxes in the mix. It was no different under Bush, when Social Security taxes constituted 37.9 percent of all taxes in 1992. In 1972, they were 25.4 percent of all taxes. Such a shift is not to the advantage of lower-income Americans.

Table 14.12
Tax Revenues (In Billions of Dollars)

	Total	Income	Corp.	SS[a]	Excise	Other[b]
1941pw	$ 8.7	$ 1.3	$ 2.1	$ 2.0	$ 2.5	$ .8
1944w	43.7	19.7	14.8	3.4	4.8	1.0
1948p	41.6	19.3	9.7	3.8	7.4	1.4
1952w	66.2	27.9	21.2	6.5	8.9	1.7
1956w	74.6	32.2	20.9	9.3	9.9	2.3
1960p	92.5	40.7	21.5	14.7	11.7	3.9
1964w	112.6	48.7	23.5	22.0	13.7	4.7
1968w	153.0	68.7	28.7	33.9	14.1	7.6
1972w	207.3	94.7	32.2	52.6	15.5	12.4
1976p	298.1	131.6	41.4	90.8	17.0	17.3
1980p	517.1	244.1	64.6	157.8	24.3	26.3
1984p	666.5	298.4	56.9	239.4	37.4	34.4
1988p	909.0	401.2	94.5	334.4	35.2	43.7
1992p	1090.5	476.0	100.3	413.7	45.5	55.0

p = mostly peace. w = mostly war.

a) Social Security. b) Estate and gift taxes, custom duties and fees, Federal Reserve earnings, sundry.

In 1990 the economy went into a downward spin, seducing Bush into the most harmful mistake of his presidency: as the economy stumbled, he increased taxes. The consequence was not impressive. In 1991, GDP growth was again negative. Over the next five years, growth in GDP averaged about 2 percent.

Ronald Reagan had faced a worse situation. The economy was sick; there were two consecutive years of negative growth in GDP (for the first time since the 1930s).

Reagan won the largest tax cut in American history. In the short term, it was harsh medicine; negative growth continued for two years. But thereafter the long expansion began—about 6 percent growth in 1983–1984 and about 3.5 percent over the next four years.

Two men faced with similar generic problems reacted in opposite ways. Bush increased taxes; Reagan reduced them. In effect, Bush joined liberals who demanded more revenue.

Reagan led conservatives who thought spending was excessive and believed that a less encumbered economy would grow and create adequate revenues through lower rates and higher employment.

If, as is maintained here, a healthy economy is the key to debt reduction, the Reagan solution increased the chances of success; the Bush solution decreased them. The economy thrived under the tax policies of Reagan and shriveled under the tax policies of Bush.

Measured as a percent of average income per capita, taxes were lower in 1992 than in 1988:

Table 14.13
Revenues and Spending

Year	Federal Dollars		Per Capita Dollars			Per Capita Percentages of Average Earnings	
	Taxes	Spending	Taxes	Spending	Avg. Earnings	Taxes	Spending
1941[a]	$ 9 bil.	$ 14 bil.	$ 65	$ 102	$ 923	7.0%	11.1%
1944[a]	44 bil.	91 bil.	326	682	1148	28.4	59.4
1948	42 bil.	30 bil.	284	203	1388	20.5	14.6
1952[a]	66 bil.	68 bil.	420	430	1653	25.4	26.0
1956	75 bil.	71 bil.	442	418	1949	22.6	21.4
1960	93 bil.	92 bil.	512	510	2219	23.1	23.0
1964[a]	113 bil.	119 bil.	587	618	2662	22.1	23.2
1968[a]	153 bil.	178 bil.	762	887	3445	22.1	25.7
1972[a]	207 bil.	231 bil.	988	1099	4677	21.1	23.5
1976[a]	298 bil.	372 bil.	1367	1705	6548	20.9	26.0
1980[a]	517 bil.	591 bil.	2271	2595	9910	22.9	26.2

Table 14.13 *(continued)*
Revenues and Spending

Year	Federal Dollars		Per Capita Dollars			Per Capita Percentages of Average Earnings	
	Taxes	Spending	Taxes	Spending	Avg. Earnings	Taxes	Spending
1984[a]	667 bil.	852 bil.	2821	3605	13114	21.5	27.5
1988[a]	909 bil.	1064 bil.	3710	4343	16615	22.3	26.1
1992[a]	1091 bil.	1381 bil.	4270	5407	20105	21.2	26.9

a) deficit year

The duty of political leaders to protect the American purse has been the underlying theme of this book. To openly propose spending, however controversial, and to fund it with a transparent tax policy is to act responsibly in a fiscal sense. The popularity that accompanies such an openfaced approach to governance justly belongs to those who practice it.

On the other hand, to win popularity by exploiting the needs and weaknesses of citizens with offerings of popular social programs, hiding in climbing debt the unpopular tax load that such fully financed plans would otherwise entail, is the act of a charlatan that is unworthy of one who chooses to lead the American people.

The above table demonstrates that since the 1960s the federal government has spent more than it has taxed and has allowed the debt to climb silently, unwatched by most of the American people, until it has reached a level that no one can hide in the closet of political mistakes and intrigues.

Such behavior during the first presidency following the introduction of Great Society programs (Richard Nixon, 1969–1972) could be excused. The legislators needed that time to study the impact of the new ideas.

But by the time Nixon's second term began, adjustments to Great Society projects should have been observable. They were not. Liberals, in full control of the 87th through the 96th Congresses, fiercely protected programs in place and, where possible, added to them.

Of the Republican presidents and congressional leaders who served in minority positions, only Ronald Reagan lifted his voice loud enough and effectively enough to awaken the people to the disgrace that our tax system had become and to the burden of debt that was piling up on a daily basis.

Bush was unable to maintain the kind of corrective momentum that his predecessor had begun. His administration spent more than it collected and, like many others, swept the difference under the rug.

What Did It?

The analysis of the deficit of 1985–1988 was the most comprehensive and difficult presented to that point, made so by the fact that controlling spending to the extent that only modest increases were allowed was no longer sufficient. The combination of *Interest* on debt and the implanted level of spending demanded by the untouched welfare state was now so huge that no reasonable level of revenue would suffice, and except for spasmodic glory years at the high end of a business cycle, the deficit was institutionalized. It was flat out unavoidable and, for all practical purposes, had been for some time. Such a situation demanded a different analytical format in considering the period in 1985–1988 that is repeated here.

DEFENSE

The cold war was over for all practical purposes when Bush took office. The need for military buildup was behind him. The opportunity for cutback opened up. For the first three years of his administration, Bush maintained an active force of about two million, but by the end of 1992, the Gulf War behind him, he dropped it below that level for the first time in more than forty years.

Table 14.14
Analysis of Defense (In Billions of Dollars)

Items	1962 (JFK)	1980 (JEC)	1984 (RWR)	1988 (RWR)	1992 (GHWB)
Personnel	$ 16.3	$ 40.9	$ 64.2	$ 76.3	$ 81.2
Operations	11.6	44.8	67.4	84.5	92.0
Material	14.5	29.0	61.9	77.2	74.9
R&D	6.3	13.1	23.1	34.8	34.6
Atomic	2.1	2.9	6.1	7.9	10.6
Other	1.5	3.3	4.7	9.7	5.1
Total	$ 52.3	$ 134.0	$ 227.4	$ 290.4	$ 298.4
1983[a]	$ 173.2	$ 162.6	$ 218.9	$ 245.5	$ 212.7
Men (millions)	2806	2051	2138	2138	1807
Per man:[b]					
Personnel	$ 19237	$ 24198	$ 28906	$ 30170	$ 32031
Other	42488	55080	73479	84657	85678
Total	$ 61725	$ 79278	$ 102385	$ 114827	$ 117709

a) Totals expressed in 1983 dollars (billions). b) 1983 dollars.

Too often in modern politics, dialogue between leaders and voters has been reduced to "spin," that is, how can the truth be distorted, short of an outright lie, so that the stated goals of the reporter appear noble and those of his opponents seem evil? In the pursuit of approval, truth becomes obscured. Voters are misinformed or bewildered.

Defense is a natural topic for such "spin" treatment.

Pre–Ronald Reagan, deficits were fashionable. Liberals seldom had to explain them. Post-Reagan, deficits were important; they had to be explained. Conservatives had no problem with that—the welfare state had run amok. But liberals could not admit that because they had invented the welfare state. What else could be blamed? Of course. *Defense*.

Reagan, they said, was a rampaging hawk who had spent America into bankruptcy with an unnecessary military buildup, and the MAD doctrine was good policy, less costly to maintain. In short, while never precisely saying so, the impression was left that *Defense* was the cost center that caused deficits. This was hardly the case.

The previous analysis of deficits during the Reagan years clearly put to rest the "spin" that *Defense* was a major cause of federal deficits. And the following table incontrovertibly demonstrates that *Defense* under Reagan and Bush was historically modest and reasonable. Furthermore, given the victorious conclusions of the cold war and the Gulf War, the buildup was long overdue, effective, and cheap at twice the price.

Table 14.15
Defense as a Share of GDP and Spending
(In Billions of Dollars)

	Defense	GDP	Spending	Percent of GDP	Percent of Spending
1960p	$ 48.1	$ 523.9	$ 92.2	9.2%	52.2%
1964w	54.8	675.1	118.5	8.1	46.2
1968w	81.9	936.8	178.1	8.7	46.0
1972w	79.2	1286.8	230.7	6.2	34.3
1976p	89.6	1880.3	371.8	4.8	24.1
1980p	134.0	2911.8	590.9	4.6	22.7
1984p	227.4	3996.7	851.8	5.7	26.7
1988p	290.4	5205.3	1064.1	5.6	27.3
1992p	298.4	6383.1	1380.9	4.7	21.6

p = mostly peace; w = mostly war

In 1989–1992, *Defense* increased 6.9 percent, well below the revenue increase (27.6 percent) for the period. This cost center was in no way responsible for the deficit during the Bush administration.

INTEREST

It is one thing to be saddled with huge debt and a worse thing to be saddled with climbing interest rates as well. Jimmy Carter and Ronald Reagan were walloped by the cost of money, but under Reagan rates moved down. Bush saw rates in the 6.0 percent range for the first time in two decades, but the effective rate (8.4%) during his presidency was above average.

Table 14.16

Prime Interest Rates[a]

President	Yr.	Rate
HST	1952	3.0%
Ike 1	1956	4.0
Ike 2	1960	5.0
JFK/LBJ	1964	4.5
LBJ	1968	6.6
RMN	1972	5.8
RMN/GRF	1976	6.4
JEC	1980	20.4
RWR 1	1984	11.1
RWR 2	1988	10.5
GHWB	1992	6.0

a) Commercial rates.

The "normal" interest rate used in this study is 6.5 percent. When the prime rate is above that mark, an unusual state of inflation is in effect. That had been the environment of the money market from Nixon/Ford through Bush.

In 1989–1992, *Interest increased 34.4 percent. Had its growth been restricted to the rate of revenue growth (27.6 percent), the cost would have been $709.5 billion, or $37.9 billion less. To that extent, this cost center added to the deficit during the period,* and the amount was a reasonable addition to public debt as a nonrecurring cost of inflation.

Interest has historical, rather than current, roots. And it will continue under future presidents as a problem of major significance until debt is finally reduced.

GOVERNMENT AND HUMAN RESOURCES

In the seven presidential periods that ended with Bush's regime, the rate of cost increase in secondary cost centers (*Government/Human Resources*) increased faster than the rate of revenue increase on six occasions—the 1985–1988 term of Ronald Reagan being the single exception.

Table 14.17

Percent Increase

Revenue, Government, Human Resources, & Debt

	Taxes	Govt.	HR	Govt. & HR	Debt
LBJ	32.9%	49.3%	46.4%	47.4%	12.7%
RMN	40.9	3.5	78.8	53.5	11.4

Table 14.17 *(continued)*
Percent Increase
Revenue, Government, Human Resources, & Debt

	Taxes	Govt.	HR	Govt. & HR	Debt
RMN/GRF	38.4	66.8	85.5	81.3	48.1
JEC	69.6	92.3	73.6	77.5	48.7
RWR	36.7	6.5	46.6	37.6	83.2
RWR2	31.5	6.0	23.6	20.5	57.7
GHWB	27.6	46.2	33.2	35.2	46.2
GHWB[a]	27.6	5.9	33.2	29.7	46.2

a) The first line for GHWB is based upon the reports of federal spending, as released. The second eliminates the "Commerce" account in *Government* which contains the results of distortive transactions related to the savings and loan bailout. George Bush absorbed about $182 billion of net costs during his watch. The second set of figures more fairly reports the true comparative cost situation. Debt figures were not adjusted for inflation.

The unaffordable cost base of the federal government was intact when Bush took office. Consequently, despite more modest *Defense* needs, a deficit was assured unless a totally unexpected surge of revenue arrived (it didn't). As the above table shows, debt continued to grow even when cost to revenue relationships improved.

In 1985–1988, funds available for *Government/Human Resources* were less than the spending totals in those cost centers during the previous four years (see p. 222). The same situation pertained in 1989–1992 (see below), and its deficit was allocated as follows:

Table 14.18
Allocation of Deficit, 1989–1992 (In Billions of Dollars)

Revenue:			Percent
1985–1988	$ 3266.3		
1989–1992	4166.8	$ 4166.8	
Increase			27.6%
Defense:			
1985–1988	$ 1098.5		
Maximum allowed (+27.6%)	1401.7		
1989–1992	1174.6	1174.6	
Variance	227.1		
Available for Interest		$ 2992.2	
Interest:			
1985–1988	$ 556.0		
Maximum allowed (+27.6%)	709.5	709.5	
1989–1992	747.4		
Variance	-37.9		
Available for other cost centers		$ 2282.7	

Table 14.18 *(continued)*
Allocation of Deficit, 1989–1992 (In Billions of Dollars)

Other cost centers:			
1985–1988	$ 2350.2		
Maximum growth rate			-2.9%
Government:			
1985–1988	$ 361.1		
Maximum allowed (-2.9%)	350.7	350.7	
1989–1992	528.1		
Variance	-177.4		
Available for Human			
Resources		$ 1932.0	
Human Resources:			
1985–1988	$ 1989.1		
Maximum allowed (-2.9%)	1932.0	1932.0	
1989–1992	2650.1		
Variance	-718.1	$ 0.0	

Even wealthy nations have limitations; they cannot borrow endlessly. However noble the motives behind Great Society programs and their offspring, and apart from the issue of federal expansion, it had been abundantly clear for some time that America had tried to do too much too soon.

States must balance budgets each year. Under those tight fiscal circumstances, had federal programs now in place (except for those funded by payroll taxes) been assumed by states, as the spirit of the Constitution would suggest, they would never have been so broad, duplicative, costly, or inefficient. And Washington, freed from extreme pressure from national lobbyists, would be a more honorable place to work.

Again, the wisdom of the Constitution has been shown. Had the desire to be all things to all people been channeled through the American system of states' rights in accordance with its terms, the filtering process would have forced a reality check and today the nation would be better off.

GOVERNMENT

Government increased by 46.2 percent in 1989–1992 (inflation was 19.2 percent). On the surface, such an increase during an era of massive structural deficits seems unconscionable. But, as usual, final conclusions must await analysis.

Table 14.19
Government Operations, Net (In Billions of Dollars)

	1989–92	1985–88	% Change
Energy	$ 12.9	$ 16.8	- 23.2%
Nat'l Resources/ Environment	71.9	55.0	30.7

Table 14.19 *(continued)*
Government Operations, Net (In Billions of Dollars)

	1989–92	1985–88	% Change
Commerce	181.8	34.1	433.1
Transportation	121.5	107.3	13.2
Community Development	27.5	25.3	8.7
International	55.4	52.5	5.5
Science	59.7	37.6	58.8
Agriculture	59.3	100.7	- 41.1
Justice	46.2	29.7	55.6
General	44.4	41.3	7.5
Total	$ 680.6	$ 500.3	36.0
Misc. Income	-152.5	-139.2	9.5
Net	$ 528.1	$ 361.1	46.2%

Under Ronald Reagan, the rate of increase in this cost center was less than the rate of inflation, meaning that in terms of equivalent dollars, costs were actually down. This was not so under Bush, according to the totals in the above table, the rate of increase being much higher than the rate of inflation (19.2 percent).

But the totals in the table must be adjusted if comparisons to other periods are to make sense. Why? Because of Commerce. That line item contains a noncomparable distortion.

As the result of corruption, mismanagement, and questionable oversight by congressional committees, hundreds of savings and loan institutions faced ruin in 1989. Bush approved a bill in 1989 that in effect bailed out the savings and loan industry and protected the deposits of a large number of people. The short-term cost to the federal government was estimated to be over $150 billion. The increase in Commerce in 1989–1992 essentially represents the first installment payment of this new cost.

When Commerce is eliminated from both totals in the above schedule, the cost increase of remaining items becomes 5.9 percent, well below the rate of inflation (19.2 percent), the third consecutive presidential period with such a positive result.

Had Commerce increased at the same rate as revenue (27.5 percent), its cost in 1989–1992 would have been $43.5 billion, or $138.3 billion less than actual, an amount that serves as a reasonable estimate of the extra costs imposed by the savings and loan problem.

Overall (Commerce aside), cost control in *Government* would have been acceptable under normal circumstances, but controlled growth of costs was no longer adequate. Shakedown was needed.

HUMAN RESOURCES

The operating deficit in 1989–1992 was $933.4 billion, of which the *Human Resources* portion ($718.1 billion) was 77.0 percent). Cost increased by 33.2 percent, well above the rate of inflation (19.2 percent).

Table 14.20
Human Resources (In Billions of Dollars)

	1989–92	1985–88	% Change
Education, Training,			
Services, Employment	$ 164.0	$ 121.5	35.0%
Health	266.8	153.9	73.4
Income security[a]	549.1	433.0	26.8
Subtotal	$ 979.9	$ 708.4	38.3
Social Security[b]	$ 1037.8	$ 814.1	27.5
Medicare[b]	406.6	290.0	40.2
Unemployment	101.2	67.7	49.5
Veterans	124.6	108.9	14.4
Subtotal	$ 1670.2	$ 1280.7	30.4
Grand total	$ 2650.1	$ 1989.1	33.2%

a) Minus unemployment compensation. b) Funded by employers and employees. Note: Major federal programs since the 1960s—Medicaid, 1961; Food Stamps, 1962; Medicare, 1967; Student Aid, 1966; Coal Miners Benefits, 1970; Commodity Donations, 1973; Supplemental Security Income, 1974; Supplemental Feeding, 1976; Earned Income Tax Credit, 1976; Legal Services, 1976; Energy Assistance, 1977.

Relative to the increase in revenue (27.6 percent), the rate of increase in the cost center of *Human Resources* as a whole (33.2 percent) was not mind-boggling, however inadvisable. Nor was the real cost increase (after inflation of 19.2 percent) of 14 percent over a four-year period shocking. But the problem had grown well beyond such terms. Even as *Defense* stabilized, huge deficits emerged.

Education, Health, Medicare, and Unemployment grew disproportionately.

Bush asserted that he wanted to be remembered as the education president. His spending reflected this objective—a 35.0 percent increase. In 1989–1992, a total of $164.0 billion was charged to this line item. In 1992 alone the expenditure was $45.2 billion, which was a four-year rate of $180.8 billion and a demonstration of a truth that makes it difficult to take Republicans seriously when they complain about spending sponsored by liberals. When the spending initiative comes from themselves, as in this case, it is supposed to be accepted as good.

They all miss the essential point. No matter how worthwhile, short of an emergency, all new spending hurts, and old programs have to be cut, consolidated, shipped to the states or junked.

Health costs were consistently driven by Medicaid, a healthcare system looking for diseases and riddled with waste. Medicare, allegedly funded in part by payroll taxes, had the "fraud, waste and abuse" characteristics of all government programs and, like the others, was badly in need of reform.

In 1992 the unemployment rate was 7.4 percent, versus 5.4 percent in 1988, a symbol of a problem Bush suffered for four years. It is said that his retreat from his tax pledge defeated him in his race for reelection. Unemployment may have damaged his chances just as much.

Had the Unemployment line item increased at the same rate as revenue (27.5 percent), cost in 1989–1992 would have been $86.3 billion, or $14.9 billion less than actual, an amount that serves as a useful estimate of the cost of unfunded and unusual spending associated with the limp recovery.

Conclusion

The foreign policies of American presidents are not the subject matter of this book and are mentioned only to the extent that they round out the profile of the man and relate to the budget deficit.

The Gulf War will symbolize Bush's international face. More than the victory itself, the challenge of organizing a response to Saddam Hussein that included Arab nations not normally counted as friends of America and always counted as enemies of Israel was one that he manfully accepted and skillfully accomplished.

Domestically, things did not go well for Bush. The positive business cycle (92 months, a peacetime record) that started in 1982 under Ronald Reagan weakened in 1989 and disappeared in 1990 and 1991 before it righted itself in 1992—too late to help Bush but convenient for his successor. Deficits increased to $933.4 billion, as follows:

Table 14.21
Unrecovered Cost (In Billions of Dollars)

Defense	$ 0.0
Interest	37.9
Government	177.4
Human Resources	718.1
Total	$ 933.4

Similar to presidents before him, Bush had a deficit that was a mixture of unfunded costs. Some could be construed as legitimate additions to debt and some could not.

Table 14.22

Analysis of Deficit, 1989–1992 (In Billions of Dollars)

Total Deficit		$ 933.4
Adjusted:		
Revenue[a]	$ 183.9	
Interest[b]	37.9	
Savings & Loan[c]	138.3	
Unemployment[d]	14.9	375.0
Net		$ 558.4

a) See *Perspectives* section, pp. 215–221. b) See *Interest* section, pp. 226–227. c) See *Government* section, pp. 215–221. d) See *Human Resources* section, pp. 231–232.

About 40 percent of the Bush deficit was a reasonable addition to public debt, a fact that makes his administration look much better than before. But the unsettling truth remains that the seeds of deficit are within the system and the system goes on and on, lurching from one revenue base to the next, hoping for a better day but doing nothing to bring about that desired result.

The foundation deficit problem in 1989–1992 was caused by *Human Resources*. Its rate of increase (33.2 percent) in current or inflation-adjusted dollars is unacceptable in any era, especially one that cannot afford the cost base from which change is measured.

Bush suffered unexpected revenue losses and costs that inflated his deficit. It is for precisely such domestic emergencies that the power to borrow should be used. And it is because emergencies will surely arise that the borrowing capacity of the nation should not be utilized for operating expenses.

Public debt is not in trouble because of highway problems, wars, banking emergencies, and economic vagaries. The portion of expanded debt related to such things that was carried by several presidents was affordable and under a sensible fiscal system could have been repaid over time. Public debt is troublesome because federal politicians will not cut operating expenses, especially *Human Resources*, to the limits of a reasonable revenue stream from a sensible tax system.

Did the economy improve in 1989–1992? To what extent did policies of Bush add to or detract from the results? As the following table shows, the four-year growth rate of GDP dropped sharply under Bush.

Table 14.23
Gross Domestic Product/Net Growth
(In Billions of Dollars)

	GDP (In Billions of Dollars)		Adjusted GDP (In Billions of Dollars)[a]		Percent Real Growth
	Beginning	End	Beginning	End	4 Yrs
Ike	$ 371	$449	$1402	$1649	17.7%
Ike 2	449	524	1649	1770	7.3
JFK/LBJ	524	675	1770	2178	23.0
LBJ	675	937	2178	2692	23.6
RMN	937	1287	2692	3079	14.4
RMN/GRF	1287	1880	3079	3305	7.3
JEC	1880	2912	3305	3534	6.9
RWR	2912	3997	3534	3847	8.9
RWR 2	3997	5205	3847	4400	14.4
GHWB	5205	6383	4400	4550	3.4

a) Expressed in 1983 dollars.

The tax increase approved by Bush in 1990 was not a positive policy relative to the debt-reduction objective. Nor was his approval of new spending on education, however admirable the projects, or his establishment of a new federal post—Secretary of Veterans Affairs. Finally, Bush failed to maintain the influential voice of presidential disapproval of Washington's fiscal mess that his predecessor had established.

George Bush met international responsibilities well and represented America honorably in the international arena. Domestically, he was a victim of bad luck and bad judgment. Bush made no contribution toward debt reduction, and following his tax increase, the growth in GDP was anemic for the next four years.

Chapter 15

William J. Clinton, 1993–1996

William Jefferson Clinton, born on August 19, 1946, in Hope, Arkansas, is the first president to be born after World War Two. Harry S Truman was president when Clinton's mother, Virginia Cassidy Blythe, saw, for the first time, her president-to-be. Three months earlier the father, William Jefferson Blythe, had died in an automobile accident.

Clinton was mostly supervised by grandparents for the first four years of his life because his mother had gone to New Orleans to earn a nursing certificate. She returned to Hope in 1950 and took charge of her son; later that year, when he was four years old, she married an automobile salesman, Roger Clinton.

The Clintons remained in Hope until 1953, when they moved to Hot Springs, Arkansas, where opportunities for work were better. The move did improve their economic standing. Roger became a service manager in an automobile dealership, and Virginia found employment as a nurse anesthetist. Clinton was seven. Dwight D. Eisenhower was president.

Clinton's home life was difficult. His stepfather was a drinker, rough with his wife. Before Roger died in 1967, however, Clinton (a student at Georgetown at that time) reconciled with him. Clinton's mother died in 1994.

Although the Clintons were Baptists, Bill Clinton received his early training in Catholic schools. Then, after two years, he transferred to the public school system of Hot Springs. Biographies, unusually lacking in specifics, state that he liked school and his grades were good.

In 1956, while Bill Clinton was still in elementary school, Virginia had a second son, Roger, Jr. In this time period, Bill dropped "Blythe" as his surname and substituted "Clinton." When he was 15, he had his name formally changed.

In high school, Clinton was known as a musician (he played the saxophone) and must have been academically and politically prominent because in 1963 he was chosen as a delegate to a citizenship training program for young people (American Legion Boys Nation). While in Washington, he got to shake the hand of President John Kennedy, an encounter that increased his political ambitions, which, his peers recall, were already evident.

Clinton graduated from high school in 1964, months after the assassination of John Kennedy. Lyndon Johnson was president, and his Great Society was taking its first baby steps into the world of the federal budget. Public debt was $256.8 billion.

Clinton finished high school with the fourth-highest academic rating in his class. That, plus musical ability, brought the scholarships that took him to Georgetown University in Washington, D.C. In his final three years, financial strain was eased with the income he earned as an intern to Senator William Fulbright, Democrat, Arkansas.

At Georgetown, Clinton majored in international affairs, serving as class president during his first two years. After he graduated in 1968, he qualified for a Rhodes scholarship and studied government for two years at Oxford, England.

After Oxford, Clinton entered Yale Law School in 1970 for his law degree. Apparently, scholarships again paid his way, assisted by income he earned from part-time jobs. During these years he met Hillary Rodham, his wife-to-be, and got his first taste of presidential politics as part of George McGovern's campaign against Richard Nixon in 1972.

After graduating from Yale in 1973, Clinton returned to Arkansas. Richard M. Nixon was president. Public debt was $340.9 billion, not yet reflecting the matured fruit of the Great Society.

In 1973, Clinton became a faculty member at the University of Arkansas Law School. Obviously, it was a temporary position because politics was his game. It was a question of when, not if, he would seek political office. For how long did he wait? Until 1974.

Clinton ran against John Paul Hammerschmidt, a Republican, for a seat in the House of Representatives. He lost, but in 1976 he was back on his feet running for attorney general of Arkansas. He won. In 1978 he was at it again, a man in a hurry, running for the governor's job. He won the election and became the youngest governor in the country, serving in 1979–80. Two years later he lost the governorship, but he won it back after another two years, serving in 1983–1992.

As a founder of the Democratic Leadership Council and as chairman of the National Governor's Association, Clinton gained some national attention, but from a pragmatic point of view, he was an unknown when he entered the presidential sweepstakes of 1992 against a field of national politicians and personalities with far more name recognition.

Despite the odds and scandalous allegations dealing with his sex life, Clinton prevailed, and assisted by the third-party candidacy of Ross Perot, he won the race against President George Bush, 43 percent to 38 percent. It was hardly a ringing endorsement, but he and Vice President Albert Gore assumed office in 1993.

From the time of Clinton's birth, public debt was in a climbing mode. When as a teenager he shook hands with John Kennedy, standing nearby was the man, Lyndon Johnson, who would create the welfare state which by the time of Clinton's inauguration had driven debt, under five presidents, to historic heights, most recently (1989–1992) to $2998.8 billion, as follows:

Table 15.1
Summary of Deficits/Debt, 1941–1992 (In Billions of Dollars)

Years		Total	Defense	Interest	Govt.	Human Resources
Before 1941		$ 42.8	$ 42.8[a]	$ 0.0	$ 0.0	$ 0.0
1941–44 (FDR)		127.8	127.8	0.0	0.0	0.0
1945–48 (FDR/HST)		47.6	37.4	5.4	0.0	4.8
1949–52 (HST)[b]		- 2.0	- 2.0	0.0	0.0	0.0
1953–56 (Ike)		6.6	6.6	0.0	0.0	0.0
1957–60 (Ike 2)		12.1	0.0	0.0	4.4	7.7
1961–64 (JFK/LBJ)		21.0	0.0	0.0	12.8	8.2
1965–68 (LBJ)		38.9	0.0	.2	14.1	24.6
1969–72 (RMN)		46.1	0.0	1.9	0.0	44.2
1973–76 (RMN/GRF)		148.0	0.0	9.2	17.0	121.8
1977–80 (JEC)		227.2	0.0	17.0	67.7	142.1
1981–84 (RWR)		600.0	133.2	125.0	0.0	341.8
1985–88 (RWR 2)		738.4	72.8	89.6	51.1	524.9
1989–92 (GHWB)		933.4	0.0	37.9	177.4	718.1
	Deficits	$ 2987.9	$ 418.6	386.2	$ 244.5	1938.6
	Adjust[c]	14.8				
	Total	$ 3002.7				
	Adjust[d]	- 3.9				
	Debt	$ 2998.8				
	Convert[e]	$ 3353.6				
	Debt 1996	$ 3732.9				
	Debt 1992					
	% of 1996	89.8%				

a) Includes cost of Great Depression (see p. 19). b) Surplus. c) See Table 11.2, note a. d) Government figures come from a variety of sources and differ somewhat. This adjustment "forces" the above total to agree with the public debt amount reported by the Office of Management and Budget, Historical Tables, 7.1. e) Convert subject debt to 1996 dollars.

Interest was now a back-breaking cost that would not go away until debt was addressed. *Government* costs were too high. And the combination of time-honored entitlements and welfare costs had become, in *Human Resources*, the political battleground upon which the struggle for America's future direction would be fought.

History had demonstrated America's ability to face and conquer international explosions and domestic tornadoes. Did it still have the character to turn away the enticements of a welfare state? And was William Jefferson Clinton the type of man to bolster, or weaken, that character?

Change in Public Debt

Clinton presided over the 103d and 104th Congresses. In the first of the two, he was supported by liberal holdovers, Thomas Foley (House) and George Mitchell (Senate). The federal deficit during those two years was $458.3 billion.

Americans always had doubts about Clinton. His majority in the 1992 election (43 percent) was the weakest since Woodrow Wilson's in 1912 (42 percent). And the people voiced their doubts again in 1993 when they gave the Republicans control of both Houses.

Table 15.2
Profile of Power, 1949–1996

Cong.	House	Senate	President
81	Rayburn (D)	Lucas (D)	Truman (D)
82	Rayburn (D)	McFarland (D)	Truman (D)
83	Martin (R)	Taft[a] (R)	Eisenhower (R)
83		Knowland (R)	
84	Rayburn (D)	Johnson (D)	Eisenhower (R)
85	Rayburn (D)	Johnson (D)	Eisenhower (R)
86	Rayburn (D)	Johnson[a] (D)	Eisenhower (R)
87	Rayburn (D)	Mansfield (D)	Kennedy (D)
87	Rayburn[b] (D)	Mansfield (D)	Kennedy (D)
87	McCormack (D)		
88	McCormack (D)	Mansfield (D)	Kennedy[c] (D)
88			Johnson[d] (D)
89	McCormack (D)	Mansfield (D)	Johnson (D)
90	McCormack (D)	Mansfield (D)	Johnson (D)
91	McCormack[a](D)	Mansfield (D)	Nixon (R)
92	Albert (D)	Mansfield (D)	Nixon (R)
93	Albert (D)	Mansfield (D)	Nixon[a] (R)
94	Albert[a] (D)	Mansfield (D)	Ford[d] (R)
95	O'Neil (D)	Mansfield[a](D)	Carter (D)
95		Byrd (D)	
96	O'Neil (D)	Byrd (D)	Carter (D)
97	O'Neil (D)	Baker (R)	Reagan (R)
98	O'Neil (D)	Baker (R)	Reagan (R)
99	O'Neil[a] (D)	Dole (R)	Reagan (R)
100	Wright (D)	Byrd[a] (D)	Reagan (R)
101	Wright[a] (D)	Mitchell (D)	Bush (R)

Table 15.2 *(continued)*
Profile of Power, 1949–1996

Cong.	House	Senate	President
101	Foley (D)		
102	Foley (D)	Mitchell (D)	Bush (R)
103	Foley (D)	Mitchell (D)	Clinton (D)
104	Gingrich (R)	Dole (R)	Clinton (D)

a) Resigned. b) Died in office. c) Assassinated. d) VP succession.

Lyndon Johnson's presidency ended in 1968 with the 90th Congress. The House thereafter was ruled by Democrats for 26 years until they lost control in 1994, and they ruled the Senate for all but six years. In every year but one (1969), there was a deficit; every president of the era passed along a greater debt than he inherited.

Clinton had all the power a president can have in 1993–1994. If he were inclined to shrink the role of the federal government, he could have led his liberal followers in that direction. Failing that, he could have developed support for the project from the Republican leaders of 1995–1996. But events show he had no intention of downsizing where it was needed—*Human Resources*. As a result, Washington's fiscal disease produced another throat-choking deficit.

Table 15.3
Change in Public Debt, 1992–1996 (In Billions of Dollars)

Public debt, 1992	$2998.8
Deficit, 1993–1996	729.6
Total	$3728.4
Adjustment[a]	4.5
Public debt, 1996	$3732.9

a) See Table 15.1, note d.

Statistics take on a verity of their own simply by being, and by lingering. Regardless of explanations, the fact that debt increased more slowly on his watch will be gradually accepted by most as an accomplishment of Clinton.

Table 15.4
Public Debt (In Billions of Dollars)

	Beginning	End	Percent
FDR	$ 42.8	$ 184.8	331.8%
FDR/HST	184.8	216.3	17.0
HST	216.3	214.8	- .7
Ike	214.8	222.2	3.4
Ike 2	222.2	236.8	6.7

Table 15.4 *(continued)*
Public Debt (In Billions of Dollars)

	Beginning	End	Percent
JFK/LBJ	236.8	256.8	8.4
LBJ	256.8	289.5	12.7
RMN	289.5	322.4	11.4
RMN/GRF	322.4	477.4	48.1
JEC	477.4	709.8	48.7
RWR	709.8	1300.5	83.2
RWR 2	1300.5	2050.8	57.7
GHWB	2050.8	2998.8	46.2
WJC	2998.8	3732.9	24.5

Perspectives

Clinton was young, but well trained, when he assumed the presidency. Behind him he had years of service in high leadership positions. To be sure, governing Arkansas was a long way from ruling the United States, but Clinton had long since broken the barriers of his state in his various positions within the Democratic party. His horizons went beyond the needs of Arkansas, and he was accustomed to the process of governance, if not the size of it, in Washington.

Clinton was not a "foreign policy" president in the sense that he was the obvious, energetic force and strategist. The Department of State held the limelight and, for the most part, articulated the administration's views.

The reputation of the United States, thanks to stunning victories in the cold war with the USSR and the Gulf War with Iraq, was at its peak. Demands placed on America's military during Clinton's watch were less dangerous, but readiness in an unsettled world was still the watchword. Tensions continued in the Middle East, North Korea was volatile, and Cuba and Haiti were chronic itches. China was unfriendly.

Breakaway states from the Soviet empire drew nervous glances from Europeans old enough to recall that an incident in Serbia (the assassination of Archduke Ferdinand of Austria in 1914) had touched off World War One. With the fall of the USSR, the old Yugoslavia disintegrated into ethnic squabbles. Essentially a European problem, America was nevertheless pulled into the peacemaking process (many say too deeply) with troops and supports—a costly enterprise with no end in view. And the continued existence and political viability of the violent leader of Iraq, Saddam Hussein, kept more American ships and troops in the Middle East than normal.

Ties between the United States and the United Nations grew closer, in part because of shared concerns. But some detected a tendency to adopt

United Nations objectives as the cornerstone of American foreign policy. Globalists liked this drift, but nationalists were appalled by it.

On domestic matters, Clinton bewildered some and frightened others. The attempt to federalize health care failed, to the relief of most of the American people. But the effort to do so was revealing. It defined Clinton, from the first moments of his presidency, as one who believed in an expanding role for government, a bad omen for a time that needed a president who would lead the effort to move in the opposite direction.

Clinton increased taxes even though he had promised to reduce them. Such a turnaround became commonplace during his presidency, a trait that didn't seem to trouble most voters or perhaps their failure to take offense simply proved again that they don't care about, or listen to, the political dialogue of the day.

On the other side of the ledger, Clinton placed several women in high government posts (cabinet, Supreme Court), a continuation of a trend that had made more inclusive the administrations of recent presidents.

Clinton's approval rating dropped, particularly after his decision to renounce a tax cut. Later, his identification with an anticrime bill and his display of a firmer hand in foreign affairs (North Korea, Iraq and Haiti) boosted his appeal. But the overall rating of his work was poor, and it set the stage for midterm congressional elections in which Democrats lost control of both houses of Congress.

The analysis of deficits from President Johnson to President Bush has made it clear that the cost of the welfare state is at the heart of the deficit problem. Since the first step in problem solving is problem identification, it was heartening to see the 104th Congress address the core issue. A welfare reform bill was passed, inadequate but a step in the right direction. Serious discussions dealing with Medicare and Social Security reform were held. In the wings, capable men and women developed plans for a complete revision of the tax system, that albatross despised by all but power-hungry politicians that had been squeezing the necks of taxpayers for decades. These were hopeful signs.

Unfortunately, and typically, the analytical spotlight that shone on Social Security and Medicare, funded programs that benefited seniors, did not shine with equal intensity on the other unfunded federal programs that fall under the rubrics of *Government* or *Human Resources.* Congressional investigations of this type will be viewed with suspicion until they embrace, openly and even-handedly, all programs that provide aid or income to citizens, including federal employees, and noncitizens.

Absent such a review, priorities cannot be set. And especially in a system that can't live within its income, priorities are absolutely essential.

The Republican Congress and the Democratic White House engaged in prolonged debate in 1995 over budget matters. In sum, Republicans won the substantive battle in that controls were imposed; some costs were cut. Clinton won the political battle in that his tactics were superior.

By the end of 1995, Republicans looked like a group of mean-spirited men determined to impose on America ruinous spending cutbacks without regard to consequences. Clinton, on the other hand, posed as protector of the people, defender of "investments" in health, children, and America's future. He was believed and his popularity surged.

Clinton supported the expansion of government, but because of his cleverness and the conservatives' clumsiness, he at least shared the credit for the general fiscal and economic improvements that came from the new conservative agenda. Over and over, Clinton demonstrated that, whatever his faults, he was a clever politician.

In terms of his programs that passed and failed to pass, Clinton emerged from his first term clearly defined as a liberal in both social and economic matters, with the dangerous ability to phrase his ideas in ways that made him sound conservative. Arguably, he was the worst possible choice for a country whose culture was in decline and whose debt was out of control.

Table 15.5
Financial Profile

	1960	**1988**	**1992**	**1996**
	(pop: 180.7 mil)[a]	(pop: 245.0 mil)	(pop: 255.4 mil)	(pop: 265.5 mil)
Federal Income and Outlay, in Billions of Dollars				
GDP[b]	$ 523.9	$ 5205.3	$ 6383.1	$ 7636.0
Taxes	92.5	909.0	1090.5	1453.1
Spending	92.2	1064.1	1380.9	1560.5
Debt	236.8	2050.8	2998.8	3732.9
Interest	6.9	151.8	199.4	241.1
Federal Income and Outlay—Proportional Comparisons, in Percentages				
Taxes/GDP	18%	17%	17%	19%
Spending/GDP	18	20	22	20
Debt/GDP	45	39	47	49
Taxes/Debt	39	44	36	39
Interest/Taxes	7	17	18	17
Federal Income and Outlay Per Capita, in Dollars				
Taxes	$ 512	$ 3710	$ 4270	$ 5473
Spending	510	4343	5407	5878
Debt	1310	8371	11742	14060
Interest	38	620	781	908
Average Per Capita Income, in Dollars[c]				
	$ 2219	$ 16615	$ 20105	$ 24231
Federal Income and Outlay as Percentage of Avg. Per Capita Income				
Taxes	23.0%	22.0%	21.0%	23.0%

Table 15.5 *(continued)*
Financial Profile

	1960	**1988**	**1992**	**1996**
	(pop: 180.7 mil)[a]	(pop: 245.0 mil)	(pop: 255.4 mil)	(pop: 265.5 mil)
Spending	23.0	26.0	27.0	24.0
Debt	59.0	50.0	58.0	58.0
Interest	1.7	3.7	3.9	3.7
Misery index, in percentages[d]				
Prime interest	5.0%	10.5%	6.0%	8.3%
Unemployment	5.5	5.4	7.4	5.3
Inflation	1.7	4.3	3.1	3.0

a) Population: U.S. Bureau of Census. b) GDP: 1940, 1942, 1944—Salem State College; other years—Federal Reserve Board, Chicago. c) Average income was not available for all years. Figures for missing years were estimated on a linear basis. d) Rates taken from several U.S. government sources.

George Bush bequeathed a 21-month growth cycle in GDP that continued throughout 1993–1996, an unending string of good luck for Clinton.

Table 15.6
Economic Indicators, 1953–1996

President	Year[a]	Cycle[b]	GDP[c]	CPI[d]	Rev.[e]
Eisenhower	1956	79%	18%	3%	39%
Eisenhower	1960	65	7	10	9
Kennedy/Johnson	1964	96	23	6	19
Johnson	1968	100	24	15	18
Nixon	1972	77	14	23	18
Nixon/Ford	1976	67	7	39	0
Carter	1980	88	7	48	14
Reagan	1984	67	9	28	15
Reagan	1988	100	14	16	16
Bush	1992	83	3	19	8
Clinton	**1996**	**100**	**7**	**13**	**13**
Range:					
High		97	19	33	24
Low		70	6	7	6
Average[f]		82	10	18	14

a) The final year of the term. b) Ratio of months of growth in GDP to 48 months. c) Real growth, four years. d) Inflation, four years. e) Real growth in federal revenue, four years. f) The working average of those within the range.

Clinton enjoyed above average growth in GDP in terms of frequency, but the upswing was not as strong as the norm (10 percent), and he paid for it, as George Bush had, in revenue increases (12.6 percent) that were similarly below average (14 percent).

Had the real increase in tax receipts in 1993–1996 reached the norm (14 percent), they would have amounted to $5279.3 billion, or $59.8 billion above actual. To that extent, Clinton was victimized by the pallid recovery.

Growth in GDP improved in 1993–1996, perhaps a sign that the economy had absorbed recent tax increases and was moving on.

Table 15.7
Adjusted Four-Year Growth (In Billions of Dollars)

	GDP		Four-Year Growth	
	Beginning	End	Actual	Real[a]
Johnson	$ 675.1	$ 936.8	38.8%	23.6%
Nixon	936.8	1286.8	37.4	14.4
Nixon/Ford	1286.8	1880.3	46.1	7.3
Carter	1880.3	2911.8	54.9	6.9
Reagan 1	2911.8	3996.7	37.3	8.9
Reagan 2	3996.7	5205.3	30.2	14.4
Bush	5205.3	6383.1	22.6	3.4
Clinton	6383.1	7636.0	19.6	7.0

a) Measured in 1983 dollars.

Federal tax revenues in 1996 were 33.2 percent more than those of 1992 (12.7 percent inflation, 1993–1996); spending was up 13.0 percent, a slower rate of increase than revenue and a hopeful sign (subject to verification) that conservative influences in Congress could be gaining ground.

Taxes per capita were 28.2 percent higher in 1996 than in 1992, an increase that outstripped the increase in average income per capita (20.5 percent). Economic recovery is not complete until it benefits the people at least as much as the government.

Public debt grew 24.5 percent under Clinton, a slower rate than usual, but higher than that of GDP (19.6 percent). In a world where a slowdown in the rate of deterioration is considered to be progress, it was good news to see that the rise in debt was relatively lower. But it was bad news to see it rise at all and worse news to see it rise faster than GDP. For the relationship between debt and GDP to tighten during periods of national emergency is expected; for it to do so during a relatively calm period is cause for alarm.

The misery index was 16.6 percent in 1996 as against 16.5 percent in 1992, a standoff, but not from a political standpoint. The change represented a public relations boost for Clinton because the unemployment rate, the most dangerous (to a politician) of the elements, dropped from 7.4 percent to 5.3 percent, while the prime interest rate (a hidden tax) moved from 6.0 percent to 8.3 percent.

To the federal government, recessions mean lower tax revenue and higher unemployment costs. The loss of revenue over four-year presidential terms because of recession has not been common. The increase in real income between four-year periods was below average (14 percent) under Eisenhower (2d term), Nixon/Ford, Bush, and Clinton. In the case of Nixon/Ford, the shortfall was severe.

But generally speaking, deficits are defined by high costs, not low taxes. In the hands of prudent men who admire the form of government prescribed by the Constitution, revenue was adequate to manage the government, to reduce blips in debt caused by recession, and at the same time fund historical social responsibilities to the unemployed, the aged, and the handicapped.

But priorities changed when the Great Society was born, when government decided to play God, seeing the solution for civil ills in terms of benefits, stamps, grants, set-asides, preferences, and subsidies.

Clinton symbolized that philosophy, perpetuated it, and backed away from it only when his highest value, personal popularity, was threatened, at which time he sounded like Edmund Burke, the father of conservatism.

Table 15.8
Spending Priorities[a]

	1960	1988	1992	1996
Defense	52.2%	27.3%	21.6%	17.0%
Interest	7.5	14.3	14.4	15.5
Total	59.7	41.6%	36.0	32.5
Government	11.9	8.3	8.0	6.1
Soc. Sec.	12.6	20.6	20.8	22.4
Medicare	0.0	7.4	8.6	11.2
Veterans	5.9	2.8	2.5	2.4
Welfare	9.9	19.3	24.1	25.4
Total	100.0%	100.0%	100.0%	100.0%

a) See discussion following Table 2.4.

Increased revenue is not enough. To most politicians, unfortunately from both major parties, the sight of a dollar incites new ideas for spending and subdues the instinct to save and conserve. If a way isn't found to restrict this urge, to force it into a cage of control, steady and acceptable growth in GDP will not ensue, and even if it does, benefits will be dissipated in higher spending and higher deficits until the bubble breaks, as it most surely will.

Under Eisenhower, classic functions of government took 93 percent of every federal dollar spent; under Reagan, a downward trend established under intervening presidents was reversed and the index came back to 82 percent; under Bush, the index was 79 percent; under Clinton, 76 percent and dropping. That which had to be done was being crowded out by the expansion of government.

Table 15.9
Summary of Federal Spending—Base vs. Other
(In Billions of Dollars)

	1960	1988	1992	1996
Defense	$ 48.1	$ 290.4	$ 298.4	$ 265.7
Interest	6.9	151.8	199.4	241.1
Soc. Sec.	11.6	219.3	287.6	349.7
Medicare	0.0	78.9	119.0	174.2
Unemployment	2.9	15.3	39.5	24.9
Veterans	5.4	29.4	34.1	37.0
Government	11.0	88.5	110.6	95.4
Base	$ 85.9	$ 873.6	$ 1088.6	$ 1188.0
Other	6.3	190.5	292.3	372.5
Total	$ 92.2	$ 1064.1	$ 1380.9	$ 1560.5

Base as percentage of total

	1960	1988	1992	1996
	93.2%	82.1%	78.8%	76.1%

Within the analysis of previous administrations, a table titled "American Social Statistics" silently reported the failure of the Great Society. There is little by way of updated figures that add to the sorry picture already painted. But a few additional observations are useful.

Are we to continually turn away from obvious failure and proceed again down the same discredited solution path? How can we study socialistic states of our era, the Soviet Union being the prime example, and conclude that what others have failed to do will, in some way, work in America—that bankrupt socioeconomic formulas will somehow prosper in the United States?

Yet the American people have accepted government policies of this stripe for the best part of four decades. Why didn't they, long ago, throw the rascals out?

Transactions

Funds available for deficit/debt reduction come from two sources: 1) increased tax revenues; 2) cost reductions. In 1993–1996, revenues increased by 25.3 percent (12.7 percent inflation) over the previous four years; *Defense* and *Government* were less expensive, and *Interest* grew at a slower rate than income. The stage was set to cut the deficit deeply and to establish a road leading to debt reduction.

Table 15.10
Transactions (In Billions of Dollars)

	1993–1996	1989–1992
Taxes	$ 5219.5	$ 4166.8

Table 15.10 *(continued)*
Transactions (In Billions of Dollars)

	1993–1996		1989–1992
Less:			
Defense	$ 1110.4	$ 1174.6	
Interest	875.1	747.4	
Total		1985.5	1922.0
Net		$ 3234.0	$ 2244.8
Less:			
Government	$ 384.6	$ 528.1	
Human Resources	3579.0	2650.1	
Total		3963.6	3178.2
Net		-$ 729.6	-$ 933.4
Debt, beginning		- 2998.8	- 2050.8
Total		-$ 3728.4	-$ 2984.2
Adjustment[a]		- 4.5	- 14.6
Debt, end		-$ 3732.9	-$ 2998.8

a) See Table 15.1, note d.

The deficit was down but given the circumstances of lower costs in *Defense* and *Government* and a slowdown in the rate of growth of *Interest*, the results for the period were disappointing. They also made it eminently clear where the problem was centered—*Human Resources.*

Taxes

GDP growth was modest (7.0 percent average real growth, four years) but steady in 1993–1996, bringing with it higher employment, higher tax revenue in Washington, and lower unemployment costs. The recovery that began in 1992 generated a steady flow of real revenue growth.

Table 15.11
Tax Revenues (In Billions of Dollars)

	Total	Income	Corp.	SS[a]	Excise	Other[b]
1941pw	$ 8.7	$ 1.3	$ 2.1	$ 2.0	$ 2.5	$ .8
1944w	43.7	19.7	14.8	3.4	4.8	1.0
1948p	41.6	19.3	9.7	3.8	7.4	1.4
1952w	66.2	27.9	21.2	6.5	8.9	1.7
1956p	74.6	32.2	20.9	9.3	9.9	2.3
1960p	92.5	40.7	21.5	14.7	11.7	3.9
1964w	112.6	48.7	23.5	22.0	13.7	4.7
1968w	153.0	68.7	28.7	33.9	14.1	7.6
1972w	207.3	94.7	32.2	52.6	15.5	12.4
1976p	298.1	131.6	41.4	90.8	17.0	17.3
1980p	517.1	244.1	64.6	157.8	24.3	26.3

Table 15.11 *(continued)*
Tax Revenues (In Billions of Dollars)

	Total	Income	Corp.	SS[a]	Excise	Other[b]
1984p	666.5	298.4	56.9	239.4	37.4	34.4
1988p	909.0	401.2	94.5	334.4	35.2	43.7
1992p	1090.5	476.0	100.3	413.7	45.5	55.0
1996p	1453.1	656.4	171.8	509.5	54.0	61.4

p = mostly peace. w = mostly war.

a) Social Security. b) Estate and gift taxes, custom duties and fees, Federal Reserve earnings, sundry.

In 1988, following the largest overhaul of the tax system in its history, federal revenue was 36.4 percent higher than it was in 1984. In 1996, after two tax increases, one under Bush and one under Clinton, federal revenue was 33.2 percent higher than it was in 1992. Federal tax receipts went up faster under Reagan's lowered rates than they did under Clinton with his higher rates.

In 1996, corporate taxes went up 71.3 percent, an increase that ends up in high prices or low paychecks. This was not good news to lower-income Americans, and it clearly didn't stimulate growth in GDP.

Taxes as a percent of average income per capita went up in 1993–1996. Why? In a period of peace, when military spending is down, why must Americans pay more in taxes?

Table 15.12
Revenues and Spending

Year	Federal Dollars		Per Capita Dollars			Per Capita Percentages of Average Earnings	
	Taxes	Spending	Taxes	Spending	Avg. Earnings	Taxes	Spending
1941[a]	$ 9 bil.	$14 bil.	$ 65	$ 102	$ 923	7.0%	11.1%
1944[a]	44 bil.	91 bil.	326	682	1148	28.4	59.4
1948	42 bil.	30 bil.	284	203	1388	20.5	14.6
1952[a]	66 bil.	68 bil.	420	430	1653	25.4	26.0
1956	75 bil.	71 bil.	442	418	1949	22.6	21.4
1960	93 bil.	92 bil.	512	510	2219	23.1	23.0
1964[a]	113 bil.	119 bil.	587	618	2662	22.1	23.2
1968[a]	153 bil.	178 bil.	762	887	3445	22.1	25.7
1972[a]	207 bil.	231 bil.	988	1099	4677	21.1	23.5
1976[a]	298 bil.	372 bil.	1367	1705	6548	20.9	26.0
1980[a]	517 bil.	591 bil.	2271	2595	9910	22.9	26.2
1984[a]	667 bil.	852 bil	2821	3605	13114	21.5	27.5
1988[a]	909 bil.	1064 bil.	3710	4343	16615	22.3	26.1
1992[a]	1091 bil.	1381 bil.	4270	5407	20105	21.2	26.9
1996[a]	1453 bil.	1561 bil.	5473	5878	24231	22.6	24.3

a) deficit year

That taxes went up was no surprise to those who knew that Clinton was a spender and that conservatives did not know how to mount effective resistance.

What Did It?

The analyses of deficits throughout this book have ranged from simple to complex. The Clinton period is one of the simplest and may be summed up as follows: *The 1993–1996 revenues were adequate to fund the increased costs of* Defense, Interest, *and* Government. *But the increase in revenues did not fully fund the cost increases in* Human Resources, *which were the ultimate source of the 1993–1996 deficit.*

DEFENSE

Defense played no part in the 1993–1996 deficit. Its cost under Clinton was less than it was under George Bush. The issue under Clinton was the degree of cutback and the adequacy of the force relative to America's place in a dangerous world.

Table 15.13
Analysis of Defense (In Billions of Dollars)

Items	1962 (JFK)	1984 (RWR)	1988 (RWR)	1992 (GHWB)	1996 (WJC)
Personnel	$ 16.3	$ 64.2	$ 76.3	$ 81.2	$ 66.7
Operations	11.6	67.4	84.5	92.0	88.7
Material	14.5	61.9	77.2	74.9	48.9
R&D	6.3	23.1	34.8	34.6	36.5
Atomic	2.1	6.1	7.9	10.6	11.6
Other	1.5	4.7	9.7	5.1	13.3
Total	$ 52.3	$ 227.4	$ 290.4	$ 298.4	$ 265.7
1983[a]	$ 173.2	$ 218.9	$ 245.5	$ 212.7	$ 169.3
Men (millions)	2806	2138	2138	1807	1472
Per man:[b]					
Personnel	$ 19237	$ 28906	$ 30170	$ 32031	$ 28873
Other	42488	73479	84657	85678	86141
Total	$ 61725	$ 102385	$ 114827	$ 117709	$ 115014

a) Totals expressed in 1983 dollars (billions). b) 1983 dollars.

The comparison of unadjusted dollars in this table suggests that Clinton spent only 12 percent less on *Defense* than President Bush did in 1992. But when the eye drifts down the table to the lines for 1983 dollars or "Men," it becomes clear that Clinton was gutting the military machine; 335 million men/women were released from duty (22.8 percent), almost as many troops as America deployed during the Gulf War. Not since 1950 under Harry Truman did America have such a small military force. Was such a cutback in 1996 appropriate for a nation that was regarded as the leader of the free world?

Clinton entered office with a questionable record relative to military affairs. Few regarded him as a friend of the military, some thought him anti-military, and his record of alleged draft evasion during the Vietnam War was well known. Mostly through speeches and ceremonial behavior, Clinton tried to persuade others that his views were more balanced. But his behavior where it counted—budget support—indicated that the original impressions were not far from the mark.

Table 15.14
Defense as a Share of GDP and Spending
(In Billions of Dollars)

	Defense	GDP	Spending	Percent of GDP	Percent of Spending
1960p	$ 48.1	$ 523.9	$ 92.2	9.2%	52.2%
1964w	54.8	675.1	118.5	8.1	46.2
1968w	81.9	936.8	178.1	8.7	46.0
1972w	79.2	1286.8	230.7	6.2	34.3
1976p	89.6	1880.3	371.8	4.8	24.1
1980p	134.0	2911.8	590.9	4.6	22.7
1984p	227.4	3996.7	851.8	5.7	26.7
1988p	290.4	5205.3	1064.1	5.6	27.3
1992p	298.4	6383.1	1380.9	4.7	21.6
1996p	265.7	7636.0	1560.5	3.5	17.0

p = mostly peace; w = mostly war

The cold war was over and the Gulf War was won. But the North Korean threat was real, especially when mixed with the attitudes and capacities of China. Iraq, Iran, Syria, Libya, and other countries in the Gulf region represented danger. The Serb/Bosnian conflict was active and continuing. Russia was tamed but armed. Every time there was a conflict of any magnitude in the world, America was called upon to serve in some capacity that usually involved the use of resources.

Some level of military cutback was indicated because the Soviet Union had been defanged. And President Bush had made some reductions. But Clinton continued to slash deeply to 3.5 percent of GDP, 17 percent of the spending pie. Was this a time for such a cutback? Was the liberal agenda under Clinton more important than *Defense*? Had it always been more important to liberals?

Interest

In 1993–1996, *Interest* grew by 17.1 percent, less than the growth rate of revenue (25.3 percent). Thus it played no role in the formation of the deficit.

Table 15.15
Prime Interest Rates[a]

President	Yr.	Rate
HST	1952	3.0%
Ike 1	1956	4.0
Ike 2	1960	5.0
JFK/LBJ	1964	4.5
LBJ	1968	6.6
RMN	1972	5.8
RMN/GRF	1976	6.4
JEC	1980	20.4
RWR 1	1984	11.1
RWR 2	1988	10.5
GHWB	1992	6.0
WJC	1996	8.3

a) Commercial rates.

Comparative rates between 1996 and 1992 are misleading. The prime rate was down to 6.0 percent in 1992, but it was 10.5 percent in 1988 and only gradually sunk to the lower level. Clinton, on the other hand, started in a cheaper money market that grew to 8.3 percent. The cost of money under George Bush was higher than it was under Clinton.

Unfunded *Interest* is a deficit problem. The size of *Interest* is a general problem; it will soon be over $1.0 trillion (for four years). Its 1993–1996 cost was almost 80 percent as much as *Defense*. It cost more than Medicare or Medicaid, more than twice as much as *Government*, more than all income security programs, more than all of the unfunded programs that politicians debate in public. Its cost had reached an obscene level.

And *Interest* was something else too, unmentionable.

At budget time, the usual cries to adjust *Defense*, Social Security, and Medicare thunder from Washington to the nation as serious-minded, cost-cutting politicians expound on their proposals to adjust these programs, but not a word is said about *Interest*, a cost that literally dwarfs most line items in the budget.

In 1996, America paid $67 billion (see Defense*) to all the troops in all the services.* Interest *was $241 billion in 1996—3.6 times more than the amount paid to the troops.*

National perspective? Where art thou?

How can political leaders remain mute before such fiscal looniness? Who are these people who run the United States government? How can they tolerate such demented fiscal relationships? Is common sense against the law in Washington?

GOVERNMENT AND HUMAN RESOURCES

Defense and *Interest* are primary costs that deserve to be fully funded when needed or subsidized by loans when situations demand it (e.g., World War Two). In 1993–1996, revenue increased by 25.3 percent over the previous four-year period. Had primary costs taken their rightful share of revenue (25.3 percent), spending would have been $2408.3 billion, or $422.8 billion more than actual, and all other things remaining equal, the deficit would have been $1152.4 billion.

What is the meaning of this?

America cannot afford a modest *Defense*, and cannot afford to pay *Interest* without generating a huge deficit. This is not a healthy situation for a world leader to be in.

GOVERNMENT

The cost of *Government* actually dropped in 1993–1996 when compared with 1989–1992. Had the message been received? Was spending under Clinton that much better controlled? Was this a sign of better things to come? If only the answer could be affirmative.

Table 15.16
Government Operations, Net
(In Billions of Dollars)

	1993–96	1989–92	% Change
Energy	$ 17.2	$ 12.9	33.3%
Nat'l Resources/ Environment	85.0	71.9	18.2
Commerce	-52.7	181.8	-129.0
Transportation	152.1	121.5	25.2
Community Development	40.8	27.5	48.4
International	64.1	55.4	15.7
Science	66.5	59.7	11.4
Agriculture	54.5	59.3	- 8.1
Justice	63.9	46.2	38.3
General	51.1	44.4	15.1
Total	$ 542.5	$ 680.6	-20.3
Misc. Income	-157.9	-152.5	3.5
Net	$ 384.6	$ 528.1	-27.2%

The inflation rate in 1992–1996 was 12.7 percent.

Some signs of restraint are observable in this table, but Energy, Commerce, Community Development, and Justice are distortive, although not to the degree formerly found. But the single element that makes *Government* look so efficient is Commerce, about which more needs to be said.

In the 1980s, savings and loan banks overextended themselves during the real estate boom. When the boom inevitably went bust, collateral was worth less than the unpaid loans. The impact of this situation was briefly described in the analysis of the George Bush regime (*Government*, 1989–1992). In the context of this book, it is only necessary to add that the United States government stood behind insured depositors, took over bank assets and disposed of them, and reorganized the industry by arranging a myriad of mergers between healthy and sick institutions.

In the analysis of George Bush, it was determined that the *Government* cost for 1989–1992 would have been $43.5 billion had it increased at the same rate as revenue. Using that amount as the natural level of Commerce for those years (instead of $181.8, above), the cost level in 1993–1996 would have been $54.5 billion if it had increased at the rate of revenue, instead of -$52.7 billion, an adjustment of $107.2 billion caused by the savings and loan problem—a cost benefit to the Clinton administration.

A fairer reading of *Government* is found when the line item Commerce is dropped from the comparison. That approach produces *Government* in 1993–1996 of $437.3 billion; in 1989–1992, $346.3 billion—an increase of 26.3 percent; slightly above the increase in revenue (25.3 percent).

In Washington, restricting growth of a subordinate cost center to the growth rate of revenue may seem wonderful, but in an era when downsizing was the apparent solution to the deficit problem, mere spending control was inadequate. Clinton did not confront the problem he was elected to solve— an overextended government.

HUMAN RESOURCES

Logic earlier revealed that *Human Resources* led to the entire deficit in 1993–1996, assuming for the moment no revenue shortfall, a truth of special importance because for once there was no other cost center that liberals could point to in an attempt to protect from pressure the hideout of its programmatic treasures—*Human Resources*.

It is worth pursuing at the same point from a different direction.

Because primary costs *(Defense/Interest)* did not need full funding, an additional $422.8 billion was available to the subordinate cost centers. *Government* did not need these funds since it had its own internal bonanza in the form of net receipts (instead of payments) on the savings and loan project. And yet, despite these fortunate developments, *Human Resources* outspent revenue by $729.6 billion.

Table 15.17
Human Resources (In Billions of Dollars)

	1993–96	1989–92	% Change
Education, Training, Services, Employment	$ 202.6	$ 164.0	23.5%
Health	441.3	266.8	65.4
Income Security[a]	752.7	549.1	37.1
Subtotal	$ 1396.6	$ 979.9	42.5
Social Security[b]	$ 1309.7	$ 1037.8	26.2
Medicare[b]	609.4	406.6	49.9
Unemployment	115.0	101.2	13.6
Veterans	148.3	124.6	19.0
Subtotal	$ 2182.4	$ 1670.2	30.6
Grand total	$ 3579.0	$ 2650.1	35.1%

a) Minus unemployment compensation. b) Funded by employers and employees. Note: Major federal programs since the 1960s—Medicaid, 1961; Food Stamps, 1962; Medicare, 1967; Student Aid, 1966; Coal Miners Benefits, 1970; Commodity Donations, 1973; Supplemental Security Income, 1974; Supplemental Feeding, 1976; Earned Income Tax Credit, 1976; Legal Services, 1976; Energy Assistance, 1977.

The inflation rate in 1992–1996 was 12.7 percent. Line items in *Human Resources* are very sensitive to inflation.

Growth in Health and Income Security, the line item that houses much of the welfare state, continued to inflate beyond reason. There was no significant sign that welfare reform had taken hold in any meaningful way.

Growth in the Medicare program, partly funded by seniors, was excessive and justified the congressional attention it was getting.

When Clinton entered office, he must have been aware of the primary causes of deficits. The cost of the welfare state was an obvious candidate for priority attention. It didn't get it. Typically, only high-profile programs like Medicare and Social Security received great public exposure. The essence of the welfare state remained hidden from view.

Conclusion

Clinton's character is not the subject matter of this book. Few will nominate him as a great moral leader. Myths about him will not grow, as they did around George Washington. But he was reelected in 1996.

Clinton is a charismatic leader, especially to females, with political talent and a knack for expressing his views in the language of his opponents. On the stump, he sounds more conservative than William F. Buckley, the renowned conservative pundit, when the occasion calls for it. But he can sound more liberal than George McGovern, his political mentor, when he addresses activists from his own party. He is untroubled by the demands of consistency.

In an age when citizens decreasingly vote and are increasingly illiterate, his brand of "all-faces-are-mine" politicking is dangerously effective.

Clinton probably will not be remembered as a foreign policy president unless he personally does, or gets involved in, something momentous in his second term. The period 1993–1996 was, perhaps, not a time for great deeds. The world was as calm as it gets. America was called upon to supervise, not fight for, its interests on Clinton's watch. The four-year deficit dropped to $729.6 billion, as follows:

Table 15.18
Unrecovered Cost (In Billions of Dollars)

Defense	$ 0.0
Interest	0.0
Government	0.0
Human Resources	729.6
Total	$ 729.6

Clinton was affected by the slow recovery and the savings and loan crisis, as was his predecessor, but not in the same way or to the same degree. Also, he was spared the need to build *Defense,* and the impact of inflated interest rates was fully financed by the revenue increase for the period.

Table 15.19
Analysis of Deficit, 1993–1996 (In Billions of Dollars)

Total Deficit		$ 729.6
Adjusted:		
Revenue[a]	-$ 59.8	
Savings & Loan[b]	107.2	47.4
Total		$ 777.0

a) See *Perspectives* section, pp. 240–246. b) See *Government* section, pp. 252–253.

Stripped of its net benefit from the savings and loan scandal, the Clinton record was unimpressive. But more important than the historical performance of a single president was the fact that *during a period of uninterrupted growth, with* Defense *spending declining, the size of the deficit went up (after adjustment).*

Presidents must be lucky as well as competent if they are to achieve great things. Clinton was extraordinarily lucky. He had an unbroken string of growth in GDP, he got benefits instead of penalties from the banking crisis, interest rates over the four years were lower, and *Defense* was cheaper—a string of goodies almost beyond belief.

Of equal importance, Republicans assumed control of Congress in 1994. Had Democrats retained power, it is highly doubtful that positive changes in budget matters would have taken place. Ironically, if Clinton earns any reputation at all in fiscal matters, it may be because his friends in Congress lost power. The table below shows the change that occurred when congressional control switched.

Table 15.20
Deficit (In Billions of Dollars)

Years	Deficit
1993–1994	$458.3
1995–1996	271.3
Total	$729.6

Allocating responsibility is important, but the true importance of the above table is its underlying message—the problem that drives deficit and debt got worse under Clinton. This late in the game, that fact is at least sad, at most dangerous. The changed circumstances that made 1993–1996 look relatively good could be swept away in an instant. Then what?

It has been a running theme in this book that growth in GDP is the essential first ingredient in the solution to the debt problem. How did the economy fare on Clinton's watch?

Table 15.21
Gross Domestic Product/Net Growth

	GDP (In Billions of Dollars)		Adjusted GDP (In Billions of Dollars)[a]		Percent Real Growth
	Beginning	End	Beginning	End	4 Yrs
Ike	$ 371	$ 449	$ 1402	$ 1649	17.7%
Ike 2	449	524	1649	1770	7.3
JFK/LBJ	524	675	1770	2178	23.0
LBJ	675	937	2178	2692	23.6
RMN	937	1287	2692	3079	14.4
RMN/GRF	1287	1880	3079	3305	7.3
JEC	1880	2912	3305	3534	6.9
RWR	2912	3997	3534	3847	8.9
RWR 2	3997	5205	3847	4400	14.4
GHWB	5205	6383	4400	4550	3.4
WJC	6383	7637	4550	4867	7.0

a) Expressed in 1983 dollars.

The American economy staggered under the tax increases of George Bush and Clinton but was gradually making its way back as 1996 closed. Time has proved that, if left alone, it has the capacity to provide the funds needed to deal with the public debt problem. Politicians must stop tinkering with an economy that works; they must fix the federal system that does not work.

Chapter 16

Conclusion

The Public Debt Problem

DEFINITION

When Franklin D. Roosevelt took office in 1941, he faced a public debt of $42.8 billion. Fifty-six years and 15 administrations later, the public debt was $3.7 trillion. What happened?

Table 16.1
Growth of Public Debt, 1941–1996 (In Billions of Dollars)

	Debt		Percent	
Events	Beginning	End	Change	Per Year
1941–1948				
Great Depression, World War Two	$ 42.8	$ 216.2	405.4%	50.7%
1949–1960				
Korea, Cold War	216.2	234.9	8.6	.7
1961–1972				
Vietnam, Cold War, Great Society	234.9	322.4	37.2	3.1
1973–1988				
Vietnam, Cold War, Great Society	322.4	2050.8	536.1	33.5
1989–1996				
Great Society	$ 2050.8	$ 3732.9	82.0%	10.2%

America had found post-war fiscal stability by 1960, and had come to terms with major federal assistance programs of Franklin Roosevelt—aid for the aged, the veterans, and the unemployed.

America's military force was strong (2.5 million men) in 1960, the budget was under control, public debt ($234.9 billion) under two presidents, Harry Truman and Dwight Eisenhower, had dropped to 45.2 percent of GDP (1946, 92.0 percent).

It is convenient, and reasonably accurate, to accept out-of-hand that 1960 debt meets Treasury's explanation of increased debt: "a legacy of war, economic recession and inflation." So doing makes the following summary possible.

Table 16.2
Allocation of Public Debt, 1941–1996
(In Billions of Dollars)

Period	Beginning	Treasury[a]	Other
Ike 2	$ 234.9	$ 234.9	
JFK/LBJ	21.0		$ 21.0
LBJ	38.9		38.9
RMN	46.1		46.1
RMN/GRF	148.0	137.6	10.4
JEC	227.2	46.6	180.6
RWR	600.0	270.8	329.2
RWR 2	738.4	162.4	576.0
GHWB	933.4	375.0	558.4
WJC	729.6	- 47.4	777.0
Total	$ 3717.5	$ 1179.9	$ 2537.6
Adjustment[b]	14.8		
Total	$ 3732.3		
Adjustment[c]	.6		
End	$ 3732.9		

a) Meets the Treasury explanation of increasing debt: "war, economic recession, inflation." b) See Table 11.2, note a. c) See Table 2.2, note a. Note: For an explanation of the allocations, see the *Conclusion* section for each president.

The explanation for rising debt given by the Treasury Department is at least self-serving and could be disingenuous. Of the total debt in 1996, 31.6 percent falls under the Treasury explanation—27.0 percent if only the debt added since 1960 is considered. One expects a more precise explanation of rising debt from the resident experts on the subject.

CAMOUFLAGED DEVELOPMENT

First, it was Vietnam. Under Lyndon Johnson, spending on *Government/Human Resources* grew by 47.4 percent, versus revenue growth of 32.9 percent; under Richard Nixon, 53.5 percent versus 40.9 percent—a formula (and, shockingly, during wartime) destined to cause future problems. But all eyes were turned toward the war. The Great Society marched on, unchallenged.

Then came the recession, made worse by the oil shortage during the Nixon/Ford administration. Spending on *Government /Human Resources* increased 81.3 percent; revenue, 38.4 percent. The ruinous combination was hardly noticed. Energy and the condition of the economy grabbed the head-lines.

The camouflage continued under Carter. Spending on *Government/ Human Resources* grew by 77.5 percent, while revenue went up 69.6 percent. This was now a 16-year unbalanced condition. And where was public atten-tion?—on the energy crisis and the hostages in Iran.

The camouflage was wearing thin when Ronald Reagan came to town but held up fairly well for one more time. Deficits could no longer be blamed on shooting wars or recession, but there were always the Russians, and Rea-gan's attitude toward them, to blame. If he were only more diplomatic, if he would stop calling them the "evil empire." If he would spend less on *Defense*, deficits would stop, so said the liberals of the day.

That spin continued until the end of Reagan's eight years. The media cooperated. Headlines were preoccupied with foreign affairs. It might have worked again but for three things: 1) Thanks to the military strength of Amer-ica, reborn under Reagan, USSR collapsed, terrorism declined, and Central America stabilized, 2) Reagan's economic policies worked—the economy was humming, and 3) Reagan would not allow the media to bury the budget/debt issue. He spoke out. Truth surfaced. When he left town, the nation knew it had a fiscal problem.

Eight years after Reagan, another $1.7 trillion has been added to debt. Deficits continue. Improvements have been made since Republicans gained control of Congress in 1994, but the core problems remain. Any number of incidents that have happened in recent years could ruin the optimism of the current hour if they revisit, as they will, at some future and unexpected time.

Is It Important?

In his 1996 work *Redeeming the Time,* Russell Kirk has written: "Eco-nomically, the position of the United States is more precarious than it was in 1929; our debt is astronomical in quantity."

There is no shortage of expressed concern about the condition of the public debt and the flawed system and philosophy that feeds it. But the opin-ion of Russell Kirk, quoted here, will be of particular significance to many since, as one of the great intellects of the twentieth century, he was a pow-erful apologist for the American system of government. One can be sure that he wrote those words with a heavy heart.

National Security—The Ability to Expand the Military

No democracy will ever maintain a military force capable of handling every possible contingency. Instead, the goal is to have enough force at the ready to hold the line until the nation mobilizes the required resources.

In budget terms, this means *Defense* goes down in peacetime and up in wartime. And it used to mean that taxes and debt drop in peace and rise in war. The same principle, in part, applies to extended economic downturns or unexpected events of consequence. Debt is allowed to rise until normal conditions resume, after which payback commences.

America's wartime strength, then, depends upon its ability to tax and borrow. "A national debt, if it is not excessive, will be to us a national blessing," said Alexander Hamilton, the brilliant Founding Father who realized the inestimable value of a good credit reputation. And America realized the merit in Hamilton's opinion when it came time to fund, for example, World War II.

Expansion of the 1940 tax base was possible—taxes were 6.5 percent of GDP. By 1944 they were up to 20.7 percent. And clearance in the debt base was available too (despite the ravages of the ongoing Great Depression); $42.8 billion in 1940; $184.8 billion in 1944. The economy was young and eager to stretch. GDP more than doubled from 1940 to 1944. And *Interest* was the insignificant expense it is supposed to be—2.4 percent of total spending in 1944.

Could America similarly expand in 1996?

Clearance in the tax base was not available in 1996 as it was in the 1940s. Revenue in 1996 was 19.0 percent of GDP, almost the 1944 level, when war was at its peak. The tax base that expanded in the 1940s to cover war costs expanded in 1961–1996 to cover (some) costs of the welfare state.

The 1996 debt base was expandable, but not to the extent it was in 1940. Then it was 42.8 percent of GDP; by 1944, 87.6 percent of a base that was more than twice as big. In 1996, debt was 48.9 percent of GDP. Can it expand to $6.6 trillion in the $7.6 trillion economy? Can America double its GDP in four years as it did in 1940–1944? increase debt by four times to $14.0 trillion?

It is at least doubtful, therefore, that *Defense* could be expanded to the extraordinary extent required by an all-out war effort through higher taxes and debt to the extent that it has been in the past.

And the expansion of the military through taxes and debt is also more limited in 1996 because of the cost of money. *Interest* in the 1940s was 2.4 percent of total spending; in 1996 it was 15.5 percent. Affordability of a major expansion of debt would be an issue in 1996 that wasn't relevant in the 1940s.

In summary, military expansion through tax increases is not possible to a significant extent, and expansion through debt is limited by factors that didn't exist in the 1940s. America's future security depends no longer on its internal ability to fund the necessary level of military strength (as was the case), but on the hope that the military strength needed in the future will be affordable.

National Security—The Need to Expand the Military

It is doubtful that America could finance military expansion in the same way as it did in the 1940s. Must it? Is the need there?

In 1980, the year before Ronald Reagan began to rebuild the military, *Defense* was 4.6 percent of GDP, and inadequate. His program took *Defense* to 5.6 percent in 1988 and involved 2.1 million troops.

In 1996, *Defense* was 3.5 percent of GDP and involved 1.5 million troops, the lowest number since Harry Truman in 1950. As Truman stripped the armed forces to the bone after World War Two, so it appears did William Clinton in 1996.

The need to rebuild the military is probable. The degree? That is a question for others to answer.

In the context of this book, it is sufficient to establish the following inference: Costs of the welfare state and the increase in public debt that follows them have become a national security issue because they abuse the nation's credit and bring to the budget process extreme pressures that cause self-serving politicians to underfund *Defense*.

THE DOLLAR

The increase in public debt experienced since the 1960s attacks the value of the U.S. currency.

America has an unanswered deficit problem that keeps pushing its debt skyward. At some point investors in U.S. securities will become concerned about the value of their holdings because of the size and the cause of America's debt. Any condition, like exploding debt, that has that potential impact on investors is a threat to the value of the dollar.

All debt in all cases represents potential pressure on the lender, and not all debt is held by friends. To the extent that America constantly needs to go to the market for funds to cover uncontrolled deficits, to the same extent it is vulnerable to pressure from debtors, some of whom are not, or may not be, friendly. In 1960 less than 10 percent of public debt was owned by foreigners. America was invulnerable to fiscal pressures from outsiders. In 1996, with 33.3 percent of public debt owned by foreigners (Office of the Under Secretary for Domestic Finance), America is more vulnerable to fiscal intimidation than ever before.

To keep U.S. securities attractive, the rate of return must be competitive. For so long as deficits drive the need for more and more debt, the incentive to keep interest rates high will continue. No system with a built-in inflationary characteristic is good for the American dollar.

The costs of the welfare state have been the source of runaway debt for four decades. If uncorrected, they will endanger the future value of America's dollar, just as they have eroded confidence in currencies of socialistic nations around the globe.

The Average American

Americans care about national security issues and, in a vague way, identify with the need to maintain sound money. But their relationship to an esoteric concept like a public debt measured in trillions escapes most. Political leaders spend little time educating them, and for good reason. They created the debt and continue to add to it.

The problem of a high public debt affects Americans personally in four very important ways: 1) job availability, 2) wages, 3) taxes, and 4) prices.

JOBS

If money supply is fixed and deficits are financed with debt, the private sector is deprived of capital to the extent that government is involved in the market. Since the 1950s the government has been pulling increasing amounts of capital away from the private sector. There are fewer jobs available as a result. To what degree? Others will supply the answer to that question. But the obvious point is made. Excessive government borrowing depresses job creation.

WAGES

High public debt sustains high interest rates. High interest rates increase the cost of doing business and threaten profit margins out of which higher wages are paid. That which decreases profits, like high interest costs, is an enemy of the wage earner. And since interest is the child of debt, the real enemy of the worker is the public debt.

TAXES

In 1996, *Interest* was 16.6 percent of all taxes collected by the federal government. If there were no *Interest*, taxes could have been 16.6 percent lower. But some level of *Interest* is natural. Back in 1956 and 1960, when the budget was under control, *Interest* was about 7 percent of federal income. Taking that as a sustainable cost level, taxes in 1996 could have been 9.6 percent lower if *Interest* cost had been "normal." High public debt causes higher taxes to the average citizen.

PRICES

The average worker spends most of his or her earnings and uses credit to finance major purchases. Using credit means exposure to interest rates.

At the end of the 1950s, the prime interest rate was 5.0 percent. In 1996 it was 8.3 percent. A climbing public debt breeds high interest rates. The penalty to consumers relative to high interest rates and common transactions appears below:

Table 16.3
Results of Interest Rates

Transaction	4-Year Automobile Loan for $15,000		30-Year Mortgage for $100,000	
	5%	8%	5%	8%
Monthly	$ 345	$ 366	$ 537	$ 734
Total	$ 16,560	$ 17,568	$ 193,320	$ 264,240

Each automobile purchased under the above terms costs $1,008 extra because of the higher interest rate—if one purchases a car four times between the ages of 30 and 60, $4,032 is added to $70,920 of extra cost that went into the lifetime house, making a total of $74,952. And this doesn't begin to count other inflated interest expense related to the purchase of household appliances, furniture, clothing, home improvement, vacations, and that big pocket buster, education loans.

Important? Yes. The debt problem is very important. The security of the nation and its currency are weakened by it. The job market is less robust and taxes are inflated because of it. And the chance of most Americans to build savings is practically destroyed by it.

Who Did It?

Eleven presidents and 24 Congresses are involved in this analysis. Four presidents stand apart: Roosevelt, the innovator; Eisenhower, the stabilizer; Johnson, the radical; Reagan, the defender.

FRANKLIN ROOSEVELT

Relative to the focus of this book, Roosevelt bears some responsibility for public debt in the sense that he showed how a tax base could be created, how the private sector could be invaded, and how certain social programs like care for the aged, veterans, and the unemployed could bring great popularity to a politician. But his enduring programs were part of the accepted federal landscape by the time Dwight Eisenhower reached the White House. It would be a stretch indeed to hang the existing strain of high debt around his patrician neck. Those who disagreed with him, after all, had more than a half-century to undo his alleged mischief.

DWIGHT EISENHOWER

The United States, its budget, its military, and its growth were under control in 1953–1960. The role of the federal government was established. It was the last period of "normalcy" that America would experience in the twentieth century.

The attitude of political leaders toward debt was orthodox through the administration of Eisenhower, although there were signs of slippage from 1955, when Lyndon Johnson became majority leader of the Senate.

LYNDON JOHNSON

Total breakaway from past disciplines didn't begin until Lyndon Johnson became president (November 22, 1963). On that day, the public debt problem was born and its momentum was thereafter unchecked until Ronald Reagan entered the Oval Office in 1981.

Public debt has grown from $254.0 billion to $3.7 trillion since 1963. It has never gone down, always up. Interim presidents, caught in the grip of entitlement programs, have been little more than spectators, watching debt mount, making little or no protest of consequence—until Reagan appeared.

Johnson didn't act alone. Presidents Nixon, Ford, and Carter could have resisted more effectively and did not. Several new welfare initiatives, including the much abused SSI (Supplemental Security Income) program, came into being under Nixon/Ford. Nixon and Ford were not major contributors to spending trends, but their opposition did not effectively reach the public. Carter added two new federal agencies and was part of the movement to expand the role of government.

The 89th through the 96th Congresses fixed the welfare state so firmly into the budget—and the national psyche—that it will take fiscal dynamite to get it out. And they did so deceitfully. The public took the benefits but never paid the piper.

Why? Because spenders did not charge for it. Excess costs slid unseen into public debt until welfare programs were so firmly established that nothing short of political revolution would dislodge them. The men who did this to America are identified below.

Table 16.4
Profile of Power, 1965–1980

Con.	House	Senate	President
89	McCormack (D)	Mansfield (D)	Johnson (D)
90	McCormack (D)	Mansfield (D)	Johnson (D)
91	McCormack (D)	Mansfield (D)	Nixon (R)
92	Albert (D)	Mansfield (D)	Nixon (R)
93	Albert (D)	Mansfield (D)	Nixon (R)
94	Albert (D)	Mansfield (D)	Ford (R)
95	O'Neill (D)	Mansfield (D)	Carter (D)
95		Byrd (D)	
96	O'Neill (D)	Byrd (D)	Carter (D)

It began with Johnson as Russell Kirk notes: "Johnson ... piled the tremendous cost of the war ... upon the staggering cost of the welfare state at home. One might have thought he could not do sums. He ruined the dollar and bequeathed to the nation an incomprehensible national debt."

But Johnson had powerful assistants in the Congress: John McCormack, Carl Albert, Thomas O'Neil, Mike Mansfield, and Robert Byrd, Democrats all. Mark the names. Remember them. They did it. Johnson and his five assistants.

Under these men, the old consensus to balance budgets was destroyed; practices of lowering taxes and debt after emergencies were abandoned. They ignored Dwight Eisenhower's doctrine relative to Vietnam (stay out of it) and wasted America's military power in a senseless war. The Soviets were thriving in the cold war. Iran thumbed its nose at Washington and held American hostages.

Ronald Reagan

Ronald Reagan did many things during his presidency but, relative to the public debt problem, his major contributions were 1) a revised tax policy that energized the economy and eliminated some of the unfairness and inefficiencies in the system, 2) the cold war victory that would benefit future presidencies in the form of lower *Defense* costs, and 3) a loud, insistent, and articulate voice describing over and over to the American people the fiscal mess in Washington.

The radical, Lyndon Johnson, started the downhill road for America that has brought the nation to the unfortunate debt position that exists in 1996. His followers have been identified. The defender, Ronald Reagan, forced the system to look at the problem. The power base changed in 1994 and brought more conservatives into play. Hope exists.

What has come of this insane fiscal journey of four decades? The table titled "American Social Statistics" that appears in the various chapters of this book clearly indicates that the Great Society has been a Great Flop.

As John Steele Gordon has pointed out: "In this period we increased the size of the national debt by a factor of seventeen. And for what? ... The answer, I'm afraid, is little more than the political self-interests of a few thousand people, Democrats and Republicans alike, who held public office during this period" (As quoted in John Steele Gordon, *Hamilton's Blessing* [New York: Walker, 1997]).

Suggestions

1) The budget is out of control; the mechanisms to correct it are not in place. The legislative and executive branches of the government must agree

on whose responsibility it is to develop a budget system that meets the control standards of 1996. Once agreement is reached, professionals should be retained to design adequate systems and the audit tests and procedures that will insure future compliance.

An acceptable control system must at least fulfill these criteria:

a) Have a spending cap

b) Recognize the primacy of *Defense* and *Interest*

c) Establish rules for the use of debt

d) Restrict debate to where to spend, not how much

e) Require a super-majority for tax increases

2) The political system is corrupt and will continue to be so for so long as a run for office is as expensive as it is. Good law will not emerge from a flawed political system. Proposals for campaign finance reform being floated by both political parties are public relations gimmicks designed to perpetuate the advantages of officeholders. They are also of questionable constitutionality. The core problem will not bend until cost is removed from the process by such steps as:

a) Shortening the campaign season

b) Designing a plan for free television time

c) Designing a plan for adequate television debates or interviews

d) Developing firm guidelines for controlling campaign spending

3) Politicians who spend a lifetime in Washington with no apparent source of income other than salary too often appear to be surprisingly wealthy after retirement. A more effective system for checking the net worth of incumbents is needed.

4) Voters should retire all politicians who were active in 1960–1980. The product of their efforts disqualifies them for further service.

5) All entitlement programs should be examined. Starting with the consensus that existed in 1960 concerning the generic interests of the federal government in such things, a plan must evolve that reduces federal costs to levels that make possible balanced budgets, debt reduction, and, in time, tax relief. The objective is to recreate an expandable tax and debt base for use during future emergency periods.

Politicians will, and should, make final decisions about where to spend *a finite amount of money.* But that isn't to say that they, by training or inclination, are capable of forming and managing a budget system involving trillions of dollars. A professional arm of the executive, probably under Treasury, should design and discipline the parameters within which politicians operate. The need to solve the problem without disturbing the balance of power between branches of government will not be a simple task.

A Word

The spending splurge since 1960 has been supported by taxpayer dollars, much of the money coming from wage earners who own little more than a house, a car, and (maybe) a small nest egg, men and women living from paycheck to paycheck, faced with parental costs increasingly beyond their ability to pay, dreaming of vacations they can't afford, and dreading retirements they don't dare face.

These people are described by some as "undertaxed" because their rates are the lowest in "the Western world," a designation that has little meaning for any individual who will lose his house if he is unemployed for six months. He does not feel undertaxed, whatever GDP relationships might be. More meaningfully, he is not undertaxed.

Just exactly who are these thinkers from Olympus who decide that 22% of a person's wages is a fair tax? Who are these people who say that the redistribution of wealth is a function of government, that the penalties associated with progressive tax rates are a morally justified practice for a government to follow? Who placed the scales of godlike justice in their hands? What is the relationship of such ideas to those of the Founding Fathers? to those of Karl Marx? When did these men stop managing the American government and start managing the lives of its citizens?

And given the results of their programs, how dare they hold themselves out as qualified to manage anything?

Taxes paid by the average person are more than mere dollars. Of the average man and his money, Petronius said: "Have and you shall be esteemed." He knew that a dollar in the pocket supports one's ego. George Bernard Shaw said: "Money ... enables life to be lived socially." Shaw knew that those with a dollar can mix with others; those without are outsiders. "Money is time," said George Gissing. He was right. Without it there is no leisure to enjoy those things that nourish the soul.

America's political leaders have unthinkingly, even stupidly, been spending for 40 years the esteem, the pride, and the leisure of Americans in pursuit of a social dream that has eluded the followers of Marx since the publication of his "Communist Manifesto" (1848). Shrouded though it might be in the language of compassion, Lyndon Johnson's Great Society was nothing more or less than the most recent failed attempt to enslave people in a bureaucratic quagmire which, when successful, reduces them to the status of dependent cogs in a well-oiled centralized machine.

The Great Society has been a monumental waste of time and money. Federal politicians of the last 40 years have violated the work of their predecessors and have abused the trust placed in them by their constituents. They must be stopped. Only the voters can do so.

Voters must get angry. They must vote. They must remove from office those who do not talk straight and elect those who will cut spending, reduce the size of government, lower debt, and return to Americans the right to live their own lives.

"I place economy among the first and most important virtues, and public debt as the greatest of dangers. To preserve our independence, we must not let our rulers load up with perpetual debt," said Thomas Jefferson.

Amen, and amen.

Afterword

"It keeps its books the way you and I keep our checkbooks."

That statement was made by John Steele Gordon in his book dealing with the national debt, *Hamilton's Blessing*. He was referring to the federal accounting system. How true. With each new edition of federal statistics comes "adjustments" of earlier-reported numbers. One such change is worth reporting here because it deals with the important economic measuring stick, "Gross Domestic Product."

Table 17.1
Gross Domestic Product, Updated (billions)

Year	Used	Change Amount	Percent
1993	$ 6688.7	$ 6704.2	.2%
1994	6951.4	7095.7	2.1
1995	7245.8	7381.9	1.9
1996	7636.0	7792.9	2.1

Current events represent an ongoing epilogue to books like *National Debt* that explore topical issues. One item of current interest is the possibility of a budget surplus in 1998 and beyond. What does this mean? Has the deficit/ debt problem been overstated? Has the magic bullet appeared?

For fiscal years 1997 and 1998, it is estimated that the deficit will be $31.9 billion; in 1999 and 2000, a surplus of $18.0 billion is expected. In effect, published numbers (OMB, Historical Tables, 1999) tell us the budget will be balanced soon. The headlines predict even rosier scenarios.

Two elements are mostly responsible for this forecast: revenue and defense. One way of showing this is to set up a comparison between Clinton's 1997 and the final years of the Reagan/Bush administrations, as follows:

Table 17.2
Reagan, Bush, Clinton Deficits
1988, 1992, 1997
(In Dollars of the Period [Billions])

	Reagan 1988	Bush 1992	Clinton 1997
Revenue	$ 909.3	$1091.3	$1579.3
Less:			
Defense	$ 290.4	$ 298.4	$ 270.5
Other	774.0	1083.2	1330.7
Total	$ 1064.4	$ 1381.6	$ 1601.2
Deficit	-$ 155.1	-$ 290.3	-$ 21.9

Table 17.3
Reagan, Bush, Clinton Deficits
1988, 1992, 1997
(1997 Dollars [Billions])

	Reagan 1988	Bush 1992	Clinton 1997
Revenue	$ 1241.2	$ 1256.1	$ 1579.3
Less:			
Defense	$ 396.4	$ 343.5	$ 270.5
Other	1056.5	1246.7	1330.7
Total	$ 1452.9	$ 1590.2	$ 1601.2
Deficit	-$ 211.7	-$ 334.1	-$ 21.9

Table 17.4
Shifting Clinton Income and Defense
to Reagan and Bush
(In 1997 Dollars [Billions])

	Reagan 1988	Bush 1992	Clinton 1997
Revenue	$ 1579.3	$ 1579.3	$ 1579.3
Less:			
Defense	$ 270.5	$ 270.5	$ 270.5
Other	1056.5	1246.7	1330.7
Total	$ 1327.0	$ 1517.2	$ 1601.2
Deficit	$ 252.3	$ 62.1	-$ 21.9

One picture is indeed worth a thousand words. Table 17.4 shows that with Clinton's income and defense numbers, Reagan and Bush would have been hailed as fiscal heroes. And it may be noted that with the *Defense* of Reagan or Bush, the 1997 deficit would have been $147.8 or $94.9 billion, and if the 1997 revenue base had been less generous, the results would have been calamitous.

Instead of serving as an example of improvement, the year 1997 is instead a vivid demonstration of the problems discussed in this book. In a peacetime year with taxes high and defense spending low, despite a revenue windfall from both amounting to $464.0 billion (vs. 1988), the result was another deficit and higher debt. What indeed will be the deficit when *Defense* is restored to the modest Reagan level (don't even think about the Roosevelt level), or when the inevitable downturn in the business cycle arrives?

President Clinton has enjoyed a lucky harvest within a business cycle that went into a positive mode under Bush in 1991. It has continued now for 87 months (to July 1998), but it will not continue forever. The Reagan boom lasted 92 months; the longest boom period since the 1930s was 106 months (1961–1969). A great window of opportunity is winding down. The welfare state stands as strong as ever, hardly dented by the ineffectual nibblings of Republicans who do not have the courage to unify behind a common program of solutions.

If a temporary budget surplus does appear, should taxes or debt be reduced or, as President Clinton would have it, Social Security protected? The last option will be discussed first.

Ironically, those who placed Social Security in jeopardy always take credit for protecting it. It was Lyndon Johnson and his apostles who set into motion the welfare state that made the affordability of Social Security an issue in the first place. And it is the "great protector" of Social Security, Senator Moynihan, who spearheaded the action to tax Social Security benefits. And here they are again, "protecting" the program by "retaining" surpluses in some nondescribed way.

Social Security is in trouble because the cost of the welfare state is crowding it out. Washingtonocrats are scrambling for a solution that makes them look good—so much the better if it fixes a few things too, but cosmetics, not substance, is what they are after. The program needs adjustment, but its future stability and affordability will essentially depend on the willingness in Washington to realign the welfare state and reestablish states' rights. Downsizing government must be the central target. Many problems, including Social Security, will shrink to manageable size when (and if) that takes place. Citizens who care will support those who advocate downsizing.

Reduce taxes? Reduce debt? Taxes are too high and, on those grounds alone, should at some point be reduced. But the only compelling argument for doing it sooner instead of later is that federal politicians cannot be trusted with the cash.

From a theoretical standpoint, debt reduction should be the first target. For every 10% reduction, an additional $2 billion to $3 billion in lower *Interest* will follow, a road that would also lead to lower money-market rates.

The "trust" argument is the most powerful. There is nothing in the recent history of debt management to suggest that federal politicians can be trusted with excess cash. Tax reduction, therefore, is the most practical short-term course to take.

At some point, circumstances may force the federal government to adopt modern procedures of budget and control. At some point, citizens may become disgusted with their representatives in Congress and elect more noble creatures who at least think of their country as much as they do their egos, incomes, and reputations. But until that time comes, take the money away from the rascals as fast as surpluses appear via tax reductions. Let debt and *Interest* shrink as a measure against a growing economy. Citizens who care will support those who sponsor such behavior.

If and when Washingtonocrats grow up and cost control systems are put into place, the absolute amount of debt could be gradually and directly lowered by making the planned reduction a line item in the annual budget.

Much is being made today about the possibility of junking the existing tax system and doing away with the Internal Revenue System as we know it. Everyone knows the system is inefficient. Those who argue for its retention, with an adjustment here and there, are concerned about power, not revenue, not fairness. The existing tax system makes politicians powerful, granting incentives here, tax breaks there, like a flower lady handing out little bouquets from her basket of goodies. Citizens who care will support those who seek to eliminate the IRS. The establishment of a new tax system that strips godlike powers from politicians is a prerequisite of government reform. When the IRS goes, much of the corruption in Washington will go with it.

Hope for the future lies in the character of the American people who believe in the dream of the Founding Fathers. The question is: Can they overcome the corrupt political system that supports a trainload of empty suits and an electorate that is increasingly immoral, ignorant, stratified, and indifferent?

The American experiment will be resolved in the next century. Either it will stamp its emblem of freedom with responsibility on the face of history more firmly that any social system ever devised, or it will join those who have tried and failed, like the Soviet Union, to buy power with benefits or preserve it with force. By acting, or failing to act, every living American will have a hand in making that decision.

Bibliography

American Almanac, 1996–1997. Tex.: Hoover's, 1996.

Axelrod, Alan, and Charles Phillips. *What Every American Should Know About American History*. Mass.: Bob Adams, 1952.

Bureau of Economic Analysis. GDP—1993–1996.

Bureau of Public Debt, Historical Information 17911939. Internet, 1998.

Chronicle of the 20th Century. New York: Dorling Kindersley, 1995.

DeGregorio, William A. *The Complete Book of U.S. Presidents*. N.J.: Wings Books, 1991.

Desk Reference, N.Y. Library. New York: Simon & Schuster, 1989.

Gordon, John Steele. *Hamilton's Blessing*. New York: Penguin Books, 1998.

Grolier Online. The American Presidency. Internet, 1998.

Information Please, Almanac, 1996, 1997, 1998. Boston: Houghton Miflin.

Kirk, Russell. *Redeeming the Time*. Delaware: Intercollegiate Studies Institute, 1996.

O'Connor, Thomas, and Alan Rogers. *This Momentus Affair*. Boston, Trustees of the Public Library, 1987.

Office of Management and Budget. Historical Tables, Fiscal Year 1997. Washington, D.C., U.S. Government Printing Office, 1996.

Office of Management and Budget. Historical Tables, Fiscal Year 1999. Washington, D.C., U.S. Government Printing Office, 1998.

Tripp, Rhoda Thomas. *Thesaurus of Quotations*. New York: Harper & Row, 1970.

Index